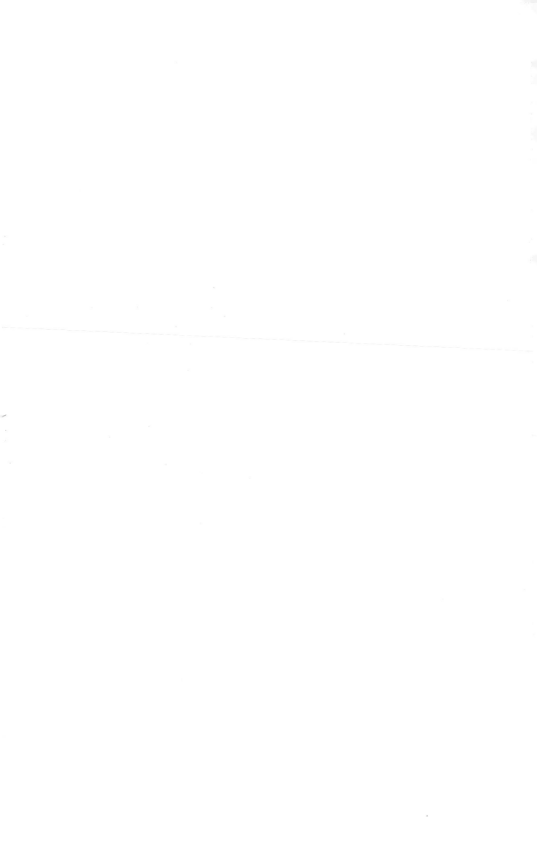

TAIL RISK KILLERS

How Math, Indeterminacy,
and Hubris Distort Markets

Jeff McGinn

New York Chicago San Francisco Lisbon London Madrid Mexico City
New Delhi San Juan Seoul Singapore Sydney Toronto

To my wife, Sena, who always gives a kind word to everyone.
There is nothing mean about her at all.

1 2 3 4 5 6 7 8 9 0   DOC/DOC   1 6 5 4 3 2 1

ISBN: 978-0-07-178490-0
MHID: 0-07-178490-X

e-ISBN: 978-0-07-178491-7
e-MHID: 0-07-178491-8

This publication is designed to provide accurate and authoritative information in regard to the subject matter covered. It is sold with the understanding that neither the author nor the publisher is engaged in rendering legal, accounting, or other professional service. If legal advice or other expert assistance is required, the services of a competent professional person should be sought.
— *From a Declaration of Principles Jointly Adopted by a Committee of the American Bar Association and a Committee of Publishers and Associations*

McGraw-Hill books are available at special quantity discounts to use as premiums and sales promotions, or for use in corporate training programs. To contact a representative, please e-mail us at bulksales@mcgraw-hill.com.

This book is printed on acid-free paper.

Contents

Acknowledgments

For knowing the world held more for me than where I came from: thanks Mom. Thank you Professor Stephen Montgomery-Smith, who helped me write a cubic spline interpolation algorithm in Mathematica in my formative years: you got me interested, and look where it led. To Larry "the Liquidator" Groves: thanks for letting me interrogate you about the old days. Thank you, Sandy Latham, for nursing my beat-up ego. Linda Hongling Xu deserves a big thank you for reading about probability, gambling, and invertible systems when she didn't always want to. Thanks to my kids, Faith, Isaac, and Ben for cautioning me to not be too serious in my writing.

Thanks to all the colleagues, bosses, and competitors that made me smarter. Thanks to the bloggers that made me tougher. Thanks to everyone over the years that shaped, formed, and twisted my views. Thanks to my agent Lynne Rabinoff. She took a chance on a newbie author and really went above and beyond the call of duty. Finally, many thanks to Zachary Gajewski, Jennifer Ashkenazy, and all the great people at McGraw-Hill who made this book possible, had so many great suggestions, and made it a lot less painful than I thought possible.

A special thank you to Aaron Brown. It may not seem like a lot to you, but your kindness meant so much to me.

Foreword

ail Risk Killers looks beneath the surface of financial news to deeper issues over longer time cycles. Some of the ideas are more controversial than others, but they are supported by data and the arguments make one think.

Tail Risk Killers has loads of surprising data sources, and each has striking relevance to current conditions. The past may be a guide for the future, but the past that matters often is little known and comes from unexpected sources. The main source of data comes from fixed income markets. This is understandable. Fixed income markets, loosely speaking, are the largest of the financial markets, and the author shows that they have survived amazing stresses over the years. In fact, bond markets are the key to understanding the concept of the modern nation state. They also figure prominently in today's economic problems because they lie at the fulcrum point of massive governmental, business, and household debt accumulation.

The message is that the world lies between massive defaults and an acceptance of the "haircuts and austerity" necessary to make the debt burden serviceable. Between these binary outcomes lies policymaker-driven "Japanification," a term Jeff explores in depth. Debt and debt resolution are key, because interest rates drive everything in finance. Functioning properly, interest rates simply determine risk and reward. But when subject to central bank policy, they reduce to instruments that distort risk and reward. This interplay between risk and risk distortion is the tension in modern finance.

One of the ways banks manage this distortion are derivatives, namely, credit and interest rate derivatives. The quadrillions of dollars in derivative exposure exist to hedge distortions in credit risk and the interest rate risk associated with decades of cheap money gushing out of the Fed's discount window. However, the ability of these credit default and interest rate swaps to effectively hedge such risk is dubious because they do not reduce risk. They serve to transfer risk to a willing buyer. As a result, the financial system is more than anything else a fragile network of interlocking liabilities—more like a house of cards than anything else. This threatens whole societies and global stability. Several chapters detail this financial architecture and its risks, some more technical and some more expository. There is a clear explanation of their purpose and how they work, including the mechanics of risk-neutral pricing, funding, and collateral management. Attention is given to understanding the information content of the prices they generate. As the author states, "The price of stability is pathology."

Risk management has never been more important, and there is a deep discussion of the core components of risk management: risk and its categories, volatility, and liquidity. While the discussion includes some necessary, technical mathematics, the bulk of the discussion is clear and informal. It highlights that much of the existing financial architecture depends on a near-perfect mathematical representation of reality. Such absolute thinking is dangerous, and mathematical deficiencies are taken on in a real tour-de-force way, supported by mathematical research.

Regardless of whether the failings of modern finance are due to old financial foes like leverage, or a slavish devotion to the more trendy models, the central message is that the real tail risk killers are not governments, central banks, or decision makers guiding things from the center. The real tail risk killers are you and I taking the sometimes painful, always reasonable steps to deal with their circumstances. Others may mitigate or provide short-term fixes, but in the end all they do is inject more long-run instability into the world.

Whether you agree with all the findings or not, *Tail Risk Killers* is an important contribution to understanding and a fast-paced, terrific read for anyone interested in the financial imbalances resulting from too much reliance on math and too little respect for indeterminacy.

—Tyler Durden

Introduction

There are only two ways of becoming a historian of the future: scientific deduction and divination or fortune-telling. But scientific deduction would disqualify itself for cognition of the future by the process of scientific deduction. For science must always be careful not to make a fool of itself. Science would scarcely go further than a computation of probabilities.

Divination and fortune-telling, on the other hand, have the inestimable advantage of looking back up on a long and venerable practice, which according to incontrovertible tradition has produced remarkably successful results. In order to be genuine, the prophetic forms of cognition must know how to wear the veil of parable and to cast the shadow of mystery.

—FRANZ WERFEL, *STAR OF THE UNBORN*

You hear it all the time: "This time is different." Sometimes it is different. Sometimes, however, this is just the mating call of the loser. The saying informs concern over hyperinflation, complete collapse, Japan-like stagnation ("Japanification"), other extremes. It sums up the psychological inclination to focus on big moves in a landscape, just as our eyes are drawn to what is moving. All these states of the world happened before, but there is a potential for things that have never happened before. It is easy to overestimate the likelihood of completely new events, because of the huge impact they carry. It is not that the concern is unreasonable: Regardless of the probabilities, it is important to grasp how different life would be if such extremes came to pass.

The opposite view has a common refrain too: "There is nothing new under the sun." This is the belief that every aberration eventually reverts back to the mean. And there is a remarkable resilience in societies, economies, and the complex financial architecture that underpins *this view*. It is a part of the human spirit to rebuild after things fall apart, to reinforce the stabilities we construct. This is exactly why credit-default interest-rate swaps exist: to hedge the credit and interest-rate risk on dealer inventories hidden behind ultralow interest rates set by the Federal Reserve. Given enough time, something new we are unprepared for comes along that makes the apparent stability evaporate, and those swaps don't work as envisioned. The result is a modern financial system with increasingly nonlinear payouts that make the system as a whole more fragile. The stability of day after day experience leads us to underestimate the likelihood of these system-threatening changes—this is where the likelihood of extremes get underestimated. These events and likelihoods depend on future events and, as a result, are impossible to know with certainty.

Mathematics, chiefly probability (the mathematics of randomness), is how people estimate such likelihoods. A probability distribution defines both the likelihood of extremes (the tails) and the likelihood of the same (the center or mass). Getting this right is the key to successful risk taking. However, the randomness of financial markets doesn't adhere to well-defined probability laws. Classical probability is based solely on history: the numerator of past occurrences over the denominator of all past events. Market conditions and even the rules change too fast for this approach. In effect, the probability distribution changes itself as market participants incorporate information. For this reason, some financial models depend on a *generalization*, where the probabilities are based on a decomposition of current prices as a sum of risk factors. This type of probability measure generates an implied volatility or similar risk premium that signals the "risk neutral" meeting of a buyer and a seller for a financial asset. Even assessment of likelihood in the risk-neutral context is sensitive to assumptions and initial conditions as well.

INDETERMINISM

At issue is something deeper than probability in its various states of undress. The issue is representation failure in a general sense meaning that there is an aspect of existence not well captured by any type of description. There is an irreducible element of indeterminism that says that not only are things Godel-incomplete, but they also can be inconsistent, contradictory.

When we say, "There is nothing new under the sun," we implicitly conceive the world as deterministic and complete—not a work in progress. It's comforting to think of the world in this way. The past is all that we know, and rules that explain the past well impart an illusion of control on the future. Sure, relaxing some rules permits some new particulars to pop up sometimes, but overall, causality is allowed to determine everything. If nothing can break the chain of causality, then there is nothing new under the sun.

Experience shows there really are new things under the sun. Everything has a first instance—all events have a starting point of creation. At some deep level, therefore, some things escape causality and determinism. Here's how it happens: We break the chains of causality with our imagination and how we recast what happened into what is to come. As long as there is historical memory and the ability to reassemble those fragments of history, it is possible to detach from causality. Creativity and spontaneity are the products of this detachment. When thought disconnects from instinctive response, we escape determinism. Something new happens under the sun when we simulate the future by blending history and interpretation to guide future actions. In this way, the narrative fallacy is no fallacy at all: it is self-fulfillment.

NARRATIVE SHAPES THE FINANCIAL WORLD

A particular view on the future can be right or wrong for a number of reasons. We can interpret data incorrectly. It may even be the case that we introduce entirely fictional events that never happened. Memory isn't a seamless tapestry of continuous events: People forget, things fade into the background, and often memory is a disconnected jumble of impressions. Information comes in packets that we recombine into a framework for deciding action.

These packets are based on the past, but they are transformed by a thought reassembly process with some randomness in it. When people take action under the influence of this thinking—whether right or wrong—new things can happen. Knowledge grows as we catalogue data, as do the possibilities for innovation and action.

History + inherent randomness in mental processing → larger range of action → indeterminism

Randomness guarantees that no rigid pattern completely determines the future from the past. Instead, there are spontaneously changing, incomplete, and otherwise screwed up rules. Finance depends on perceiving the future correctly and having the courage of your convictions. Math is the natural way to categorize, develop the rules, and establish control. It seems foolproof, but the relationship is conflicted.

This is why finance and mathematics have a special place in their hearts for one another. Finance lends to mathematics a field of application and a set of problems with which to busy itself. Mathematics lends to finance an aura of certainty and precision and a way to engender confidence in those cautious of risk. The mathematician finds application, and the trader gets new trading systems. The combination generates returns for a time and moves "sure things" onto awed retail investors. It seems like a win, but the relationship is conflicted.

The Conflict Between Finance and Mathematics

The conflict between finance and mathematics is due to the inherent indeterminacy in finance, which mathematics can't handle well. The mathematical approach is to eliminate indeterminacy entirely one way or another. For examples, dynamical systems subject reality to inviolable rules. The rules are valid distillations only because they agree with the past. Such models are captured by the past and simply repeat old patterns of behavior. We find in these systems all kinds of behaviors ranging from convergence to a resting point, to endless repetition, even to complexity so severe that it looks completely random. In fact, mathematician Sheldon Newhouse found that by far the most common behavior for dynamical systems is instability: A system can never decide between an infinity of possible outcomes.[1] A dynamical system can be so unstable that there is no hope for understanding it at all.

Likewise, much of probability eliminates memory effects entirely for the sake of tractability. Probability reduces to moving through time in an independent way that makes learning impossible. Everything there is to know about the past is assumed to lie in the present, as is everything there is to know about the future. These assumptions are necessary for mathematical modeling because without them, the methods won't fit the problems they attempt to resolve. But the assumptions often distort some essential aspect of reality. The models sterilize the randomness found in real life.

So the meeting of math and finance is where inevitable, seamless mathematical self-definition inadequately encounters a reality constantly rethinking itself. The product is contrived and fragile. What you get is the irony of office buildings engineered to withstand tsunamis, but the tsunamis instead rip out power lines, and nuclear reactor cores melt down. Financial markets evolve in the same way: always a work in progress, never complete, constantly expanding and collapsing in ways that confound our efforts at control.

There is a totalitarian urge in math to impose order and symmetry on an indeterminate chaos at odds with it. But it is far more than an imposition on the universe: It *recreates* the world by linking solid empirical observation to logical precision. Nowhere else are truth and beauty so well blended. This is why reality so often obeys well-established rules, why pure mathematics is applicable in so many ways.

And yet periods of success are mingled with punctuated failure. Things that make no sense persist in this world. Swap spreads at duration can remain persistently negative, opening clear arbitrage to Treasuries. Because the persistently irrational cannot be captured by optimizing technique, irrationality escapes such deductive models. Also, things can be individually rational but irrational in the aggregate. Short-term funding at floating rates can lever long-term trades. But interest payments do not stay low forever, and when floating rates spike, deleveraging ensues as everyone sells in size. When everyone rushes for the exits, there is no clear idea of valuation, creating illiquidity. There is a level of debt beyond which income and cash on hand cannot support interest payments. Beyond this point, deleveraging goes into reverse to the point of default, causing insolvency. We all know these two twin evils, illiquidity and insolvency, because they brought down Bear Sterns, then Lehman Brothers, then AIG, and countless others in the past.

CHANGE, PERSPECTIVE, AND FINANCE

There is no other way but to enlarge our frame of reference, apply rules that remain free of counterexample, and be open and receptive to change. Change depends on one's perspective. To a child born in Shanghai in 2000, nothing seems remarkably different at all in 2011. To a guy born in Shanghai in 1978, China's economic progress may be spectacular, but it is a smooth evolution in rising living standards. To someone who remembers the fragmented Shanghai in the aftermath of a dead Ching Dynasty in the 1920s, then to become a Japanese colonial possession in the 1930s and 1940s, then ground underfoot by a maniac bent on the destruction of Chinese culture in the 1950s and 1960s, then to emerge as a geopolitical epicenter in the 1990s and noughties—yeah, China is revolutionary. In this example, history has three equally important flavors of change: discontinuity, evolution, and stationarity.

And the three constantly work at cross-purposes, as shown in some examples. Getting struck by lightning is a rare, unpredictable extreme. In contrast, the chance of a 60-year-old man dying from a heart attack is well captured by actuarial tables. Numbers of people die because of concentrated bursts of wars throughout history. But the people who die of sickness and malnutrition eclipse that number. Change can be so slow and negligible that it escapes our notice. Even in finance, the mundane constantly nullifies the extreme. For every company that successfully markets a new medication, there are four costly failures at the clinical trial stage. An investor diversified across a large number of drug companies doesn't feel extreme gains or losses nearly as much.

The law of averages may well make our lives more stable and controlled, but it doesn't always work. Every action can have unintended consequences. For example, overuse of antibiotics allowed microbes to repopulate their decimated legions with more resistant attackers. Bacteria strong enough to survive the parasites survive at the expense of weaker ones. Once this happens, widespread antibiotic usage increases the number of antibiotic-resistant bacteria, making these strains dominate all other variants. Antibiotics represent an unsuccessful attempt at revolution, a failed attempt at creating a world free of certain diseases and a reduction in pain and death. Such efforts at control have unintended consequences. Antibiotic usage exerts selective pressure in favor of antibiotic-resistant microorganisms that lead humankind to greater pain, misfortune, and sickness.

The financial world teems with examples of punctuated motion, slow-fast unfolding change, and same-old, same-old. The take-home message is this: We never will figure out everything under the sun. We can go so high that we are just a touch from the angels and then fall into catastrophe. And there is no envisioning all possible ways complex systems can take us there. We can only search the ruins of the forgotten past for answers, imagine what we think they mean for the world, and hope that indeterminate chance works in our favor.

THE NEW WORLD FINANCE

Chance never gets much credit, especially on Wall Street. To admit it was just dumb luck diminishes the cultivated image of a complexity and sophistication needed to grow assets under management. This holds more true of quantitative finance than anywhere else. Quant people held a unique place between academia and Wall Street. They had a somewhat otherworldly persona, like the offspring of some ephemeral math goddess and a ruthless barbarian trader. They boasted market-beating returns on the presumption of clever models and expert deployment of them.

Late 2008 made good short-term returns into an illusion. Long term, there is little reason to believe that quants are any more successful than a market index. And performance is often based on an inadequate timeline for performance measurement. Selling earthquake insurance in a risky area such as the San Andreas fault line does generate a fortune in premiums until an earthquake strikes. However, if this fortune is moved into untouchable accounts when it is time to settle up the claims, it doesn't really matter. One simply files for bankruptcy, heads for the good life in Boca Raton, and leaves a mess for others to clean up. Further, the performance is seldom based on absolute returns. It is a comparative benchmark, similar to grading people on a curve.

The explanations for apparent short-term success most often relate to information or trading execution advantage. First, some firms are at an advantage to others because their nature and scale of activity create a cozy relationship with regulators. Thus they can bend the rules everyone else has to follow. There is regulatory arbitrage: Banks loan money to hedge funds to make trades they cannot because of regulatory constraints. This is the much discussed "shadow banking system" that continues to implode. They can even break the rules. This is called *front-running/special privileges*, where prop desk trading is advantaged by the flow business going on under the same roof. A part of the profits made in financial markets comes from access to information and instruments closed to retail investors.

There are also reputational effects: Some firms work hard to convey an appearance of method, model, and mental superiority. If successful, the perception actually can work for a time. People herd in imitation of the trades if the trader *appears* better than others. These traders, in turn, are the first to leave the crowded trades. It is hard to get a herd to follow after a meltdown, and some carry an air of eclecticism and even outright weirdness. Now it is a tall order to restore that persona.

Hard work makes survival possible. It is an unending quest for understanding the dark risks hidden in the footnotes of the modern, derivative-laden financial system. It is the discovery of mispriced risk and taking appropriate exposures. There is liquidity management. Finally, there is luck, and it can matter more than anything sometimes.

When models fail and expectations prove wrong, search for perspective. Find reference points for the outliers that blew up the mathematical machinery. Imagine how those reference points translate across time. This is why I wrote this book—to give people some insights in the new world finance and to show at the same time how often forgotten history has a bearing on the future.

CHAPTER 1

Default-Cost Asymmetry: Humpty Dumpty Was Pushed

Even in discounting economic conditions, people have a tendency to think in terms of extremes. For this reason, the outcomes investors assign to the future are pretty binary: über-deflationary collapse or hyperinflationary explosion. Why does everything have to be so über and hyper? Whatever happened to flat prices and high inflation?

It is true that the world's financial tail-risk killers—central banks and politicos—do everything they can to preserve the status quo, but in the end, all their effort amounts to jousting with windmills? Nature is too complicated, crafty, and feral for policy to fix everything. Time and the path of least resistance are the only cures. Determining just where those paths go is a tricky matter.

Mother Nature either will be allowed to get her groove on or she'll burn the club to the ground.

THE PRIMORDIAL SOUP KITCHEN

Objective reality is the basic structure of the entire universe. It consists of particles in fields of force. Human beings regulate their interface (i.e., cold, hunger, hardship, joy, satiety, comfort) with objective reality by constructing *social* reality. This reality adheres to or deviates from a set of reference rules generated by human-created institutions. These institutions, under normal circumstances, self-regulate (for example, legislatures, Federal Open Market Committee) and react to changes in human preferences (for example, as democracy places an upper bound on corruption and transfers power). The interaction of these institutions is where things get complicated and interesting. From human social interactions emerge new *self-renewing* institutions such as legislatures that create and interpret laws as circumstances change. Legislatures and courts interact with each other in ways that can sustain each other. Either institutions are sufficiently rigid to endure the stresses of time and path resistance without change, or they have enough flexibility to adapt and go with the flow.

Complex Adaptive Dynamical Systems

People adapt, learn, and react in ways that make their behavior non-linear and complicated. This makes society a complex adaptive dynamical system—an unstable system with unique and interesting features. Complex adaptive systems are self-organizing—interconnected in ways that create vicious and virtuous cycles. The people and institutions they create mediate objective reality by constantly adapting behavior. The evolutionary purpose of individual parts of such systems is to find deficiencies and to fill niches that remedy these problems. If successful, they replicate—as when bureaucracies grow and expand their sphere of influence by becoming more interconnected to other parts of the system. In turn, the system itself gains properties that the people and institutions making it up don't have when viewed in isolation.

These kinds of systems explicitly work to reduce complexity. For example, humans live in groups, and group life is regulated by institutions that stabilize social interactions. This is why there are stop lights. The alternative is daily auto pileups on the drive to work every morning, capital structure instead of pervasive theft, and hopefully, elections instead of revolutions. The system itself generates rules to make interactions durable and predictable because it transforms data into the knowledge on which interactions are based. In turn, it supports more complex rule-generating institutions.

All complex adaptive systems require this type of complexity reduction, and it coincides with variance reduction in the behavior of parts of the system. There are unspoken norms and rules of behavior for just about every circumstance in polite society.

When interacting parts of systems have too rigid regularities, though, aggregate behavior can become uncontrolled because the system as a whole loses flexibility. Rigidity increases system entropy. In effect, entropy makes things more predictable and robust to small shocks at the level of personal behavior but makes an aggregate response to large-scale condition changes unpredictable. Here is where expectations cluster around a single viewpoint. Society rewards members who adapt and do not cling to past reference points without reservation until disaster ensues.

Social realities are structurally unstable because of this rigidity. This means that certain shock events, such as the default of a small municipality or country, dramatically affect the nature of the *entire* system, not just a small part of it. For example, financial markets exhibit an ever-increasing degree of interaction among participants. Correlated behavior between different participants of the system becomes so strong that even a small shock to a few participants causes them to act in a certain way. Because of the correlation, it will lead to the same action coordinated among others. The coordinated action cascades through the market like falling dominos, resulting in at least a greater possibility of an extreme outcome, such as a crash or a melt-up.

Shocks can come out of the blue, such as North Korea detonating a nuclear device in a ship docked in Singapore. Other shocks can occur when institutions internal to the system reach a critical mass, such as the London Interbank Offered Rate (LIBOR) exceeding 2-year yields past a threshold. When shocks such as these happen, the system has potential to undergo bifurcation—when transitions from state to state quickly evolve in increasingly complicated evolutions for a time and then collapse into simpler behavior. Depending on the flexibility of the system, larger shocks can be disruptive, painful, rejuvenating, or all three.

The Potential for Collapse

Whether or not a system collapses depends on its attained complexity and how close that level of complexity is to the system's threshold limit for handling complexity, beyond which it collapses. For such unstable systems, chaos is what lies between order and collapse. Human systems need complexity in order to use resources efficiently, but that complexity needs to be balanced and controlled—otherwise, it will destroy itself.

Progress depends on the "right" amount of innovation. When innovation is too low, societies stagnate. Populations containing erratically acting members are often at an advantage when interacting with members who rigidly adhere to existing rules because they are more predictable. When there are too many crazies on the loose, innovation becomes too high, and the system breaks down because it is impossible to know the best possible actions.

What lies between order and chaos is the internal tension between self-regulating behavior that enhances stability and destabilizing mutation that exploits predictable behavior successfully. A common intuition is that systems of this type have the best outcomes when they are at the "edge of chaos"—meaning not too rigid when change is needed and not so fluid that good ideas can't be identified.

Humans produce risk as a by-product of progress. It emerges from within the system itself as it adapts to favorable and unfavorable circumstances. Therefore, as complexity increases, risk increases. As risk increases, the power of history as a predictive framework fades. At the threshold between order and chaos, there is no adequate way to identify how the future will take shape and where punctuated, game-changing events emerge.

There's no stopping this. Fed policy, your senator, Zhu Rongji, me—we're all a part of it. Time is going to take us where it wants to. Enjoy Mother Nature, and hope that she enjoys you.

INTERCONNECTIVITY AND THE SYNTHETIC GOLD STANDARD

Societal changes that appear tiny on the surface can have the most impact because of exponential effects over time. For example, the gold standard of a century ago was a basic parameterization of all other values in terms of gold, plus or minus some cost-of-carry fuzz. Thus gold was the starting point for speaking about valuation: It provided a basic balance point. Gold was recognized as underlying currency only because enough people viewed it as such. This assignment of value is no more or less fragile than anything else. The gold standard is dead.

The monetary standard we have now is much more complicated and beautiful: It's like a Caribbean colony of jellyfish with sunlight shining through them as swimmers pass underneath. The arbitrary nature of valuation is now explicit and breathtakingly fluid. Everything changes in a day: yen valuation, U.S. dollars (USD), Canadian dollars (CAD). The starting point is the valuation of one currency to other currencies. It is remiss to call this system fragile: Jellyfish like this can kill a human being in a matter of seconds with one sting.

The system's dangerous sting is its complexity and interconnectedness. Complex adaptive systems are volatile, and the volatility causes instabilities in other things, such as labor and capital markets. Central banks have created a "bend but don't break" kind of stability through currency swaps. Currency swaps fix valuation between currencies on a relative basis because the most interconnected central banks also have the most freedom to use the printing press (see Figure 1.1).

This system is robust because it enables variance reduction without excessive rigidity. The extent of the network itself makes it robust. However, if one of the central nodes dies (e.g., USD, EUR, ECH, or JPY), then every node dies. Currency swap arrangements hold the world together.

THE PATH OF LEAST RESISTANCE IS SHARED SACRIFICE

Everyone knows a busted Treasury market when the economy is on life support would be more than bad. But it isn't hopeless. Default doesn't

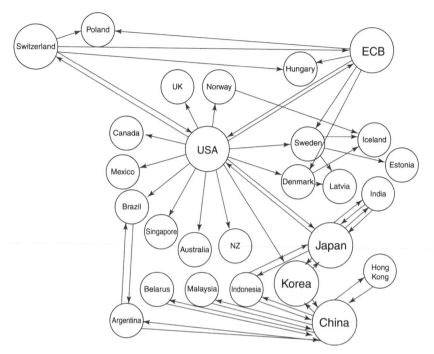

Figure 1.1 **Degree of Connectedness in the Financial System.**
Source: Alea.

necessarily mean that the debtor summarily pays nothing. In fact, such a case is extremely rare. It's just not how things work.

In default, both debtors and creditors must absorb costs. This is especially true in the case of sovereign default. There has to be hope of getting out from under a mountain of debt before a population will agree even in theory to years of high taxation. And to prevent societies from unraveling, austerity cannot completely absorb the cost. Creditors, who must always be prudent of risk, should not be rewarded with a bailout. At the same time, creditor haircuts so extreme that they are perceived as theft leave everyone worse off.

Moderation almost always works out for the best. It's messy, confusing, and unfair to everyone. But it works. There is a clear symmetry in this middle path: Debtors and creditors share the pain. *Debtors take steps that make them financially sound, creditors take haircuts to make this possible, and everybody else stays out of it.*

In case of corporate default, time and due process convert debt into equity and enable credible restructuring in an orderly way. This concept is deep and shouldn't be trifled with by fools. Law is not something artificial or imposed. It is the product of natural selection because it has stood the test of time and is inherently capable of change. Government breaking these rules is cheating that distorts risk perception among debtors and creditors by applying guarantees. Markets work well when risk is understood. A market where debtors and creditors both have claim to a guarantee is the theater of the absurd.

Too much debt and too much capacity mean that the endgame of deleveraging is wealth destruction. The way out is wholly unconnected to theory or policies. It is decentralized. Millions of complicated adaptive families acting in their own best interest determine reality. Not Bernanke and not Goldman Sachs.

In nature, the lucky thrive, which is the strongest case for diversification out there. The majority survive, wiser and poorer for the experience. The unlucky get crushed.

HUMPTY-DUMPTY WAS PUSHED: HAIRCUTS AND AUSTERITY

Let's look at Latvia's recent situation because Latvia's problem is the global problem: a massive run-up in private-sector debt that led to a massive out-scaling of productive capacity (see Figure 1.2). For Latvia, it wasn't a government problem. Government debt went from frugal to prodigal because it was the only thing keeping society from coming apart at the seams. Meanwhile, the private sector is in full debt-reduction mode.

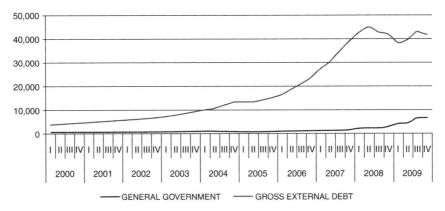

Figure 1.2 **Latvian General Government and Total Net External Debt (million USD), 2000–2009.**

The Latvian tail-risk killer objective of LT/EUR stability implies that adjustment comes via the labor market and not inflation. Cutting the peg and devaluing the currency imply that savers and currency longs take the brunt of the pain. Either way, the result of adjustment is income reduction. The world is in the process of figuring out how the costs will be shared among creditors and debtors— the mix of haircuts and austerity. How it plays out in Latvia may be prophetic.

THE REALITY OF LOSS IS UNAVOIDABLE

The only workable remedies are organic ones: They are robust to specific circumstance, hopefully gradual, and the winners of natural selection against alternatives. However, there needs to be some symmetry in the inevitable restructuring, and this is where government can play a role—to assist in making adjustment gradual and ensuring that both debtors and creditors absorb costs. Push too hard, and the whole system will crash. Successful debt restructuring enables the survival of debtors and enforces to a degree the rights of creditors.

This is not sunshine and rainbows. Haircuts can be disguised as an extension of maturity, lower interest rates, or inflation, but they leave stinging damage that won't be forgotten the next time. Government extraction of high taxes from the profitable and the poor alike leaves citizens with difficult choices about how to survive without government assistance. The elderly eat grass soup gathered from their backyards. Stoical wives make hard evening decisions about who to spend the night with so as to feed their children. Jobless husbands are quiet and numb about these things.

Take note: All those sure of those hyper- and über-outcomes: Reality is more dreary and colorless than some blaze of glory on the way to hell, but it grinds you into dirt like nothing else. Policy fixer-uppers: Be careful what you wish for. You never know when total failure will strike.

Such failure can show up when you least expect it, as demonstrated in Figure 1.3.

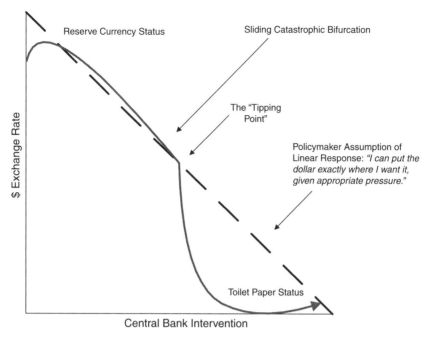

Figure 1.3 **Linear Policy Framework Versus Nonlinear Realities.**

Central bankers, within certain parameters, have latitude to affect exchange rates. The relationship can look very predictable and controlled until a critical point is reached. Then all bets are off on what happens. A currency can go from a medium of exchange to strips of paper very quickly indeed.

CHAPTER 2

Risk-Minimal Trade Construction: Treasuries Since 1798 and Gold

As long as human societies have been complex enough to store wealth and mine shiny metals, gold has been a friend to humankind. Gold has been on a good bull run for a decade now, starting even before the year 2000. Gold will persist in being a good trade because the most powerful central bank in the world wants inflation. Ultimately, when the Fed wants something in its power to affect, it gets it. However, the U.S. government, insofar as it represents the interests of wealthy insiders who do not want to take massive haircuts, has sufficient political will to keep it from going too far. Hopefully.

Gold (and other commodities) are doing well in the uncertainty. Because current interest rates are artificially low through government intervention and economic activity is lackluster, the benefitting commodity is the bellwether store of value, gold. Further, the answer to debt deflation has been nationalization by governments of the world. This moves the center of pain to sovereign debt in time. As result of these factors, we're in the middle of a big multiyear ramp in gold prices.

Pain in sovereign debt doesn't imply complete destruction of sovereign debt. It implies a rise in the risk-free rate of return and convergence to the historical mean in risk premia. But this is not the end of days: It is nothing more or less than the end of a great bull market in Treasuries. It will be the death of the "Great Moderation" circa 1980. This bear market will feed fears about many massive changes for humankind: deglobalization, the hand of justice closing into an iron fist, a slackening in the pace of technological change, on and on. To me, it just means that duration can't be a portfolio anchor anymore.

There is good reason for the Federal Reserve to revive inflation in the economy, but it is clear that the Fed doesn't want a bear market in Treasuries as a result of its policies. It may be a foregone conclusion, though. The two objectives of monetization and strong debt prices aren't compatible at this point. Monetary policy can't control what inflates and what doesn't, and if times get really tough, either the Fed reinflates and a bear market in Treasuries ensues, or the U.S. government has insufficient political will to reinflate, and we enter a Japanese spiral of deflationary hell or worse.

Make no mistake: Ultimately, the United States will get its fiscal house in order simply because it must, and the Treasury market bear will take the Standard & Poor's (S&P) to the some grave and deep lows. I theorize that this will decimate high-yield (HY) and leveraged loans, but these instruments haven't seen much outside of a 24-year Treasury bull market, so who knows? Consumer credit will be in a constant downtrend. The financial system will suffer and downsize. A bear market in Treasuries *is* deleveraging manifested. In a more positive sense, the bear market will begin the process of creative destruction.

Gold screaming higher doesn't necessarily imply a doomsday scenario, a currency crisis, or a variant apocalyptic vision. Gold is just a straddle option to hedge government recklessness and theft. It is an instrument to clip the tail risk in otherwise risk-minimal trades because it is an excellent long in times of inflation and deflation. But it's not enough. It generates no income, and it is certainly not without risk itself.

THINKING ABOUT RISKS

Turning even a benign zeitgeist into a trade often doesn't profit because of time inconsistency (noise around the trend nulls the trend over the investment duration), and the information and computational power needed to make a fair prophet is not possible. Sometimes the best remedy for not knowing what is going to happen is to follow Aristotle: Moderation in everything. Have the humility to understand that things don't always work out the way you think. In short, seek minimal risk positions, and make good guesses about the "center" of cross-asset return distributions.

Think about this theoretical example with two risky investments. In box 1, your return is $1 million with 0.5 probability, and you lose $500,000 with 0.5 probability for each of the 365 days of the year. In box 2, you instead get a return of $1 million with 0.9985 probability and lose $500 million with 0.0015 probability each day.

Note that the mean returns for each investment are the same: 365×0.5 in both situations. For the second investment, however, the mean has little value for stating risk. The concentration of risk is completely different. The probability distributions in Figure 2.1 show this.

The world is in Box 2, with losses and gains a function of context-specific shocks. Gold is an instrument to trim risks in the extremes. You also need something to cover in-the-money events.

The U.S. Treasury market is a real-world example of this situation. From a couple of sources I gathered up data on long-dated Treasury yields going back to 1798. Yes, 1798. You find evidence of the kind of

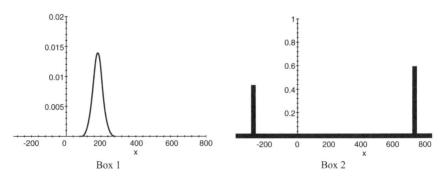

Figure 2.1 Very Different Probability Distributions on Risky Investments.

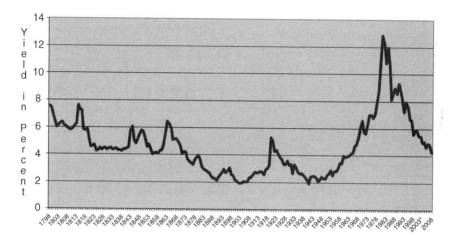

Figure 2.2 **Annual 30-Year Treasury Yields, Constant Maturities, 1789–2008.**
Note: When 30 maturities are unavailable, the nearest maturity yield is used.
Source: Sidney Homer and Richard Sylla, *A History of Interest Rates* (New Brunswick, NJ: Rutgers University Press, 1996). Available at www.federalreserve.gov/releases/h15/data/Annual/H15_TCMNOM_Y30.txt.

probability distribution mixing found in Box 2. Note that yields start becoming 3σ outliers after 1971, after Bretton Woods, but a secular bear market in Treasuries actually began around 1946 (see Figure 2.2).

By examining higher moments using pre/post-1971 as a structural break, there is even more indication of distribution mixing across yields from different time periods. I calculated other points (such as 1935 and 1946) as structural breaks too. Table 2.1 delivers the goods.

Table 2.1 **Moment Statistics for 30-Year Treasury Maturities, Whole History and Selected Structural Breaks**

	1798–2008	1798–1934	Post–Bretton Woods	1935–	1946–
N	211	151	35	71	60
Mean	4.66	4.12	7.73	5.45	6.00
Median	4.37	4.25	4.9	4.91	5.69
Variance	4.35	2.06	7.22	8.16	7.69
Standard deviation	2.09	1.43	2.21	2.86	2.77
Skewness	1.24	0.37	0.7	0.74	0.59
Kurtosis	2.03	−0.70	−0.17	−0.25	−0.30
Coefficient of variation	44.77	34.77	28.62	52.40	46.20

Note that the pre/post statistics vary little in the higher moments, but the first and second moment differences (the mean and variance) completely transform the distribution of Treasury yield history into something with a sharper peak and bigger tail risk than the normal distribution (see the kurtosis stat). The recent high yields also skew the distribution so that it is less symmetric. Such wide within-sample differences are a sign of being in box 2. More to the point, even the de-risking trade du jour has embedded tail risks. Risk minimization demands a hedge against these tail risks, and a preferred trade should have few moving parts, like gold.

RISK ONTOLOGY

Some rules of thumb addressing essential properties for a risk-free trade:

- There should be zero default risk.
- Actual return must equal expected return.
- Liquidity should be robust to reasonable levels of panic and greed.

The first piece of my risk-minimized trade is gold. Gold as a commodity certainly has zero default risk. Supply considerations make its fundamentals impaired: Scarcity conditions are inherent to commodities. But gold possesses something worse than reinvestment risk. It generates no income. Further, the transactions costs associated with gold (less so exchange-traded funds) make it somewhat illiquid. This is why gold is always a good hedge in a fiat money system. As a monetary metal, sustained deflation drives people to buy it as the soundest money possible. It is also a good inflation hedge.

The second part is U.S. Treasuries. Treasuries are not exactly free of default risk, but they are close. This is not because they have superior fundamentals. It is because the Federal Reserve controls currency printing and acts in concert with the U.S. Treasury in a crisis. In nominal terms, they will always be able to fulfill their obligations, and a default event is replaced by an inflationary dilution. Treasuries have inherent reinvestment risk, but this risk is lessened by their coupons, which commodities do not have. Finally, as far as liquidity goes, Treasuries exhibit much more than gold.

That said, technical factors (mainly issuance) for Treasuries are absolutely terrible. The U.S. Treasury market is the necessary liquidity sump pump that glues the current system together. Unlimited capital flows are absorbed within it, and no amount of American planned economic transformation has put much dent in it (so far). It is an architectural wonder of the modern world.

One could make the case that Treasuries are rendered more risk-free through credit-default swaps (CDS). But I believe that long CDS trades on Treasuries are not safe because counterparties will be hard pressed to pay if a default triggers the CDS. These trades have many moving parts, such as daily marking and collateral management. Simplicity that balances the complexity of the financial system is desirable.

There is fundamental and technical strength in the two forces that drive human systems: hierarchical redistribution and interpersonal exchange. Treasuries are shaking hands with a system that has concentrated acid for blood. Face it, the world economic system is shaped by raw exercise of power as much as by mutually advantageous economic exchange. You cannot escape the fact that the dollar—with all its faults—is the reserve currency of the world by virtue of the U.S. government's military power and its ability to tax the living daylights out of its subjects.

Your straddle, gold, impersonally tells the existing system to kiss your derriere. This trade is satisfying in so many ways.

There is no perfectly risk-free asset. Gold may have been a store of value for 5,000 years, but Treasuries have remarkable resilience as well. The full force and ability of the United States is based on a functioning Treasury market. Quantitative easing is the mechanism used to protect the Treasury market from costly propping up of bank cronies who have captured the state in a bread-and-circuses-late-Roman-Empire-kill-the-middle-class gambit, but when it comes down to it, easing will end.

TREASURIES AREN'T GREY GOOSE, BUT THEY AREN'T POPOV IN A PLASTIC BOTTLE EITHER

If foreign countries stop buying our debt, yields will rise, and domestic buyers will incrementally increase Treasuries in their portfolios. This will compensate for some of the rising inventory of this paper. At the same time, federal, state, and municipal bonds will go on a well-needed austerity budget because there is no alternative. Mind you, "austere" only compared with the current insane levels of government spending we now burn through. Current trends are unsustainable, so they'll change. Hopefully in the ways I indicated.

Treasuries aren't the best investment in the world. I won't argue with you there, but I am looking at the issue from the perspective of existence. Some economic institutions will implode or atrophy, but that doesn't mean everything will be wiped away. Treasuries have a good shot at staying around. With unemployment at 10 percent, record delinquencies, credit imploding, and crude close to nominal highs, there's probably going to be another demand shock and collapse. Treasuries with a coupon certainly aren't the worst investment.

Given tremendous deflationary forces, a bear market in Treasuries isn't set in stone, nor is it necessarily imminent. It is also very likely that foreign countries won't stop buying our Treasuries. Countries that run an export surplus will not change strategy when global demand is fragile, and exports will suffer when a currency becomes too strong. So exchange-rate targeting will persist as the primary end of monetary policy in emerging markets. Make no mistake, a rise in the risk-free rate (Treasury yields of some maturity) will unravel the whole world. Whether you are pricing an AAA CDO or a roadside food vendor in Thailand, the U.S. Treasury yield is embedded in the calculation. I believe that policymakers understand this. In the short-term, therefore, expect self-interest to keep Treasury yields propped up in the following ways:

- Foreign central bank support for Treasuries will remain as long as exchange-rate targeting remains.
- Treasury volatility usually doesn't explode like equity volatility (crossed fingers)—it builds inertia over time with slower decay.
- Taylor rule considerations apply whether quantitative easing (QE) stays or goes.

Simply because a situation is grim doesn't mean that the causes of the trouble can't change. Governments often remedy fiscal imbalances by cutting spending and raising taxes. It is not because they want to or because it is the right thing to do but because they must. The merciless logic of markets demands it if they want access to capital.

CAPITAL DECONSTRUCTION

There is little creative destruction—much less deleveraging—to be seen in the developed world in the recession of the first decade of the 2000s. Instead, governments of the world responded to the threat with nationalization and capital dilution. So their hapless subjects will take the divine hammer in the end.

But nothing, nothing escapes the Dao. Excessive government debt issuance will end the bureaucratic manipulation of Treasuries one way or another. With the Congressional Budget Office (CBO) projecting $14 trillion in Treasury securities held by the public in 2019,[1] it is unlikely that foreign purchasers will fill the financing gap. More likely, foreign purchasers will foster internal domestic consumption because the U.S. consumer is in the process of paying down debt, repairing balance sheets, and saving money. This will reduce external surpluses, reduce the need to force down exchange rates, and accumulate Treasury reserves.

So what is a crooked government to do? It will follow the centuries-old pattern of history: stealing from bondholders, of course. The modern, preferred method of theft is inflation. Since so many foreign central bank are the bondholders, there is little political pressure to protect their rights. China knows this and has moved in the past few months from short maturities to reducing Treasury holdings outright.[2]

A TREASURY BEAR MARKET WITH QE CREATING AN EXTENDED TOP

It is true that we've never seen such a massive display of government recklessness and engineered capital destruction to write down debt burdens. But I've also not seen such an unstable termite mound of Ponzi finance poised to collapse and smother everyone and everything in deflation faster than a million printing presses.

For these reasons, a good risk-minimal position is gold and 10-year Treasuries (10s). The 5s/10s range on the yield curve got

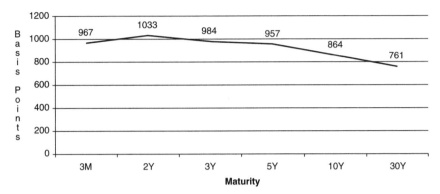

Figure 2.3 **Peak-to-Trough Yield Changes in February 1997 to September 1981 Treasury Bear Market.**

slaughtered the least on a relative basis in the truly awful bear market of 1977–1981, which holds cognitive bias for me. From trough to peak, in the 1977–1981 bear market, yields on 10s exploded by 864 basis points (see Figure 2.3). But it was worse for shorter maturities. Treasury inflation-protected securities (TIPS) issuance, if increased significantly, introduces tangible default risk in the trade.

There is also real risk in gold too because it is leveraged through the nose. However, as the ultimate convergence point for hedging government action, you really can't get too far away from it.

I'm open-minded about tinkering with the duration. Taking on a long-maturity steepener lowers certain risks, but this depends on timing. Alternatively, one could take a position in more pure inflation commodity hedges (such as oil or sugar). On the deflation side, one could long Treasuries further on the yield curve and add commodity hedges uncorrelated to gross domestic product (GDP) change (do your research).

There is real risk in Treasuries. There is real risk in gold. Together they work well.

Should one hoard Hormel and ammo and default on every obligation except the Nevada cave dwelling? Only if you think you can handle it without losing your mind. The rest of us grasshoppers should aim for humility, calm, and balance. Even abrupt change is evolution not revolution, and risk-minimized trades help to make it all look normal-ish as time goes by.

CHAPTER 3

Par Value during the Black Plague: Treasuries Are Financial Teflon

Silver has its place. It's an industrial metal, has a nice correlation with equities, and has been used as money for thousands of years. This combination of industrial demand and investment demand makes its price somewhat erratic. But don't think that silver currency (or the gold standard) is an effective way to handcuff government theft. As long as there have been silver coins circulating, there was a crooked mint debasing them to its advantage. The *Tungsten effect* (where tungsten bars are plated with gold and passed off as bullion bars) is the rule, not the exception. Historically, the most common metal in coinage was lead. This is simply the nature of things. Cash of any kind exhibits exponential decay, a half-life.

Currency functions as a way to pay off liabilities so that your real assets stay yours and don't revert to someone else. Real safety is found in paying your taxes.

The strongest discipline imposed on a state is not connected to its currency. Iron discipline stems from credit. The government bond market is the crown jewel of any state. A state will torch its constitution before it lets its bond market get crushed. Choosing between bond market creditors and a statutory obligation is like choosing to repair a ruptured jugular instead of getting a face lift. Treasury paper default shouldn't be a worry to anyone just yet. As long as the United States is around, there will be Treasuries paper earning income, however meager. Let me say this in another way: If the Treasury market goes, so does the United States—and pretty much everything else with it.

Whence flows this confidence? Because government bond markets have seen much worse than anything you or I have known in our lifetimes. Government bond markets have seen things a thousand times worse than the Great Depression. Ditto the Great Panic of 1873. In fact, they show incredible resilience in a hell's-coming-with-me scenario that most people probably can't easily imagine. More than resilience, they follow a predictable dynamic (and did even 700 years ago). You see, there was a penultimate black swan at the very top of the capital structure in a period when just about everything from the human forge was destroyed.

Since the commercial revolution began, the interbank market has always been the quiet and demure core of the world economy, but it is government bond markets that dominate everything economic, and they are the ones full of interesting memory.

THE REAL WORST-CASE SCENARIO

Start with superbanks that produced financial innovation in loans, bonds, insurance, and equity markets. A legal system equipped them with capital structure and freedom of contract. There was a carry trade optionalized by forward contracts and arbitraged in Antwerp and London[1]: the Venedetto ducat/Genovesi pound. Derivatives were written by the Bardi and Peruzzi investment houses, two megacompanies that had the combined business lines of Goldman Sachs, Exxon Mobil, and Newmont Mining, only 10 times the relative net worth.[2] These banks were embedded in an integrated world economy with persistent trade imbalances between Europe and Asia. These imbalances doggedly threatened to destroy everything. Welcome to the medieval Venetian Republic circa 1285–1400.

The complexity of the Medieval Mediterranean economy was comparable with our own time. And then the system went into pure meltdown. For starters, one third of Europe's humans died from the black plague. World trade collapsed for generations. Supply chains that provided raw materials were completely destroyed by Mongols. Although the ducat was a great reserve currency, the hoarded silver coins still lost 20 percent of their silver content within one's lifetime.[3] Foreign nations threatened the existence of the republic multiple times. For a century, Venetian military power wasted itself in a never-ending series of small-scale conflicts to gain commercial concessions. Radical political change made a council of 10 tyrants the rulers of the republic, and they, in turn, used a doge to enforce martial law. Civil war culminated in execution of the doge on the palace lawn. Nations that imported Venetian manufactured goods became protectionist and forbade foreigners from retailing goods.

All these factors led to utter financial collapse. There were only a handful of mind-bogglingly powerful international banks, and the two largest went bankrupt because of leveraged loans to the emerging markets of England and France, who used the loans to kill each other. Although Venice remained an unquestioned world-class military, financial, and commercial power, there were only two large-scale social institutions that avoided systemic meltdown and complete reconfiguration: property rights and the bond market.

PAR-VALUE LAWS OF MOTION

Guess what? Despite it all, you just couldn't kill Venetian "govvies." Sure, there were bear markets that make ours look like kid stuff, but there also were times when the debt traded for higher than par value. I charted the worst century in recorded economic history for you in Figure 3.1. Records are incomplete, but there are enough data for a human eyeball to see trends. Cubic spline interpolation using *Mathematica* didn't add anything. Owing to the missing data, I didn't attempt to extract any information about the process's sequence distribution.

There are no known records of the yield on these securities.[4] Rates may have been uniform across time, making the yield a function of par discounting; determined by the amount of paper creditors'

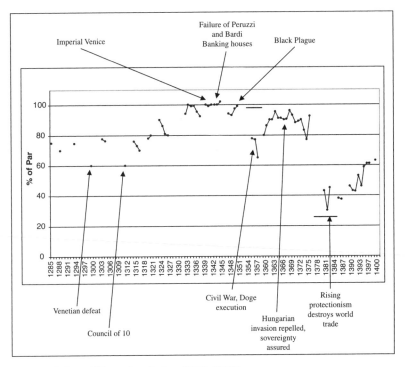

Figure 3.1 **Price of Venetian Debt, 1285–1400.**
Source: G. LUZZATTO, Il debito pubblico della Repubblica di Venezia (Milan 1963).

assumed; or set by one's political status. Term maturity was one year, which explains some of the volatility. Longer-term debt was securitized (*compera*) or had an annuity structure (*renta*). As such, there was no yield curve, but there was a roll that traders kept their eyes on.

It was a completely domestic market. Foreigners were not allowed, in theory, to be creditors to the state. While this did not optimize liquidity, it did create strong mechanisms to ensure creditor rights and (as far as I know) made default rare.

Venetian sovereign debt had bear markets, hitting generational lows in times of *extreme sovereign risk*, from 1285 to 1310 and in the late 1350s. Debt traded at a low 60 percent of par when Venice was decisively defeated by its rival Genoa at Curzola and also when the Council of Ten took over. It dropped close to this when near civil war got their equivalent of a president executed on the palace lawn.

Secular bull markets occurred during times of political stability. Following imposition of oligarchy, the bond market began a 35-year secular bull market, peaking at the height of Venetian commercial/colonial power.

Extreme financial stress (more than you've ever seen) even can smash the top tier of capital structure (1345-1360). Starting sometime around 1345, total systemic collapse of the financial system, the realization of human depopulation, and political strife culminating in civil war didn't drop bond prices to historic lows! The four horsemen of the apocalypse hate bonds but less so than most other human contrivances. Maybe it's coincidence, but bonds never recovered, even 60 years after the financial system died.

Deflation makes risk-free risky. Even though there is no knowledge of yields on these securities, it seems reasonable that in periods of ultra-deflation, cash [α (lead) + (1 − α)(silver), $0 \leq \alpha \leq 1$] outperformed bonds, and bondholders had their asses handed to them medieval-style. Even controlled devaluation of currency value by the issuers can't keep up with strong deflation effects. I theorize that this due to default risk or outright defaults, but there is no recorded evidence of default.

It took politically engineered destruction of world trade to take bond prices to their all-time lows (1375–1400). In 1392, it became officially forbidden for foreigners to retail goods in England, but such was unofficially common across Western Europe. This pretty much ensured the destruction of trade-based maritime economies, as well as worker-bee living standards.

EXTREME DEFLATION'S NASTY SURPRISE: U.S. TREASURIES ARE THE BEST ASSET CLASS, BUT THEY'RE NOT VINTAGE VALPOLICELLA EITHER

Then, as now, derivative contracts existed to control swings in prices of the underlying. However, most contracts were settled by physical delivery, not cash. They existed because of high costs in transporting goods, for example, from Constantinople to Venice via Florentine letter of credit to transact in Antwerp to London. Today, this is not so. Cash settlement in derivatives exceeds the underlying physical market, and the divergence is of such a magnitude that derivatives are increasingly more important to prices than actual supply and demand. This is the profoundly deflationary driver of modern finance because it diverts money from hoarding oil, gold, and real stuff into paper.

Then, as now, having a reserve currency (and Venice had a good one, too) means that your sovereign debt is capital structure king—the safest place to park cash. However, U.S. Treasury auctions are different from any other government bond market ever in existence: They are the most rigged in history. They have to be—Treasuries are the liquidity sump pump for the whole galaxy. Pricing is artificial in that Treasuries are instruments to target export-oriented economy exchange rates relative to the dollar. Par value is completely unconnected to yield or risk considerations. This is just the nonderivative side of the trade.

Further, modern Brownian motion finance has one-upped anything that has come before it. It is not just commodities that are manipulated by speculative flows. Because minimal-risk trades are positions of minute advantage, incredible leverage is used to maximize return. This is one reason why over-the-counter (OTC) interest-rate derivatives are around $420 trillion notional.[5] The sheer size of the collapse makes the whole thing too big to fail and, at the same time, a scary failure if it happened.

Rigged markets can last more than a human lifespan. *Since the whole world has skin in the game, a Treasury default is an extremely low-probability event with high damage potential.* Even if it suddenly became unrigged, the Treasury market won't die, although a lot of institutions surrounding it might. No apocalypse here, ladies and gentlemen. It will just align to fundamentals, and bondholders will get the divine hammer.

Instead, government stupidity renders Treasury paper fundamentals like Swiss cheese—full of holes. The ball and chain of fundamentals imply that bond prices are going down because there's not enough capital to absorb a Congressional Budget Office (CBO)–projected $19 trillion in Treasury issuance by 2019. U.S. Treasuries may outperform anything else, but percent of par still will go down. Soon after, issuance will drop and tax rates rise. "QEasing" sufficient to make a difference will only drive bond prices lower because of inflation expectations and currency risk. The Treasury market will survive just fine and do better than just about anything else. It is government-provided services that will be on the receiving end of a transformation.

The worst historical stress test I could find shows that in extreme deflation, cash (read $) can beat even the best credit. It doesn't matter if cash is silver or goldfish or pancakes. Nanosecond maturity on the yield curve is king when the system is in complete meltdown.

One can throw out North Korea or Pol Pot or Juenger's *Der Arbeiter* as a thought experiment in how bad things can get, but there is negligible "caveman risk" in our collective future. Accept difficult, complicated realities with painful, unsatisfying solutions. Silver coins won't fix the problem because (1) governments monopolize currency, (2) governments always screw over the honeybees and drones for their gain, and last but not least, (3) power always finds a way. So shake hands with it and hope that it doesn't mug you.

CHAPTER 4

Stretch to Farthest Point Known: Thoughts on a Hyperinflation Event

At most points in time and space, predictions tend to fail—except the lucky ones. So it's good to think through scenarios that one would even consider *extremely* remote. Active risk management means that low-probability, high-catastrophic-outcome tail events must be hedged and, just as important, gain exposure to those pesky black swans in ways that lead to advantage. To accomplish this, it helps to obtain a quantitative sense of their impact—to get a "feel for the cloth," as a wise former boss of mine used to say. So let's try here.

HYPERINFLATION AND CURRENCY CRISIS

What if the Fed more than succeeds in reflating and the end result is *hyperinflation*? As remote a possibility as I think this is, the Fed really *could* print a way to another, completely inflationary type of economic destruction. All it has to do is print proactively, not reactively.

Hyperinflation is rare but not inconceivable. It happened on multiple occasions in the last century alone. It is indicative of extreme government failure as the state fails to perform a most basic function: monopoly provision of acceptable currency.

Above all, hyperinflation shows that humankind holds closely some constants that will endure, even though the world around us never stops changing. Even in hyperinflation, life doesn't lose all its familiar contours.

FORGET ARGENTINA 2002 . . .

Imagine a country carrying a crippling amount of external debt. Its core financial intermediary system remains on life support at best; at worst, it is an explicit arm of government policy. The central government and its affiliates control a large portfolio of residential and commercial real estate and further subsidize the housing market through administratively controlled interest rates.

Banks with large loan books and scale are iteratively recapitalized as losses are realized and become wards of the state, with increased political control over their operations. Smaller banking entities increasingly do not exist through liquidation or absorption into a special-purpose vehicle that allocates credit on an uneconomic basis to specialized industries.

Industries with "strategic value" (read political connections) are completely nationalized, with taxpayer-forced liability to cover the cash burn. Further, these socialized businesses compete with private businesses with smaller economies of scale that do not have the luxury of taxpayer-funded advertising budgets or a creditor that doesn't care about funding loss-making enterprises through tax revenues.

To cover the increasing losses of all these commitments—in particular, government losses on assets related to the mortgage market—the central government resorts to the printing press in real force. A market forms to price in capital and exchange controls. The currency is no longer used, and people practice *currency substitution*, the use of another nation's currency as a store of value and, in some cases, the medium of exchange. The combined mass exodus from the currency and hypermonetized national debt causes the inevitable—hyperinflation.

Is this the story of the United States in 2012 or Poland in 1989?

There's a lot of difference, of course. The United States doesn't have exchange-rate and capital controls (yet). The degree of nationalization isn't as endemic to our economy. There is a thin veneer glossing over similar aspects of our political culture. But there are some strong similarities as well.

Importantly, the Poles realized that there was something unique and historic about their macroeconomics of decontrol/disintegration. To record knowledge of their fate—and to preserve the jobs of as many bureaucrats as possible—the government statistical service preserved the minutest details on a monthly basis.

The data source is various issues of the *Biuletyn Statystyczny*, the Polish household budgetary survey that consisted of a rotating 8,000 households in Poland. Just so you know, through 1990, it excluded the self-employed as well as households of persons involved in military or police service, so there was an underreporting of self-employed entrepreneurs.

READING THE BONES IN POLAND 1989 . . .

The Polish hyperinflation was a short-lived event, but in the space of one year, inflation rocketed up 300 percent. After the huge acceleration shock, price increases only decelerate, but they don't decline. Note in Figure 4.1 that there were only seven months of real hyperinflationary explosion. After that, prices stubbornly increased, but there were no seismic events.

The data suggest that *modern currency collapses don't mean that dollars or zlotys or any other bearer bond with no coupon goes the way of the dodo completely, even in hyperinflation*. What you get instead is currency reform—a "new and improved" bearer bond with no coupon in exchange for the old one (an extreme haircut at redemption) and high real and nominal interest rates (if there isn't currency reform, that toilet paper can hang around as a unit of account for some time).

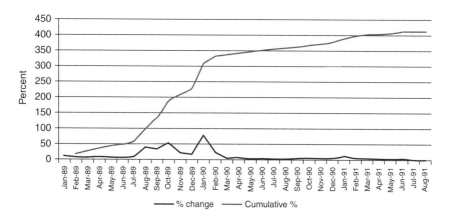

Figure 4.1 **What Hyperinflation Looks Like: Poland in Collapse.**

Exchange Rates and Capital Controls

Shorting the currency would seem to be a no-brainer here. However, there's a high probability of a snag: capital controls and "official" exchange rates—currency inconvertibility (see Figure 4.2). Such measures would screw up straightforward and profitable currency shorting, but the data show that they don't work to dampen inflation. People are cunning, and they develop work-arounds to a dying currency. Even if citizens must accept said currency as legal tender, they

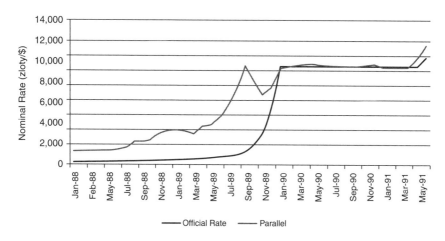

Figure 4.2 **Capital Controls Are Ineffective: Poland 1988–May 1991.**

develop efficient ways to off-load it using market mechanisms. Note the price discovery on the black market for zlotys (Polish currency) before and after the exchange rate finds a hard peg, when interest rates start to bite.

Cost of Living

This is where the "minute detail" comes in. The household survey discussed earlier captured consumer prices by category during hyperinflation. The results show that hyperinflation is the ultimate in living for the now. As prices for basic necessities go through the roof, the prices of nonessentials collapse. Not only is capital stored in currency destroyed, but the cost for food outstrips other consumer categories. For the record, *nonfoodstuffs* means clothing and shoes and electrical/mechanical goods for the home; *entertainment* means newspaper expenditures, books (including school books), movies, and related items such as concerts; fuel (heating oil and gasoline) is not included. Subsidies and usage differences make such comparisons inadequate anyway because few had a car when Polish communism collapsed. Take a look at Figure 4.3, which shows the main budgetary categories of consumer prices in hyperinflation in Poland in 1989, 1990, and 1991.

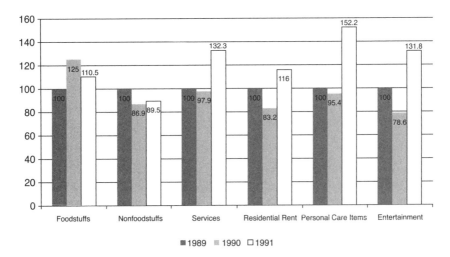

Figure 4.3 **Consumer Prices in Hyperinflation: Main Budgetary Categories.**

There are some clear and profitable conclusions to this section. Food (and fuel) is how one will profit in the initial stages of a hyperinflation, even as rents and nonfood consumer goods collapse. This is due to the fixed nature of rental arrangements, and the "immiserizing"[1] effect whereby inflation takes luxury goods out of reach. Items for immediate consumption are the ones that really jack up. After the initial inflation shock, returns on other goods surpass those on foodstuffs.

The biggest defect of the comparison is the exclusion of petrochemical usage because it was a heavily subsidized and differently used commodity in communist and transitional Poland. It is safe to assume that gasoline and distillates in general would be most sensitive to any type of inflation shock.

INFLATION EQUATIONS

However, you could hedge inflation risk through U.S. consumer price index (CPI) futures settled in another currency over the counter (OTC). So let's assume that one is associated with Taleb's Universa Investments[2] and wants an explicit hedge to a hyperinflation event. Consider the following inflation option-like product: a nonstream cap security with a strike at x percent inflation. Think of such a cap as a call option on the inflation rate implied by the CPI. I know, I know, it is not exactly an option in that the CPI isn't a tradable product.

Using some modified Royal Bank of Scotland (RBS) methodology[3] or Barclay's[4] for less exotic inflation caps, the payout is

$$N\psi i \left\{ \omega \left[\frac{I(T_i)}{I(T_{i-1})} - 1 - \kappa \right] \right\}^{+}$$

where N is the notional, κ is the strike, ω is 1 for a cap (–1 for a floor), and θ is the contract-year fraction for the interval T_{i-1} to T_i. Retrofitting with the data earlier shows that quarterly fractioning is efficient. $I(T)$ is inflation at time T, measured by CPI. In the case of a nonstream cap such as here, T_{i-1} resolves to T_0.

For pricing, assume away counterparty, institutional, rounding, and seasonality risk. The pricing formula is rather complicated, similar to a cliquet option.

$$
\omega N \psi_i P_n(t,\,T_i) E_n^{T_i} \left\{ \frac{\mathcal{G}_i(T_{i-1})}{\mathcal{G}_{i-1}(T_{i-1})} \; \Phi\left[\omega \; \frac{\ln \dfrac{\mathcal{G}_i(T_{i-1})}{K\mathcal{G}_{i-1}(T_{i-1})} + \dfrac{1}{2}\sigma^2_{I,i}(T_i - T_{i-1})}{\sigma_{I,i}\sqrt{T_i - T_{i-1}}} \right] \right.
$$

$$
\left. - K\Phi\left[\omega \; \frac{\ln \dfrac{\mathcal{G}_i(T_{i-1})}{K\mathcal{G}_{i-1}(T_{i-1})} - \dfrac{1}{2}\sigma^2_{I,i}(T_i - T_{i-1})}{\sigma_{I,i}\sqrt{T_i - T_{i-1}}} \right] \,\middle|\, \mathcal{F}_t \right\}
$$

Formula aside, I'm not sure what kind of quote you would get from a derivatives broker for a hyperinflation cap. For options on inflation, one generally has to rely on quotes from brokers such as ICAP,[5] and brokers apply a mark-up.

CHAPTER 5

The Macreconomics of Decontrol: Multisigma Sovereign Risk

Everyone knows the current global economic order and that the global imbalancing act is unsustainable. So it will change. The most interesting aspect of the coming change is its nature, which is unclear. What can be counted on is that unsustainable phenomena such as current account imbalances, negative savings rates, and seeming infinite asset price appreciation will correct. One way or another, falling savings rates and rising deficits become rising savings and falling deficits.

The tail-risk killers at the Fed and other central banks are conditioned by training and organizational culture to think they are all-powerful. They are not. Nor are they able to influence all economic effects as they intend. More often than not, the major result of monetary policy is unintended consequences. Their power rests in their ability to transfer financial-system risk into a category of sovereign risk and the sovereign risk of one country onto another country. Nothing more magical than that. This transfer ability is finite and

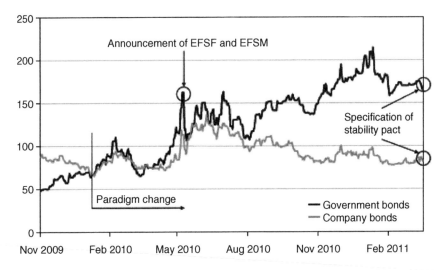

Figure 5.1   **Credit-Default Swaps (CDSs) on Government and Company Bonds (Europe).**

ultimately self-defeating when wealth is eroded past a certain threshold. In fact, the unintended consequences of such policies are clear in the European Union: The credit risk of government bonds is greater than the credit risk of corporate bonds embodied in credit-default swaps (see Figure 5.1).

When quants have to price complicated assets, they start by finding an asset most like the one to be priced and then applying risk premia to it based on the perceived differences. This approach makes it possible to extrapolate from the present to the future: One finds comparable past behavior, identifies differences, and follows future trajectories. It doesn't always work, but it provides a reference point with which to tinker. Thus, in this case, the approach is to find a time and place where sovereign credit risk exceeds corporate credit risk.

Newer measures such as credit-default swap (CDS) spreads have information content but also limitations: Counterparty risk, cross-hedging, and market-maker behavior jointly determine CDS spreads to some extent. But the widening in selected sovereign CDS spreads is also in part the result of government guarantees on domestic financial liabilities and not just the guarantees of other sovereign liabilities.

Another measure for this is bond yields. It is clear that sovereign bond yields exceeding same maturity corporate paper is a historical signal of a sovereign exceeding its limits. Policies that attempt to distort pricing of credit-sensitive assets only transfer risk, but there is always a payback.

TAKE-AWAYS

The past provides a prologue for these kinds of paybacks, and its message is clear:

- Sovereigns shouldn't take their privilege for granted because sovereign irresponsibility makes high-grade corporate debt more attractive than government paper.
- Government policy normalization is inevitable and restores sovereign credit spread norms. The "commitment to irresponsibility" is a farce.
- In an age of austerity budgets, one should get used to seeing inverted yield curves.
- You don't need negative inflation to invert the yield curve. Decelerating price expectations appear to be sufficient.
- A democracy can and does endure inverted yield curves for extended periods of time.

Governments always have a trump card up their sleeve with respect to their domiciled businesses: the ability to tax them whether business is good or bad. This is the core reason why only in short-lived extremes do corporate bonds trade rich to sovereigns.

ISSUE: YIELD-CURVE INVERSION

When talking about bond term structures, an inverted curve typically is viewed as a problem. This is understandable because inversion often means the present is a disaster—but it doesn't necessarily mean that. It simply can mean that the present looks better than a dreary future. Maybe the real problem with curve inversions is that we aren't used to them anymore. Such inversions were the rule, not the exception, for a chunk of the nineteenth century. That chunk in many ways resembles our own difficult present—and maybe our future. Shades of the "new" normal lie in this past.

By definition, an inverted curve means that there is a lower yield on longer-term bonds than on shorter-term bonds. Inside our plastic-fantastic world, we are conditioned to think that inversion simply implies an expectation of persistent deflation. Looking outside conventional wisdom, an inverted yield curve speaks to larger issues. Inflation expectations are a part of the matter, but significant change to any factor that affects an economy's capacity to profitably absorb capital drives interest rates just as much. Among these factors are

- Government's role in allocating resources
- Capital and labor mobility
- Changes in demography
- Technological innovation and its diffusion
- Policy rates, liquidity conditions, and the monetary standard

When these factors work together to generate a steep yield curve, they create positive feedback and can generate bubble valuations. Also, invariably, such bubbles burst, and negative feedback takes over. The nineteenth-century United States frequently saw such boom and bust cycles: 1866, 1873, 1878, and 1890. The last century had a bust that everyone knows from grandpa's stories: the Great Depression.

CONTEXT

Let's take a look at the time period of 1862–1879: the greenback era. The United States recovery from a destructive Civil War was incomplete. Post–Civil War reconstruction and economic expansion to the West created massive capital investments in railroads. Overinvestment and overleverage resulted in multiple panics and crashes. Banks suspended gold redemption in 1861–1862 and resumed gold redemption only by federal mandate in 1879.

Aside from massive government budget deficits and quantitative easing, there were a number of similarities to our own time. The monetary regime differed little from our own post–Bretton Woods system. The greenback era was a time of decelerating inflation, diminishing profits, wholesale prices, and *massive sovereign risk.*

When reviewing the published records of the middle to late 1800s, you get a sense of the entrepreneurship of the data collectors, even at the government level. In many cases, they reported only data that made sense for the conditions immediately at hand, not for the sake of posterity. As a result, definitions changed, and time series ran for a few years and then were never seen again. Frederick Macauley (of "Macauley duration" fame) and David Durand deserve a great deal of credit for reconstructing much of the data presented in this chapter.

The United States was an industrializing economy absorbing massive international and domestic capital inflows. But *the productivity of this capital, measured by increased earnings, diminished over the entire period, as shown in Figure 5.2.*

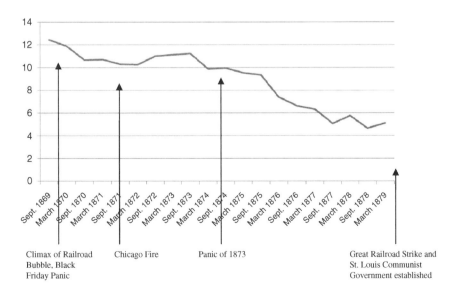

Figure 5.2   **Earnings-to-Capital Ratios, 1869–1879.**
Source: Annual Report of the Comptroller of the Currency, 1879.

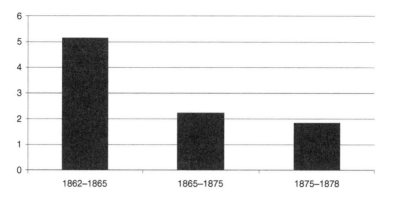

Figure 5.3 **Percent Growth Rate of Wholesale Prices, 1862–1878.**
Source: Historical Statistics of the United States, 1st ed., series app. 24.

DIMINISHING PROFITABILITY AND INCREASING SOCIETAL PRESSURES

While inflation was very high during the Civil War, it decelerated dramatically on the war's conclusion, along with declining capital productivity. The Warren-Pearson Index of Wholesale Prices demonstrates that after what appears to be a rapid price deceleration spell, wholesale prices were pretty stable over the period from 1865 to 1875. From 1875 to 1878, wholesale prices again decelerated (see Figure 5.3). *Overall, the secular trend was not deflation: It was sometimes hard and fast, sometimes a slow grind of price increase deceleration.*

As for bonds, the longest standard duration was six years. From 1867 to 1878, *there was a long secular trend of declining yields on the long end of government and corporate debt. Corporate debt had lower yields than government debt* (mainly the Pennsylvania, Hudson River, New York Central, and Camden & Amboy railroads) for several years following the Civil War and had equivalent yields for a good chunk of the time period.

PERVERSE CREDIT RISK, REVERSE CROWDING OUT

As for yield curves, constructing a yield curve is not straightforward when you don't have a Treasury market to soak up every possible free dollar (see Figure 5.4).

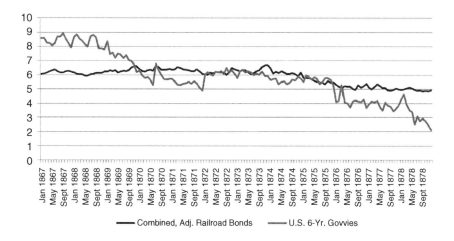

Figure 5.4   Yields on 6-Year Railroad Bonds and 6-Year Treasuries.
Source: Frederick Macauley, *Some Theoretical Problems Suggested by the Movement of Interest Rates, Bond Yields, and Stock Price in the United States Since 1856* (New York: National Bureau of Economic Research, 1938).

The aforementioned Frederick Macauley (of Macauley duration fame) and David Durand constructed annual yield curves using the most liquid paper available within the 1862–1879 and 1880–1929 time frames. How Macauley did it makes sense, but there were difficulties. Rating agencies didn't exist. Treasury issuance was chaotic, going from bursts of quantitative easing to finance the Civil War to sporadic auctions of an austerity budget. All debt was illiquid because the United States was an emerging market at the time. So Macauley used commercial paper yields as a reasonably liquid representation of the short end of the debt market and six-year railroad bond yields as representative of the long end. Durand in 1900 to 1929 had a simpler task. He looked at the yields on one-year-maturity investment-grade corporate bonds and the yield curves associated with them.

History may rhyme, but every generation has its novel wrinkles. Here we see the prevalence of inverted yield curves.

SO HOW COMMON WAS AN INVERTED YIELD CURVE?

From 1862 to 1878, the median interest rate on one-year commercial paper was 7.56 percent. Yields higher than this were associated with an

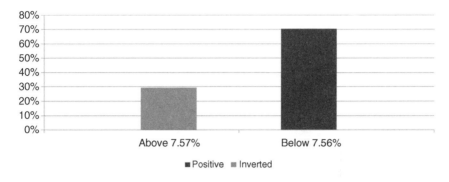

Figure 5.5   **Type of Yield Curve Associated with One-Year Commercial Paper Yields, 1862–1879.**

Source: Frederick Macauley, *Some Theoretical Problems Suggested by the Movement of Interest Rates, Bond Yields, and Stock Price in the United States Since 1856* (New York: National Bureau of Economic Research, 1938).

inverted yield curve. When yields were below this median, the associated yield curve was typically positive.

Over the 17 years of this period, yield curves inverted 29.4 percent of the time (see Figure 5.5).

The period 1880 to 1929 has its own share of ups and downs, but it was structurally different from the greenback era. It had a stable gold standard. Reconstruction was complete. The economy was slowly working through the epic panic and resulting bust of 1873. Policymaker pandering was of the "never again" variety.

For this period, the interquartile range on one-year commercial paper yields was 4.21 to –5.4 percent. When commercial paper yields were higher than 5.4 percent, the yield curve inverted. When yields were below 4.21 percent, the yield curve was positive. Within the interquartile range, the yield curve was inverted 76.4 percent of the time. Across the entire range, the yield curve was inverted 64.7 percent of the time (see Figure 5.6).

One-year investment-grade debt during 1900–1929 shows the same general features (see Figure 5.7). However, the yields on the investment-grade (IG) debt continued to compress. (Caution: We should exercise great care in making historical comparisons, as there can be duration

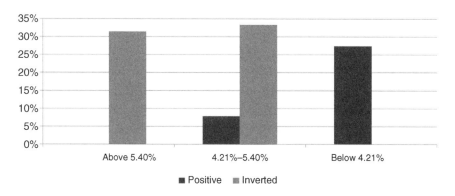

Figure 5.6   **Type of Yield Curve Associated with One-Year Commercial Paper Yields, 1880–1929.**
Source: Frederick Macauley, *Some Theoretical Problems Suggested by the Movement of Interest Rates, Bond Yields, and Stock Price in the United States Since 1856* (New York: National Bureau of Economic Research, 1938).

mismatches and inaccuracies in data from the nineteenth century.) Yield-curve inversion isn't as common using these data points (it occurs around 35 percent of the time).

Keep in mind that the United States was an emerging market at the time. Now it is at the epicenter of the global economy. The railroad

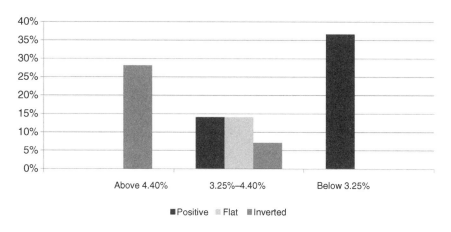

Figure 5.7   **Type of Yield Curve Associated with One-Year, Investment-Grade (IG) Bond Yields, 1900–1929.**
Source: David Durand, "Basic Yields of Corporate Bonds, 1900–1942," *NBER Technical Paper No. 3,* 1942.

bonds at the time were the most liquid high-quality paper around, but one can't extrapolate what their corresponding credit rating would be equivalent to today.

Above all, there is a powerful reversion to the mean effect to be observed. Governments can remain reckless only for so long before they collapse, or democratic process saves the day. The longer the delay, the more painful mean reversion becomes.

CHAPTER 6

Weightless Waiting for the Deflation Descent

Way-back machines don't just offer visions of the extremes. They set a framework for understanding reality. Simple pattern recognition can be right or wrong. Combined with logic and human reason, it is a powerful way to summon the muse. If inflation is fiery and vibratory, then deflation is cold and numbing. Get ready for an icy forecast.

DEFLATION AND CARRY TRADE: FROZEN EAST

A *carry trade* is a short funding currency, long target currency position that takes advantage of interest-rate differentials. Unfortunately, high interest rates typically go hand in hand with interest-rate and exchange-rate volatility, creating conditions for an unwind crash as the money heads out of risk and back home. A return crash in financial terms typically means that volatility is low for a long time and then spikes in short order.

Low inflation makes for low interest-rate returns and a weak currency, which are the essential ingredients for a carry trade in the first place. Kurtosis and skewness specify the nature of how such a carry trade will unwind. The skewness in interest-rate differentials shows

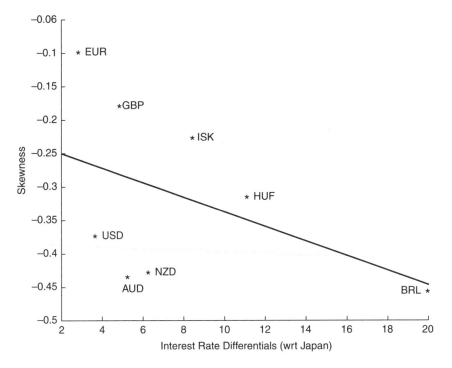

Figure 6.1   **Interest-Rate Differential Skewness, Japanese Yen to a Currency Basket, 1996–2008.**

how symmetric the probability measure is (see Figure 6.1). Options traders understand skew well because it affects the price of buying a call to offset the price of buying a put.

Kurtosis measures the thickness of probability distribution tails. Thicker tails imply greater likelihood of extreme events. Positive kurtosis implies a peaked probability measure and higher chances of an extreme event going down. Using data from the Japanese carry trade, the negative skewness shows that the impact of the unwind is negative for a number of target currencies from 1996 to 2008. You also see the currencies with the highest kurtosis in Figure 6.2.

Combining positive kurtosis with negative skewness is the worst of all possible setups, but it is the fundamental nature of a carry-trade dynamic: The combo with the highest return on the carry also has the highest probability of an unwind crash.

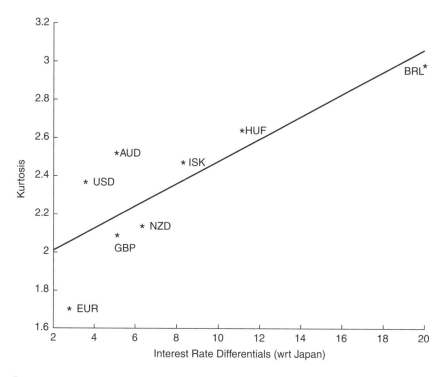

Figure 6.2   **Interest-Rate Differential Kurtosis, Japanese Yen to a Currency Basket, 1996–2008.**

Source: Sy and Tabarraei, www.pse.ens.fr/document/wp200914.pdf.

DARK ANGELS CIRCLING FROZEN REFLECTIONS

There has been much discussion about the possibility of a dollar carry trade. Although I've resisted it, it seems clear at this point that there is full-on dollar carry trade. This means bad, bad news for every other asset, and I've nicknamed it "the Unwind."

It is the Unwind because the dollar shouldn't be a carry currency: It is volatile anyway, and that, combined with its reserve-currency status, makes it like playing with gasoline and matches. Wild swings in exchange rates and asset markets are the result of an incremental leveraging and then a violent unwinding when dollar funding rates rise. Get ready for some dollar love that will burst many bubbles and illusions.

The Unwind will initiate the next iteration of debt deflation. Don't let the current optimism and propaganda dull your wits: Optimism prevailed from 1929 to the spring of 1931. Just such an unwind prevailed then, as described in the authoritative *The Crash and Its Aftermath*[1]:

- By 1931, *interest-rate spreads declined to their lowest levels* since the market crash.
- The *Sterling currency crisis* drove interest rates to new high levels.
- South American *country defaults* destroyed the foreign bond market.
- Investment-grade bonds collapsed. *Utility bonds* became the premier investment.

I selected these bullets (from the *dozens* available) for a reason: Currency unwinds are the triggers to pure economic carnage. Emerging markets literally can just "sudden stop" without a stream of dollars coming in the coffers; if a return crash did this to their bond markets, what do you think it did to their equity markets? Even high-grade bonds got smashed, except utilities.

These events aren't unique to the United States after the crash. The Japanese "Lost Decades" show the same pattern. The Unwind will generate the same kind of crash.

If the United States has to raise interest rates to protect the dollar, it's all over. If target countries default off bad fundamentals, it's all over. The Unwind begins like Shiva smiling on Alamogordo.

BENEATH THE ICY FLOE: POSTBUBBLE PRICE CONVERGENCE

Pricing power and, to a lesser extent, debt profile determine survival in even mild deflation. For example, Japan's real estate and rents under-performed the general price level for more than 20 years after the event horizon, as shown in Figure 6.3.

Japanese petroleum product prices (distillates and crude quotes) proxy the commodity complex in their Lost Decades, and it doesn't bode well for the commodity melt-up going on right now. Roughly two years after the real estate crash of 2008, petroleum products in Japan saw a hefty spike—and then utter collapse. It took 15 years for it

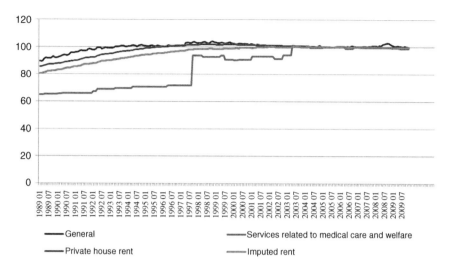

Figure 6.3 **Consumer Prices in Deflation, Japan, January 1989–November 2009.**

to recover. We saw another megaspike in 2007—and then implosion. Past is prologue.

Note what outperformed the general price index over the whole time period consistently in Figure 6.4: electricity, gas, and water charges.

For utilities, the premier investment in deflation.

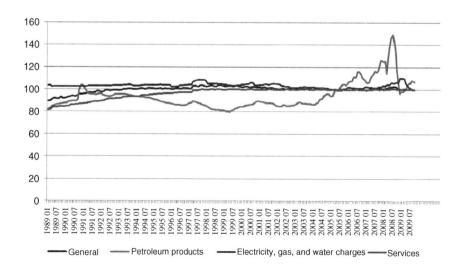

Figure 6.4 **Input Prices in Deflation, Japan, January 1989–November 2009.**

ECLECTIC SWAPS IN FROZEN INTERVALS: DEBT-DEFLATION POSITIONING

Selected credit-default swaps (CDS) spreads are popping already, but there is a way to use them that is correlated to the business cycle. This is the lab-works idea: trading a view on recovery rates.

This view is constructed by bundling a standard CDS with a digital-default swap (DDS). If there is a credit event over the tenor, the short-recovery-rate side will profit from buying defaulted debt at a lower price than the implied recovery rate. Thus, if the implied recovery rate on the trade date is 40 percent, and the reference entity experiences a credit event, buy the bonds on the market at, say, 20 percent of par. Receive 40 percent implied notional, deliver the bonds into contract, and net 20 percent times notional on the trade. This strategy could be traded on credit-derivative indices.

Don't expect an economic ice age—such extreme deflation is too dark and troubled to ponder anyway—but do expect years of silent fields and pale winter light. Remember that when snowflakes dance under bleak cloudy skies, they are still beautiful when you look at them.

CHAPTER 7

Disintegration and Securitization

...When Silenus had finally fallen into his clutches, the king asked him what was the best and most desirous thing of all for mankind. The daemon stood silent, stiff and motionless, until at last, forced by the king, he a gave shrill laugh and spoke these words:

"Miserable, ephemeral race, children of hazard and hardship, why do you force me to say what would be more fruitful for you not to hear? The best of all things is something entirely out of your grasp: not to be born, not to be, to be nothing. But the second best for you—to die soon."

—F. NIETZSCHE, *The Birth of Tragedy*

What would happen if stock markets and bond markets blew up at the same time? I'm assuming that the most likely way this could happen is via massive bond defaults. Certainly I am not saying this is *necessarily going* to happen, but it is worthwhile to consider extreme events. And it's not a stretch to think that Greece and Latvia, with a debt-to-gross-domestic-product (GDP) ratio of around 500 percent, and U.S. states such as California and Illinois are expecting—defaults, that is. It is worth understanding how people and institutions respond to an unsustainable debt burden on a societal scale and how to make money on it. The unexpected results of a promiscuous consequence-free debt binge will have extreme consequences for shaken money makers.

TAKE-AWAYS

The basic jist of what to expect is *adaptation*: using existing financial instruments in novel ways in interaction with extreme changes in an economic environment. This includes

- Pervasive reduction of leverage. Syndicated loans and dependence on short-term bank financing will be reduced. Longer-term financing (bonds) will be viewed as less risky.
- Deleveraging means that retained earnings will be an increasing source of financing. As a result of this dividend reduction, equity issuance will be a funding source for few companies. This will be harsh on equities.
- There will be big changes in the mergers and acquisitions (M&A) landscape. Disintermediation will place companies with pricing power in an enviable position. They will create integrated conglomerate industries that pair businesses that throw off cash with other, less profitable complementary business lines.
- Household, business, and central bank behavior will innovate to survive. Firms will fragment their risk exposures. Household strategic default will become rather common. As far as central banking is concerned, it may not be legal for the Fed to purchase corporate debt, but there are no current restrictions on purchases of credit-linked obligations or collateralized bond obligations (CLOs, CBOs).
- Securitization is a powerful cipher of decontrol and is going nowhere. Owing to large liability overhangs, intractable government commitments far in excess of tax outlays, and a desire for institutional portfolios to off-load exposures,

securitization arranger and originator businesses will endure. Future securitization will bundle new raw material (e.g., bundled tax/payment arrears). This is the ancient practice of tax farming in new clothes.

- Unwinding securitization is a powerful cipher of disintegration. Expect securitization unwinds of some existing products. Toxicity going forward will be controlled by more stringent collateral standards and aggressive discounting.

WHERE WE ARE, WHERE WE GO

The setup is a hangover from a liquidity binge. Sovereign bond issuance will drive sovereign govvie yields up, and weaker sovereign credit spreads will blow out. Corporate credits, both IG and HY, will follow as tax rates rise. Any improvement in the top line likely will be insufficient to avoid higher default rates. There will be less residual earnings, so equities will underperform.

This is a well-known story, agree or not. How people and organizations behave in such an extreme environment is the unknown issue. It is important to anticipate the strategies that people develop in extreme situations to improve their circumstances.

There is an entrenched *insolvency* problem in the United States, and a picture is worth a thousand words. Insolvency is not illiquidity; insolvency is about income that can't service debt burden. Notice where things fall off the cliff: I believe that we are getting close to this point. We just need a catalyst. Sequential bond auction failures here, a sovereign default there, massive liquidity drain all around, worse—whatever. The fumes running the engine (QE or credit easing) are dwindling.

DON'T GO CHASING WATERFALLS . . .

In the absence of organic revenue growth, asset prices rise and fall with central bank liquidity provision (see Figure 7.1). The effect of this liquidity is not symmetric, though. There is a gradual rise that moves with liquidity, followed by a catastrophic drop-off in which asset prices settle at a low ground state.

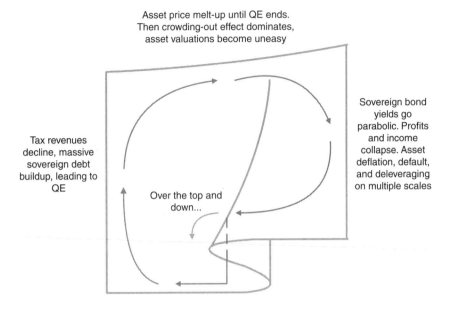

Figure 7.1 **Liquidity-Driven Asset Price Cycles.**

The ingredients are already in place for a much-needed solution to hubris. One can observe top-down government economic reengineering interacting with moral hazard–induced behavior adaptation in bad ways. The potential outcomes are shown in Figure 7.2. There is any range of possibilities, but I can assure you that good intentions mean nothing where survival of the fittest is written explicitly into the cosmic gene code. History does provide a template for how this sort of political reengineering will shape the next few years. Buckle up!

A powerful neutralizer of nihilism is data to look at how these adverse policy effects—payment arrears, ambiguous property rights, zombie banks, and such—reconfigure society. It may take years to work through, but this is nothing new under the sun.

The data suggest something of note: *Humans can slip out of the noose for some time through innovative behavior. In meltdown situations, liquidity is generated when firms and households adapt and develop work-arounds to an unsustainable debt burden. Government turning a blind eye and ignoring basic corporate law (creditor rights) is more inflationary than any fiscal*

The Intention	Method	Implementation	Adverse Effect
Goverment Intervention to Mitigate Deleveraging and Insolvency	Fiscal Policy	Direct Stimulus (expanded unemployment benefits, food stamps, other transfer payments)	Firm and Taxpayer Payment Arrears
		Direct Industrial Subsidies (GM, AIG)	
		Financial System Capital Injection	Ambiguous Property Rights
	Monetary Policy: Collapse of asset prices destroys balance sheets. Excess liabilities force everyone to go into debt minimization mode. Monetary policy becomes largely useless, no matter how much money is printed.	Liquidity Injection	Creates Zombie Banks
		Weaker Dollar	Geopolitical Risk: Import capacity is suppressed
			Reserve Currency Risk: OPEC rejects denomination of oil price in dollars

Figure 7.2   **Exhibit A: Good Intentions Mean Nothing.**

or monetary policy. However, it is unsustainable and only magnifies systemic risk. When chaos dominates order, things fall apart. Stability resumes when illusions burn away, and all things must live within their means.

I found an out-of–the-way laboratory to observe these rules, one with a certain back-to-basics charisma: Romania. After all, Transylvania is an ideal place to study undead zombies. The time: Right after a real vampire, Vlad Ceaucescu, was killed in a bloody revolution months after the iron curtain fell.

Indeed, there are few more glamorous locales for a Lovecraftian scene. Sure the United States is different. But note that there is a global dynamic going on that is bigger than any single country—a dynamic of decontrol. Political and social structures are all in flux. The ascendant autonomy of the individual to act in his or her best interests independent of other considerations is the decisive element of contemporary history. Where better to observe this dynamic than at a punctuated equilibrium point between communism and capitalism? What enterprise arrears were to a smokestack satrap economy churning out wholesome proletarian smoke is what mortgage squatters are to an economy driven by central bank liquidity.

For example, Romanian corporations under the pressure of unsustainable debt levels, declining revenue, and threats of bankruptcy broke their firms up along divisional or factory lines. It was an effective way to both avoid balance-sheet stresses and increase autonomy against government regulators. How is this different from a Wall Street structured investment vehicle (SIV)? Human systems and human nature really have changed little since Athens and Ur.

Let's start with the disintegration of the existing Romanian government in 1991, resulting in a stop-go approach to law and order. Then observe a demand implosion and a massive unemployment spike. Next, prices were liberalized, meaning that basic goods prices went through the roof. Monetary policy in the sense we understand it didn't exist. Banks were simple accounting entities commanded by the center, not mechanisms that profited from taking credit risk.

The government was disintegrating, and there was no existing financial structure to administer conventional fiscal and monetary policy. How could real wages—the most reliable measure of household well-being in a command society—possibly hold together and even increase in 1995 and 1996? See Figure 7.3.

The answer to the preceding question is: Because people and social phenomena survive extreme limit situations by (1) fragmenting risk exposures and (2) searching intensely for better options outside the box.

RISK MANAGEMENT BY RISK FRAGMENTATION: WHAT LIQUIDITY INJECTION REALLY DOES

In the United States, capital infusions by purchase of preferred stock (this purchase was diluted to common stock in due time), liquidity injections, and organized mortgage-backed security (MBS) purchases

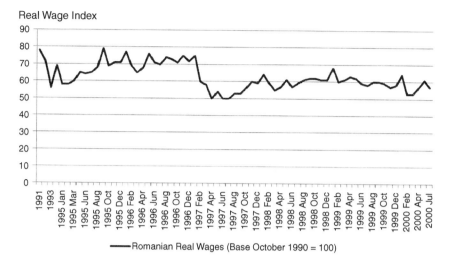

Figure 7.3   **Real Romanian Wages: No Sign of Apocalypse in Collapse.**

enable an entire financial system to hunker down in extremes. The entire system reorganized assets in a decentralized way to SIVs or other off-balance-sheet conduits outside regulator purview, whereas liabilities were managed at the on-balance-sheet center to create a "too big to fail" entity. This created a maze of theoretically independent legal entities whose status is, by design, semiautonomous in practice.

This attempt to hold liabilities on balance sheets is what enabled banks to enjoy "too big to fail" status using that standard of measurement. At the same time, holding assets that could be regarded as good money using another valuation method is a tactic to escape the reach of regulators. I know that the Financial Accounting Standards Board (FASB) may change this situation, only to change it back again should the need arise.

So the best case for both Romania and Wall Street is that they got a bailout. Socialized versus private-enterprise distinctions are meaningless when the state holds a big equity stake. It may be true that the U.S. government will not exercise its right regarding disposal of property, but it could. And the government does have rights over residual income streams and business decisions.

There are also fortunate businesses that have cash flow when others don't. In such cases, risk fragmentation of assets and liabilities creates interlocking business conglomerates. If a business can't collect on receivables, then its suppliers will exchange debt for equity, creating conglomerates whose centers generate cash. This isn't about Wall Street. This happens in any economic downturn.

THINKING OUTSIDE THE BOX: STRATEGIC MASS DEFAULT

Thinking outside the box in Romania meant ceasing payment of interest and principal. Not paying interest and principal as a debtor's *unilateral decision* independent of legal recourse is what makes a payment arrear. And arrears explain how businesses kept going and employing people. Remember that rising real wage in 1995–1996? State and firm arrears exploded in 1995–1996 to make it happen.

Capital and liquidity injections to banks in the United States create incentives for bank forbearance and mortgage delinquencies. Delinquency is just a type of payment arrear. Whether this is an intended transfer payment or an unintended consequence of a direct subsidy, the result is damaging if it becomes a perceived free ride. How pervasive could arrears become? Business and state/local government arrears approached 50 percent of GDP in Romania (Figure 7.4).

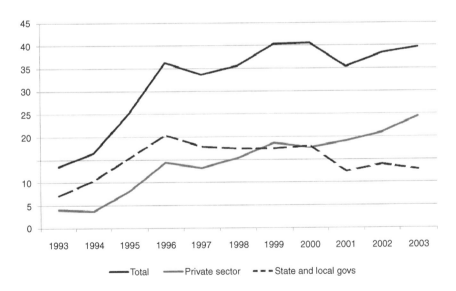

Figure 7.4 **Unpaid Arrears as a Percent of GDP, Romania, 1993–2003.**
Source: IMF Statistical Annex (various issues).

Table 7.1   Sources of Funds for Romanian Firms, Percent of Total Financing

Source	1999	2000	2001
Retained earnings	6.8	8.9	11.9
Company reserves	0.6	1.1	0.9
Equity capital	35.6	29.2	28.3
Bank credit	23.2	22.6	24.2
Tax arrears	19.2	22.6	15.2
Payment arrears	6	5.7	7.2

Arrears created a persistent dynamic for business funding in Romania (see Table 7.1). Tax and payment arrears still accounted for over 20 percent of the total financing for corporations almost 10 years after the arrears problem first presented. Note also that retained earnings formed a growing share of financing even as equity financing declined. This should be expected in any deleveraging context.

ENDGAME

One should not fault these "Romanian" behaviors. Arrears kept possibly solvent businesses under intense liquidity pressure from buckling entirely. They kept people employed. They kept household wages supported. They kept people from starving and freezing in the streets. However, the behaviors become negative when they become entrenched, leading to incentives to downsize living standards are negated by a government-sponsored sense of entitlement.

In the United States, if mortgage delinquencies become a bigger source of retained income for the unemployed than bank credit or transfer payments, then enforcing payment discipline will become very difficult. Debt issuance needed to finance government spending on transfer payments will crowd out business and household credit needs, making profitability and asset devaluations even worse. This will magnify the extent of payment and tax arrears even more.

The Romanian situation highlights the dangers of direct government intervention outside the parameters of established law, coupled with a lack of control in other areas. It makes business arrears larger and creates more instability. *The trigger to arrears is a liquidity squeeze combined with ambiguous property rights.*

Further, it is difficult for government to disentangle itself from direct subsidies and bail-outs of favored industries because of the special interests that profit from them. At the extreme margin, further economic difficulties accompanied by government inability to act pressures the central banks to purchase all types of assets. We are already on this track. The purchase of Treasuries is a relatively impartial method of reflation. The purchase of MBS is *credit easing* that favors the financial system in general and the weakest links in particular. The logical conclusion of credit easing is the purchase of corporate debt via collateralized loan obligations (CLOs) and collateralized debt obligations (CDOs). Note that this policy would be different from U.S. government AIG and GM capital injections only in scale and method.

All such government policies are in the end self-defeating. They enable unprofitable businesses to continue cash burn. The implicitly approved payment arrears inevitably will lead to explicit *tax arrears of both businesses and households*. As a massive source of corruption and fraud, it is only a matter of time before arrears manifest themselves as tax evasion.

The positive spin on this is how resilient people are in the face of shocks. They become tough and resolute when it is needed.

CHAPTER 8

Coming to Grips
with Austerity

Talk of *austerity* is all the rage. The problem is that we don't even know the meaning of the word. Let's face it, most of us are pretty coddled when it comes to belt tightening.

Austerity is not flashy. Nor is it fun. But it isn't hopeless. People get angry, get sad, and then they move forward. It is characterized by

- Ambiguous property rights
- Extreme income inequality
- And, often enough, violence

I found some data, long forgotten and collecting dust, to shed some light on the subject.[1] The data come from a survey of 2,910 households randomly chosen in clusters of 30 households and stratified across 32 of the 39 provinces of South Vietnam in 1964. The only region of this country not included in the survey was the central highlands because the surveyors surely would have been killed as soon as night fell. Half the hamlets surveyed were "secure," meaning that it was reasonably safe to travel there in daylight hours. Whether or not the hamlets surveyed were under tight Viet Cong control is unknown, but they averaged around 16 miles from the nearest provincial town. The survey covered all rice-growing areas and most areas of commercial activity.

SOUTH VIETNAM, 1964

What clarity do these data provide? *They give you a glimpse of a world where people live without safety nets and a sense of how similar economic life is across a bread range of settings.* More important, they show that austerity does not mean hopelessness. Life goes on after a debt binge. In terms of income distribution, Vietnam is not much different from the United States, except that it is more egalitarian (see Figure 8.1). Richer people live in urban areas, and the poor live out in the sticks.

There was a heavier reliance on agriculture in Vietnam in the 1960s, of course. But the majority of income came from wages and salaries, business income (entrepreneurship), and return on capital (Figure 8.2).

Even in a politically unstable, poverty-stricken, and violent environment, life goes on. Even the poorest people spend money; some even sacrifice (7 percent of income) to educate their children (Figure 8.3). Americans do this mostly through indirect subsidies via tax policy.

People buy big things even when ownership rights are tenuous. Take a look at the percent of total income spent on consumer durables by South Vietnamese at the time (Figure 8.4).

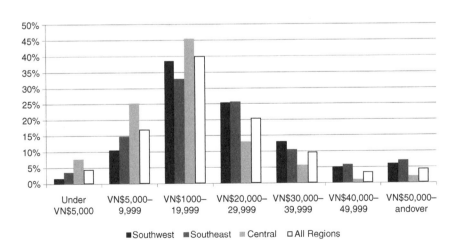

Figure 8.1 **Household by Income Class and Region (Vietnam Dollars).**

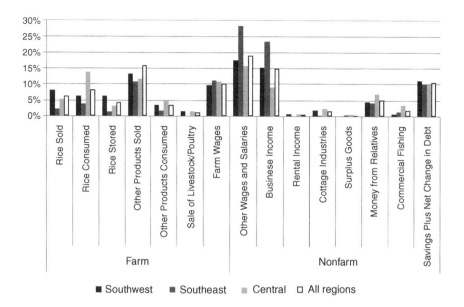

Figure 8.2   **Sources of Income, Percent of Total.**

The take-away message here is that austerity means little leverage, which implies that people spend most of their money on subsistence goods such as food and beverages. Even the richest people in South Vietnam spent nothing near the affordability thresholds that banks use in issuing home loans.

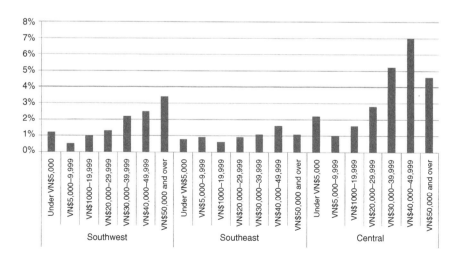

Figure 8.3   **Education Spending, Percent of Total Income.**

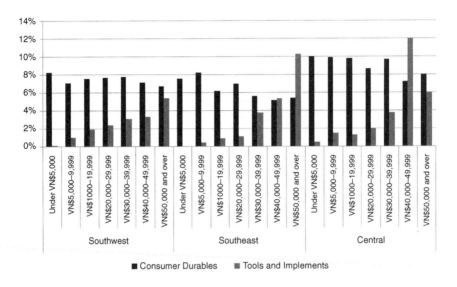

Figure 8.4   **Consumer Durables Spending, Percent of Total Income.**

Note that the poorest people spent relatively more of their income on subsistence goods (Figure 8.5).

Most people spent less than 15 percent of their total income on housing, and even the wealthiest people spent only 20 percent of their

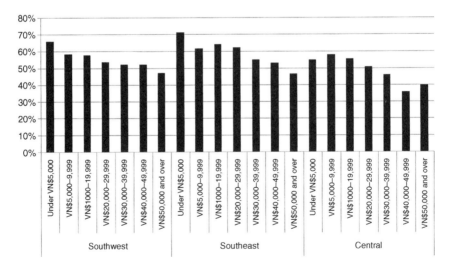

Figure 8.5   **Food and Beverage Spending, Percent of Total Income.**

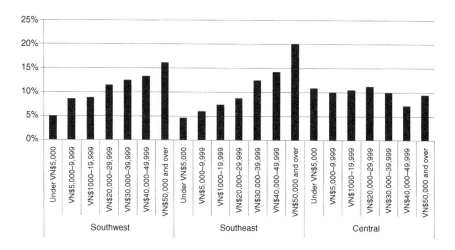

Figure 8.6 **Housing Spending, Percent of Total Income.**

income on housing (Figure 8.6). This is a function of the depth of financing or the lack of it. Banking matters to everyone, and a banking system that takes credit risk and manages that risk (without backstops) increases societal wealth. Financial *intermediation* makes everyone better off.

While we are on the subject, the most substantive difference between South Vietnam and the United States—the "emerging" versus the "developed" worlds—lies in the finanical system. The developed world is a coddled world that won't understand austerity until it crushes the life out of our naivety. At the same time, modern banks have been so used to easy money that they don't really understand the origins of intermediation anymore. For the record, intermediation didn't begin or end with a central banking cartel.

Financial intermediation begins with funding modes.

WHOLESALE BANK FUNDING AND ROLL RISK

Financial intermediation is premised on acquiring pools of cheap funding and a lending-to-credit risk/reward profile that create profits. In the United States, this funding consisted of deposits in a time long before we got a nutty professor as Fed chairman. Things have changed since then. Now funding comes from money markets. This change in funding radically affects financial intermediation.

Intermediation was funding via savings deposits, combined with assets held to maturity. When these assets were loans and government securities, it was a safe business with reasonable margins. As margins compressed, leverage became the common method to sustain bank profits. And there was an intense search for additional sources of financing that drove down funding costs. Wholesale funding eclipsed deposits as a funding source.

Wholesale funding providers are money-market mutual funds (households), corporations, and other financial institutions with excess cash to deploy on a short-term basis. Wholesale funding instruments are repos, commercial paper, certificates of deposit (CDs), Fed fund borrowings, and the like. These instruments fueled a lending model that borrowed at short durations with implied low risk and lent at longer term to higher credit-risk profiles. The crisis of 2007 was set when banks extended leverage by accepting collateral that had value only so long as interest rates remained low. Keeping them low was the chief reason for credit easing—the only way to control the long end of the yield curve. To fall back on bank deposits as the chief funding source implies deleveraging: The pool isn't large enough to sustain current lending levels.

When bank solvency is assumed and the funding roll is assured at refinancing, wholesale funds are similar to deposit funds. When this house built of tarot cards collapses, though, refinancing aggressive short-term funding becomes incrementally more costly for banks.

Wholesale funding markets become sensitive to information and often are subject to maturity mismatches. Information-sensitive money markets mean the potential for acute roll risk. Default implies that money-market investors know that they are not immune to loss of capital and liquidity. Without precise information about specific institutions, refinancing becomes more difficult for all banks. This can be seen when interbank rates, paper-bill spreads, and other spreads blow out.

Bear Stearns is a case in point. Forty-eight percent of its liabilities were short-term collateralized funds. *When refinancing became impossible, high-quality liquid assets plunged from $18.1 billion (March 2008) to $2 billion three days later.*

Why do you think *tail risk killers are so fearful of a freeze in money-market accounts?*

The problem is somewhat intractable because banks hide their dirty linen. Thus the tail-risk killers do what they do best: throw money at the problem, hoping that it allows for sufficient healing time before there is no more chance to kick the can down the road.

THE GEORGE COSTANZA MOMENT[2]

Perhaps the best course of action for Bernanke, given these risks, is a George Costanza moment: doing exactly the opposite of what is expected. The benefits of market-based interest rates are clear and obvious to everyone but the guys in charge of propping up the status quo. It is probably clear to them too; not even they believe their own BS anymore. You may just get an "Asian miracle," meaning

- Savings will rise. If you compensate depositors for their risk, deposit pools and wholesale funding will stabilize, minimizing roll risk.
- Institutions levered in all the wrong places will go the way of the dodo.
- Things will heal in time, maybe sooner than anyone thinks.

South Korea was one of the poorest countries in the world in the mid-twentieth century. It was absolutely impoverished by colonial powers and then devastated by civil war. When Park Chung Hi acquired power, he went about subsidizing heavy industry and trying the then-conventional economic reconstruction programs.

Maybe it worked after enough time elapsed, but all the data suggest that all it created was inflation and misallocation. Perhaps out of despair of anything better, Korean interest rates on deposits were allowed to rise (see Figure 8.7). The de-reconstruction and return to the basics of rewarding risk and helping the prudent was the real start of the Asian miracle.

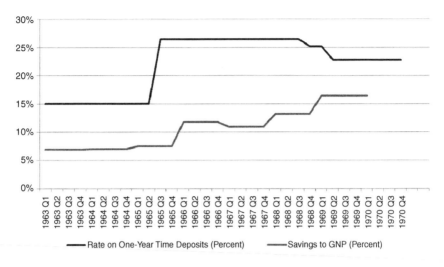

Figure 8.7   **Korean Response to Higher Market Interest Rates.**

Capital accumulation outstripped money-supply growth and inflation (Figure 8.8).

When you take away all the flashy models and techniques, finance is and always will be about intermediation: the meeting of buyers and sellers willing to take counterparty and credit risk where an intermediary stands between them. When intermediation doesn't work well because there is insufficient capital, you have bare-bones austerity, and

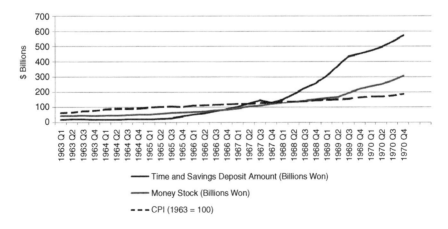

Figure 8.8   **Korean Capital Accumulation Outstrips Inflation.**

the focus is on day-to-day subsistence. Intermediation can fail in the other direction as well: There is capital, but insufficient return on it makes for an unstable source of funding. Balancing this dynamic is the razor's edge on which capitalism depends. When intermediation blows up, the best thing to do is to let funding grow organically by letting interest rates rise such that they will attract capital. In a world where central banks distort risk as a matter of course, interest rates that reward savings can lead to the unexpected—maybe even a miracle.

CHAPTER 9

Carry Trade II: Extremely Long Dollar Love

Revolutions happen when broken parts of existing structures reassemble themselves in novel ways. Today's Japanese carry trade will become something completely new: currency jettison—fundamentally changing Japan. The revolution will be driven by exchange-rate volatility hedging, handcuffing the government, and going for full-on dollarization. When that happens, shorting yen will be the best trick on the planet.

Dollarization to control currency volatility happens often. It is not even a radically new event[1] in Japan, but it will go viral and mutate into something not seen in generations. The utter abandonment of the yen as a *derisk* will end any return crashes. And the Japanese semidemocracy (this designation applies to all nations, not just Japan) won't be able to do much about it. Aging pensioners are both *creditors* and *voters*: The only possible adjustment they can make to any coming sovereign crisis[2] is to get entirely out of the yen. Only if the aging population in charge lets all that is parasitic in the financial system crumble will dollarization be averted. Either way, the Gordian debt knot will find resolution. Creditors will take it hard.

Spurned creditors get their pound of flesh in the end. And this is why in the end the dollarization of Japan will not be a short-term affair. Not only will deposits be dollarized, so will liabilities and claims. Monetary policy itself will be reinitialized to dollars. The idiot-elite in charge will want to get some turf back, but the handcuffs won't be coming off for a long time.

I don't need to tell you that this has import far beyond Japanese shores. Japan won't be the only country to dollarize, and to possibly abuse a term, the world dynamical system will be coupled with even greater synchronicity. Get ready—the dollar love you are going to feast your eyes on will be revolutionary in and of itself.

TRANSLATING DOLLARIZATION INTO OTHER IDIOMS

Dollarization is just an extreme form of exchange-rate pegging that strips a state of its monetary authority but leaves unchanged its fiscal authority. It's sort of like a gold standard, but the currency is based on multidimensional faith, not a pricey rock. At its essence, dollarization is just another riddle of globalization. In one way, it centralizes power; in another, it devolves it. To understand this idea, let's look at an example of dollarization in another currency.

This other country is very old and was once known as the land of the scorpion-men and Pazuzu.[3] Its culture is infused with millennia-old social structures that do their thing independent of late-comer add-ons, such as government. Its society is intensely conservative and hesitant to discard anything from the hallowed past, and as a result, it is Black Swan–resistant. Arabic provides a common language, psychology, and overtone shared with its neighbors. Political organization is centralized, with a tendency for competing rulers to harness the power of society by controlling the religious, military, economic, and other forces that constitute the state.

The country is Lebanon. Despite its ancient rhythms, it is also intractably *Français*, with a long tradition as a financial crossroads. Lebanon is also a contemporary senseless tragedy: once the financial center of the Middle East—sophisticated, elegant, and clever—utterly destroyed by civil war.

DOLLARIZATION IN DEPTH

Before the Lebanese Civil War (1975–1990), Lebanon was an international financial hub, dealing in petrodollars. Few, if any, restrictions were placed on capital movements. Its sophisticated banking system offered foreign-currency accounts to residents and foreigners alike, but the service really took off when a large bank run in the late 1960s wiped out about 20 percent of total deposits.

Throughout the 1970s, dollars stayed around 20 percent of total deposits, even when the civil war started, and households hoarded cash as basic financial architectures started to break down. Serious inflation and currency depreciation started as a result of government failure. By 1979, there was a secular shift out of Lebanese pounds and into dollars. At the time, foreign currency was used as a store of value against inflation or exchange-rate depreciation.

When Israel intervened in 1982, pretty radical swings in the exchange rate changed the motive for dollarization to *volatility hedging*. After the Israelis withdrew, the rush out of pounds began. The weakened central government did not inspire confidence in a stable future. This government also co-opted the country's savings to finance its deficits through quantitative easing (QE). Within two years, the dollarization ratio skyrocketed from around 35 percent to 70 percent of all deposits.

History Lesson: Exchange Rate and Treasury Yields

A credible government was established in Lebanon around 1992, and the situation normalized in approximately 1996. This historical prelude is embedded in the USD/LBP exchange rate shown in Figure 9.1.

There is more information than is shown in the exchange rate. The real nerve cord of even rudimentary market economies is the yield curve. Since 36 months is Lebanon's version of the long bond, the 3-month bond functions like 2-year U.S. govvies (see Figure 9.2).

All the way through 2009, yields were in secular decline. This was good news for a country coming out of a 15-year civil war. There was not a well-functioning secondary market for T-bills, and the rate in the primary market acted as the key reference rate for the nominal

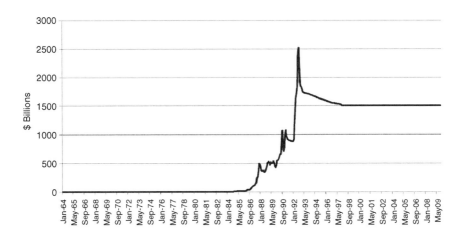

Figure 9.1   **USD/LBP Monthly Average, January 1964–November 2009.**

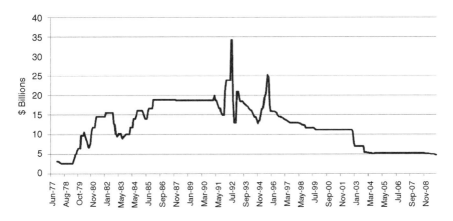

Figure 9.2   **Yields on 3-Month Treasury Bills (Primary Market).**

economy. However, the thoroughgoing dollarization of the economy ensured that it remained a nominal benchmark.

Still, stability has made only a little dent in Lebanese dollarization. In fact, dollarization is largely unchanged because creditors contract in dollars now, not Lebanese pounds. The term nature of debt combined with creditor aversion to inflation creates strong reinforcement of dollarization. Deposit dollarization may be more sensitive to inflation at times, but the relationship (particularly from 1997 to 2002) demonstrates that dollarization is entrenched despite falling inflation rates. Lebanese dollarization rates are overlaid with annual inflation-rate data are available for Lebanon, and the monthly data points are interpolated.

From 1994 to 2009, the ratio of liabilities and claims denominated in foreign currencies (mostly dollars) ranged from 90 to 82 percent. Dollarized private-sector deposits ranged from 50 to 80 percent. The data suggest that these deposits are sensitive to changes in inflation up to a threshold. These ratios are key adjustment mechanisms within the Lebanese economy.

Remember what I said about creditors getting their pound of flesh? Well, anybody who lends capital just before massive currency devaluation gets their tail handed to them, period. As a result, they tend to denominate credits in another currency. This is profoundly destabilizing because it could trigger waves of bankruptcy, as wages and revenue would collapse in local currency terms. It is ironic how "debt jubilee" plans make no difference at all in the end.

Note that there is a lot of sophisticated behavior going on in lebanon. Figure 9.3 shows that the Lebanese hold somewhere around 50

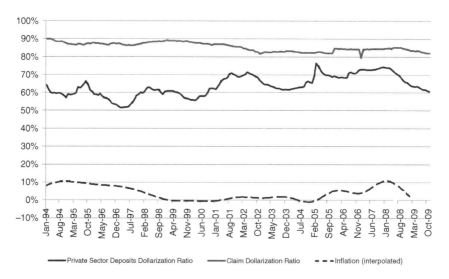

Figure 9.3 Entrenched Lebanese Credit Claim and Deposit Dollarization, 1994–2009.
Source: Bank du Liban, www.bdl.gov.lb/. Interpolation employed a natural spline executed with *Mathematica.*

to 80 percent of their liquid capital in dollar deposits, and Lebanese creditors denominate nearly all their capital in dollars as risk-minimal investments that generate real return unconnected to domestic inflation.

This is not to say that the Lebanese aren't sensitive to other macroeconomic factors, in particular monetary shocks emanating from the United States or global benchmark interest rates. Some banks in Lebanon link foreign-currency deposit rates to London Interbank Overnight Rate (LIBOR) plus a margin. Lebanese pound deposits are linked to certificate of deposit (CD) rates and ultimately U.S. Treasury bills.

With the other 20 to 50 percent of their liquid capital, Lebanese seek nominal returns generated from speculative positioning with respect to domestic inflation and keep a portion of capital (checking deposits) in liquid domestic currency even if it sometimes delivers a negative return just to pay the bills (see Figure 9.4).

Humans are cunning and supremely adaptive to changes in environment. The environment of Lebanon required return to be measured in *real, not nominal, terms* (see Figure 9.5).

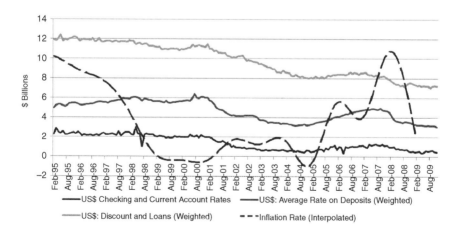

Figure 9.4 **Dollarized Assets Don't Care about Domestic Inflation.**

Source: Bank du Liban, www.bdl.gov.lb/. Interpolation employed a natural spine executed with *Mathematica.*

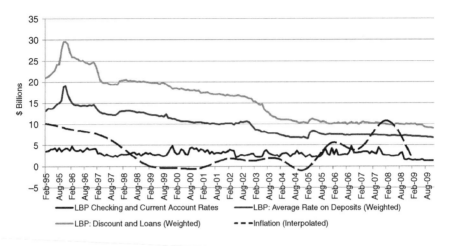

Figure 9.5   **Domestic Currency Assets Implies Nominal Return Seeking.**
Source: Bank du Liban, www.bdl.gov.lb/.

GENERALIZED EMPIRICISM

Japan has not experienced a 15-year civil war, but it stoically endured 15 years of policy hell that has destroyed credit ratings at every level, immiserizing nearly everyone, and has forced destabilizing carry trades on the world. Japanese society is also strongly predisposed toward consensus building and adherence to hierarchy. In this way, it has similarities to Middle Eastern society. And just as Lebanon is Francophile, Japanese society is intractably Americanized—uniquely where the tea ceremony and the Styrofoam cup coexist in harmony.[4]

Just as the Lebanese adapted to their environment, so will the Japanese, and it will mean that they will look for *liquid stores of wealth and a stable medium of exchange. Since dollar assets provide exchange-rate volatility hedging and real return, they won't look back.* Creditors, because of their economic necessity, and currency holders—with what remaining political influence they have—will dollarize the Japanese economy.

Discarding a local currency in exchange for another currency is a response to central bank suppression of interest rates. It depends on liquidity needs, real return, and cultural factors such as how quickly debtors and creditors absorb innovations. Thus . . .

1. There is a close link between big, persistent currency depreciation and dollarization. Once bitten, twice shy.
2. Under persistent government policy abuse, human beings become cunning, and they adapt by ignoring nominal returns and focusing on real return. Dollarization is a consequence of this.
3. Human beings develop sophisticated behavior to both maximize and hedge returns.
4. Creditors initialize dollarization and make it nearly irreversible because they anchor their claims independent of government intrusion and well in advance of any potential inflation increases.
5. Currencies may plummet, but if the state doesn't die, the currency won't die. It just becomes a ghost of its former self, relegated to a simple unit of account and marginalized transactions.
6. People and businesses dollarize, with or without tacit sovereign approval.
7. The world interest rates and asset prices will be even more tightly correlated after dollarization.

The human race is truly marvelous. Only humans can adapt to the Arctic, the Sahara, the Himalayas, the jungle. Only humans can reconstruct complexity on the smoldering ruins of war, pestilence, and famine. We rival rats and cockroaches in the survival game because our collective strategy is to reshape the world to our preferences.

POSTMODERN ENDGAME

For the last 5,000 years, the central problem of this planet has been civilization. This will continue in the twenty-first century through globalization. The core of the problem is that governance models are in flux and weakening. Power is devolving down from states toward the individual, even as the state struggles for retrenchment. There is a decisive balance needed between state order and personal freedom. This continuous tension is the defining characteristic of social existence. Lebanon's short-lived Cedar Revolution[5] was just another manifestation.

The tension is dangerous in that risks and threats are less domesticated. They are ambiguous in kind and imprecise in degree. The associated large-scale and persistent economic volatility implies widespread social contract breakdown. Dollarization is an expression of this situation. People decentralize away from localized nation-state influence, but the increased interconnection of all people and places dramatically reduces the variance of possible behaviors at the global scale. The world looks more "extremist" by the day.

There will be attempts and pretexts to justify state retrenchment, to constrict territorial state's coils around human desire for life without legalized extortion. Trading this or any worldview, for that matter, will be difficult.

And it is true that government encroachment on living things is not nearly as burdensome as it once was. The course of state diminishment can continue on unimpeded. The state may not be able to get much turf back.

CHAPTER 10

Japanification: Some Asset Behaviors When the Government Is at War with the Natural Order of the Universe

Reducing risk should be a primary objective because Japan's economic situation is a likely history of future. Not just for the United States—the whole world. There are market forces bigger than any government action in play now, and in fact, policymakers trying to save the world only cement the difficulties. Some call it the "new normal." I call it "Japanification"—the slow entropy of leverage in semicontrolled reverse. The alternative is to let it all go in one smoldering champagne supernova. But all the hyperspeed money printing and World War II–grade stimulus just falls in a financial black hole so strong that not one penny will ever escape.

I'm surprised that so many people disagree about Japanification. It's been going on in the United States for nearly a decade. There are variations from country to country, but here's what it means in broad brushstrokes:

- Bursting of an *equity* bubble triggers an economic shock.
- Policymakers react by lowering interest rates to increase liquidity.
- Resulting *credit* bubble in real estate (RE) and commercial real estate (CRE) bursts.
- Policymakers respond by printing and throwing money at the problem.
- Financial system instability persists because *money printing is reactive, not proactive.*
- Bankruptcy of major banks triggers a financial meltdown.
- This results in a *sovereign* debt explosion.
- Policymakers respond by quantitative easing (QE).
- The central bank balance sheet indicates a debt bubble.
- Rising Treasury yields (despite deflation) pretty much crush everything.
- Government firewalls off its own credit risk by cutting spending and raising taxes.

This does not preclude bursts of economic growth. Real growth is possible, albeit with quick reverses into contraction. And periodic inflation is possible too. Japanification—from aging developed-economy demographics to consumer debt reduction, to the drying up of corporate free cash flow, to banks not lending, to unemployment rises all over the globe—really does work against inflationary trends. Inflation can only occur in earnest after bubbles stop popping.

Governments are fighting Japanification in various ways. For example, Ben Bernanke actually *pays* banks interest on their excess reserves, possibly guaranteeing a deeper credit crunch.[1] Sweden, on the other hand, actually *charges* banks via negative interest rates[2] to park excess reserves. As creative and decisive as Sweden is from a policy perspective, it really just shows how difficult the situation is.

PRINTING MONEY DOESN'T HALT ASSET DEFLATION FOR LONG

Money printing won't halt deflation because printing enough money to actually reverse deleveraging is self-defeating. Printing money is a pure shot of inflationary Everclear, but the gains seen in reinflating expectations will be in the extreme more than offset by inflationary destruction of asset performance. The only lasting cure for asset deflation is organic recovery in demand. For this, you need economic growth and employment. Given an economy in financial crisis and high unemployment, demand for real estate won't recover until a severe enough drop in prices significantly reduces the downside risk of holding property. Artificial attempts to pump prices don't work.

DELEVERAGING: A VICIOUS DOWNWARD CYCLE

Companies and people are insolvent when falling prices (labor compensation or revenue) make them unable to service their existing debt obligations and so force default or liquidation of assets. These defaults and liquidations reinforce deflation and credit contraction in ever greater waves. These contractions do not happen in a gradual fashion—they happen in sudden bursts of volatility. This volatility in currencies, equities, and commodities can be absolutely breathtaking.

As for gold, anybody who has held a gold coin in his or her hand feels the draw. Anybody who held gold in 2008 knows how effortlessly poised it is in great crises. It is with regret that I bash gold, bugs. Respectfully, I don't think you understand gold. When things are at their worst, it is lively, wise, and beautiful. But things never remain so in great crises (see Figure 10.1).

Every intensity eases into mediocrity. In times of mediocrity, gold doesn't do much. Gold isn't a good risk asset for those inclined to surf liquidity, either— it's a pretty weak wave most of the time.

Deflation safety is not found in owning high-priced things; rather, safety is found in *highly credible* promises of future income. Like to know Japan's decade-plus performer, aka, Kimiko's very special friend (Figure 10.2). This shows that government securities are your friend.

If you think that the bull market in U.S. Treasuries is at a top right now (2011), well, I really can't blame you. I respectfully disagree despite the irresponsible issuance coming on deck simply because

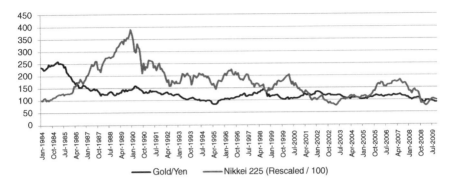

Figure 10.1 **Watanabe's Bane: Risk Assets and the Shiny Metal with Weird Cointegration.**

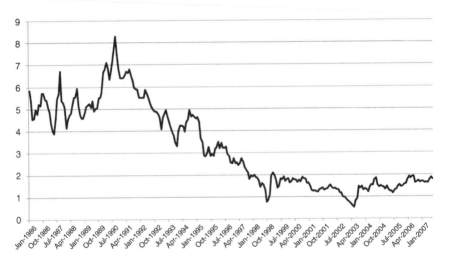

Figure 10.2 **Kimiko's Utsukusheen Tomodachi: JGB-10 Yields.**

conditions are really that bad in my view. Notice that *yields were less than 1 percent for 10-year Japanese government bonds despite exploding debt/gross domestic product (GDP) ratios!* Also, quantitative easing (money printing) didn't drive yields down more—it only created an extended and what will ultimately be an unsustainable top. It is the crushing effect of insolvency further down the capital structure that bids govvie bond prices up. As of late 2011, 30-year yields touched former highs.

EXPENSES ≤ REVENUES ENDS JAPANIFICATION

Speaking of capital structure, governments are the final domino. Government finances deteriorate owing to fiscal spending during the crisis and a decrease in tax revenues amid the economic downturn. There is no choice: Governments must triage the basket cases, rationally distribute the pain, and firewall off the essential financial structures that can be saved, or the market does the same with a colder, more merciless precision.

Some ancient wisdom applies here. Lao-tzu has an answer for Aristotle: Don't defeat the irresistible object by being immovable against it: Yield to it. All the Dao of heaven wants is for things to return to reality and exist within their means. Fighting what can't be beaten only makes the end bloodier. My view is that the Fed will not win its battle to reverse deleveraging. This does not mean that the world will look like a woodcut from Gallerie St. Etienne. Frankly, excepting Wall Street and the financial world, there's not much loss for the United States. Do what you can, Ben. Nothing escapes the Dao.

FOR DISCERNING PALATES: LEAST SQUARES

I was curious about how gold will perform in the future. To examine it, I took a lesser-traveled road via the Japanese experience. I did find that its lack of correlation (and cointegration) with the Nikkei and Japanese government bonds (JGBs) over any time horizons actually could make it desirable as risk-minimizing seasoning in some kinds of postbubble soufflés.

I have built a linear model to shed some light on the subject. The results are reported in Tables 10.1, 10.2, and 10.3.

The model:

$$(\text{Spot gold in yen}_t) = \alpha + \beta_1(\text{Nikkei225}_t) + \beta_2(\text{Jap10s}_t) + \varepsilon_t$$

Table 10.1 Analysis of Variance and Model Parameters, 1986–2009

Source	F Value	Pr > F	R^2	Variable	Parameter estimate	Pr > |t|
Model	41.59	<0.0001	0.2452	Jap10s	4.82641	<0.0001
				Nikkei225	−0.00012691	0.5746

Table 10.2 Analysis of Variance and Model Parameters: Prebubble, 1986–December 1989

Source	F Value	Pr > F	R^2	Label	Parameter estimate	Pr > |t|
Model	23.93	<0.0001	0.521	Jap10s	6.72937	0.046
				Nikkei225	−0.00175	<0.0001

Table 10.3 Analysis of Variance and Model Parameters: Prebubble, January 1990–2007

Source	F Value	Pr > F	R^2	Label	Parameter estimate	Pr > |t|
Model	16.72	<0.0001	0.1379	Jap10s	1.38159	0.0755
				Nikkei225	0.00049301	0.0677

Here are the conclusions that I draw from the model outputs:

- Before the Japanese equity bubble burst, gold price was positively correlated with rising yields. In other words, it acted like a good inflation hedge. Significance is good enough (Pr > t: 0.046), the slope estimate shows a lively response, and I won't complain about the R^2 (0.521).
- After the bubble, gold loses its luster. With no inflation, the correlation to rising or falling bond yields broke down. There's no significance at the 5 percent level, and the parameter estimate is skunky. The whole model fit sucks ($R^2 = 0.137$). For this time interval, gold remains mysterious, and further research (cointegration) says that it doesn't make a good pair trade.
- Over the whole time series, gold is not a good-risk asset. You want risk exposure? Go for long equities or something else.

CHAPTER 11

The Narrow Road to the Deep North: Fixed-Income Skew and Signatures of Japanification

What ails Japan, the United States, and many other countries is financial deleveraging. There has been much talk about "Japanification" because the Federal Reserve response to deleveraging is to follow the Bank of Japan (BOJ) policies but compressed into a shorter overlapping time frame. This imparts the look and feel of the Japanese experience. Aside from this policy compression, there's nothing new in the policy brew. The monetary policy compression and fiscal excesses arguably have made the next step—a tax increase—even more imminent than when Japan instituted its consumption tax.

Central banks can salve financial system wounds, but the wounds must heal on their own, and the problems of the financial sector reflect adjustments going on at the household level. The implication is that these problems must be resolved organically by debt reduction, capital losses, and rescaling of capacity.

Heal they will. Most people will be poorer to show for it, but economic decline happens according to economic time, and that is often s-l-o-w when measured against clock time. It may take decades for deleveraging to work fully through, but the change likely will be so gradual that people will observe it clearly only in hindsight.

Of course, this slow change is not always the case. 1989 shows two paths of collapse: Japan and the former Soviet Union. In economic time, we are too close to the initial conditions to know which will dominate. In time, however, we reach a bottom and then resume the climb ever higher.

Dark indicators / a cold winter wind that spreads / clouds on autumn sky.

This is Japanification in a haiku.

DELEVERAGING FROM A BANKING PERSPECTIVE

The basic issue is how financial crunches work themselves through to resolution against a backdrop of demographic change. The rapier point is the decline in bank return on equity (ROE) relative to the terrific ROE of the last couple of decades owing to the following factors:

1. Net long Treasury positions, steep yield curve → good Treasury profit contribution
2. Strong home price appreciation → high borrowing demand
3. Sustained high employment → capacity to borrow
4. Secondary market liquidity for loans → ability to lend
5. Strong deposit growth → low funding costs
6. Fee income → high profits for bank branches

Deleveraging happens when enough of these factors are reversed, leading to credit losses and forcing banks into heavy write-downs and losses. Banks increasingly can't unwind their book, which causes a lack of liquidity, and interbank lending freezes up. This creates the well-known self-feeding cycle seen in dark economic clouds all over the world.

A CLOSER LOOK AT JAPANESE ECONOMIC TIME

Since the beginning of the twentieth century, fixed income never had a particularly good home in Japan. Bond and bill performance was

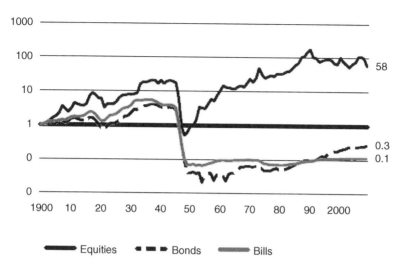

Figure 11.1   **Japanese Asset Class Annualized Performance, 1900–2008.**
Source: Elroy Dimson, Paul Marsh, and Mike Staunton, *Credit Suisse Global Investment Returns Sourcebook,* 2009.

completely dismal right after World War II up to the equity bubble burst in 1989. Bill and bond returns went from miserable to pathetic in the nineties and noughties (Figure 11.1).

Equities have been stuck in a negatively skewed holding pattern since 1989. This backdrop makes the Japanese policy even more intriguing.

GOAL-LESS SURREAL ACTIVITIES: SOME REMARKS ON POLICY

When bank ROE is crushed, the whole equity market suffers. This is so because banks act in many ways as coordinators of economic activity given how they allocate credit.

In a world dominated by technocrats, the perfectly Daoist policy of "letting it be" through inaction is unacceptable. And Japanese citizens failed to recognize that much economic theory is justification of the status quo. This translates into: Provide liquidity given a solvency problem, commit to the liquidity morphine drip whenever needed, and keep a floor on asset prices though central bank purchases.

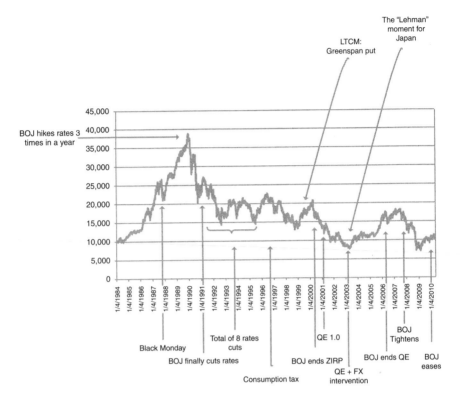

Figure 11.2   **Nikkei 225 Index, 1984–2010.**

The Fed policy response has been little different. In fact, monetary policy in the "developed" world is reduced to bald political tactics that have pretty much discarded the trappings of coherent theory. The whole point is to sustain banks given horrendous headwinds. This reduces to three things: *shaping interest-rate expectations, altering the composition of the central bank's balance sheets, and expanding the central bank's balance sheets.*

The Bank for International Settlements (BIS) and the International Monetary Fund (IMF) have some good papers on the Japanese macroeconomic experience. Much can also be inferred from directly observed data (Figure 11.2). Over this span of time, the Nikkei 225 (analogous to the Standard & Poor's 500 Stock Index in the United States) initiated a massive liquidity-fueled ramp, only to collapse to ever-lower levels. Let's look at its effect on rates and government debt.

THE SIGNATURE OF QUANTITATIVE EASING: NEGATIVE SKEWNESS

Short-term interest rates in Japan remain a study in minimalism. Japan forced investors to search for higher returns by taking risks in other markets, spawning the well-known yen carry trade. Low interest-rate policies also forced investors to increase term risk in long-term government bonds. The decline in long-term interest rates also raised expectations of large potential capital losses in the event of a reversal of interest-rate movements, and this caused negative skew and kurtosis to increase in the empirical yield distribution (Table 11.1).

The long solid line in Figure 11.3 is an assumed normally distributed line fitted to the mean and variance of daily yields before and after QE began in 2003. I customized the histogram buckets so that you can get a better feeling for the spread distribution.

Figure 11.4 shows probability plots for these yields. Probability plots are a good way to get a feel for the shape of the yield distribution. If the plot doesn't deviate much from the diagonal reference line, then the distribution is well approximated by the normal distribution.

Probabilty plots before QE stay much closer to the reference line. Probability plots after QE show greater skew (the deviation in the middle of the reference line), but in either case the tails aren't fat (Figure 11.5). This means that QE imparts bigger risks on bond-yield moves, but these moves are more likely to express themselves gradually and not in a big move.

Table 11.1 Ten-Year Japanese Government Bonds (JGBs), Before and After Quantitative Easing (QE)

10-Year JGBs	Before QE (January 1986– February 2003)	After QE (March 2003–)
Mean	4.068	1.397
Standard deviation	1.734	0.262
Skew	−0.038	−0.713
Kurtosis	−1.010	1.451

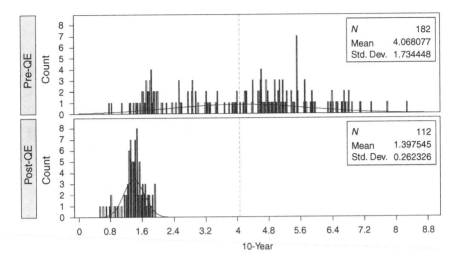

Figure 11.3 **Comparison of 10-Year JGBs Before and After QE.**

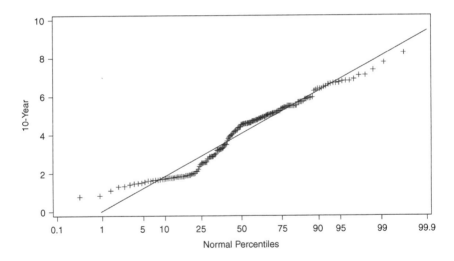

Figure 11.4 **Probability Plots, 10-Year JGBs Before QE.**

SO DO WE SEE ANY INDICATIONS OF THE SAME IN US TREASURIES?

It may be too early to tell for sure because of the short time frame, but the evidence immediately prior to QE and immediately following QE is reported in Table 11.2. The financial collapse during the

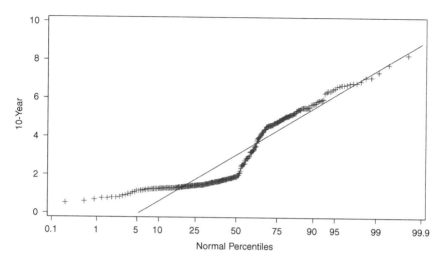

Figure 11.5 **Probability Plots, 10-Year JGBs After QE.**

period shifted mean yields far lower after QE. The standard deviation compressed as well. There is a change in the skew from positive
to negative but little change in kurtosis. That negative skew indicates
that if the Fed takes the bid off Treasuries, the risk rises that the
Fed-sponsored party in Treasuries will be over, and yields are likely
to rise.

Kurtosis statistics on Treasuries measure the fat tails of their yield
distribution—the likelihood of an extreme move. Like Japanese bond
yields, 10-year U.S. Treasury yields are not fat-tailed (Figure 11.6).
The Kolomogorov-Smirnov test rejects normality as well.

Table 11.2 **10-Year Treasuries, Before and After QE**

10-Year Treasuries	Before QE (January 1986–March 2009)	After QE (March 2009–)
Mean	6.1252	3.4017
Standard deviation	1.6603	0.3409
Skew	0.2131	−0.5156
Kurtosis	−0.9592	−0.6046
Kolmogorov-Smirnov normality test	Reject at $p < 0.010$	Reject at $p < 0.010$

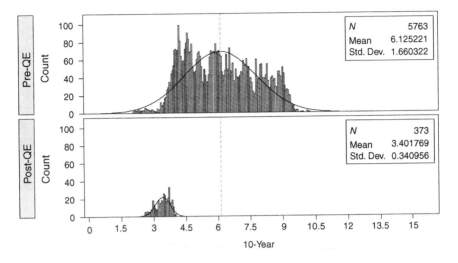

Figure 11.6   **10-Year Bond Returns, Before and After QE.**

SO WHEN WILL THE PARTY BE OVER?

The liquidity provision Bank of Japan (BOJ)–style was closely connected to the zero interest rate policy (ZIRP) cycle. For example, commercial paper operations were carried out in a repo manner and thus are not outright purchases by the BOJ. The BOJ liquidity, providing operations in bank bills and commercial paper (CP), works essentially as the BOJ lending to financial institutions with eligible securities as collateral. In contrast, in the operations in asset-backed commercial paper (ABCP), asset-backed securities (ABS), and government securities, which began in 2003, the BOJ bought these assets outright. These purchases had big effects on money markets.

The overnight indexed swap (OIS) call rate declined to at most 0.01 percent, whereas in the quantitative easing period (QEP), the rate declined further to 0.001 percent. Differences in interest rates for individual financial institutions also declined to minimal levels, at least at the short end of the money market.

On July 14, 2006, the BOJ changed the guidelines for its money-market operations, and the uncollateralized overnight call-rate target went from 0 to 25 basis points. The loan rate on the BOJ's version of the discount window went from 10 to 40 basis points. This may not seem like much, but it signaled normalization in Japan.

Even before the policy interest-rate rises, spot/next-day (S/N) repo rates and implied rates for yen funding tomorrow/next-day (T/N) transactions through foreign exchange (FX) swaps temporarily exceeded the complementary lending facility loan rate. Repo rates rose in May and June 2006, increasing the upward pressure on rates in other markets, such as the overnight/next-day (O/N) call market.

If the Japanese experience provides any guide, it seems that repo rates and the London Interbank Offering Rate (LIBOR) will telegraph an impending rate rise, combined with overnight indexed swap (OIS) rates moving in tandem. So spikes in LIBOR may signal to the Fed it is okay to provide less, or maintain, support for the banks. I suppose that it also could mean something more sinister too.

CHAPTER 12

The Price of Stability Is Pathology: Thoughts on Some Default Intervals

Hat tip: Kay Giesecke, Francis A. Longstaff, Stephen Schaefer, Ilya Strebulaev, "Corporate Bond Default Risk: A 150-Year Perspective"[1]

The authors of the paper referenced above focus on structural model building and dynamics and attempt to explain the business cycle through default rates. They largely skirt around the issue of whether corporate bond defaults going back to the Civil War are relevant to current financial research at all. Have times changed so much that the differences outweigh the similarities?

The authors do attempt somewhat of an answer in two ways:

1. "[W]hile the names of the bond issuers and the industries they represent may change and evolve over the centuries, the applicability of financial theory to the determinants of default risk and the pricing of corporate bonds should not change."
2. ". . . [I]n coming to grips with the current financial market situation which has been termed a 'historic crisis' or 'the worst

financial crisis since the Great Depression,' nothing is so valuable as actually having a long-term historical perspective."

In short, they assume an extremely consistent theory and reversion to the mean to justify building more sophisticated models. I have some reservations with these answers. The theory assumes that there are constant laws of motion that hold in all cases. Given this assumption, a successful theory explains phenomena and is robust to known initial conditions. But there is a second assumption at work: mean reversion. On one level, this implies that initial conditions don't matter because the laws of motion are invariant to them. In short, the starting point doesn't matter because all observed cases converge to the same final outcome in time. This is a core intuition behind all kinds of credit modeling and relative pricing models, and it has a formal characterization.

AN ERGODIC WORLDVIEW

Consider a law of motion T on a state space X. If $T: \underline{X} \rightarrow X$ is measure-preserving, then almost every point in any set of positive measure must return to the set under the action of T. The average value of a function f along the range of T, that is,

$$\frac{1}{n}[f(x) + f(Tx) + f(T^2x) + \cdots + f(T^{n-1}x)]$$

has a convergent limit if T preserves a finite measure and if the (real-valued) function f is integrable. The notions of $f(Tx)$ and $f(x)$ have an intuitive meaning. $f(x)$ is the physically observed space of a dynamical system. $f(Tx)$ constitutes a representation space where each point Tx corresponds to a point x in X. This representation is a way to trace out a law of motion starting from a point of initial conditions and passing through the collection of points that represents how the system evolves over time.

The set of points $f(Tx)$ reveals deep properties of dynamical systems. For example, when you collect all possible paths initiating from a collection of starting points, the set is called a *dynamical flow*. These flows often show clearer patterns of behavior than $f(x)$ itself. Instead of having to process the sometimes jagged ups and downs of $f(x)$, $f(Tx)$ can describe the behavior of $f(x)$ as converging to a point, as a circle (periodicity), a spiral (almost periodicity), a doughnut (quasi-periodicity), or some other three-dimensional attractors that can be so complex as to be practically unpredictable (chaotic motion). Sometimes these sets of points can be self-similar, meaning that one observes recurring behavior but on different time scales—when people talk about fractals, this is what they mean. The simplest case is where flows converge to a state of rest (a fixed point).

Mean reversion really implies something about how a given law of motion evolves over time. It means that for almost all initial conditions x in X, the average value of $f(T^i x)$ of the dynamical flow as it evolves through time is the same as the average value of $f(x)$. Such laws of motion are called *ergodic*: One can recover almost all the information about a process from almost every "adequate" subsequence of the process. It is here where probability becomes equivalent to frequency.

It is clear how the ergodicity concept provides some logical support for the "mean reversion" worldview. This implies that a *"typical" corporate bond of the same maturity will behave like other bonds regardless of whether they were issued in Thailand a month ago or in Manchester, England, a hundred years ago.*

There are, however, only a few ways to implement ergodic concepts in a concrete situation. Where these methods finds closest connection in finance is with entropy measures of random variables. These measures tend to zero for random processes that are mean reverting but random (like white noise) or bounded and deterministic (like the sine function over the interval 0 to 2π). There are a variety of ways to calculate entropy. But they require a very large number of data points to calculate entropy or stability via Lyapunov exponents. Therefore, in most financial applications, entropy remains a logical construction upon which theory rests.

DIVERGENCE

Given the short length of historical time series, ergodicity of historical bond defaults can't be demonstrated mathematically. Mean reversion is just a claim that must be evaluated on the basis of strength of evidence. There's some evidence against it.

It is true that bonds have been around since ancient Ur,[2] and if there is a bond, then there is credit risk. Credit risk can be assessed with simple intuitive rules of thumb, such as how pool players make amazing shots without knowing the physics behind them. There are also more quantitative frameworks like the Hull-White model to assess credit risk. The latter method works very well for pricing hedge ratios and trading when the bid is liquid.

However, there are very significant differences that alter credit risk across time. The concept of a lender of last resort didn't exist in ancient Mesopotamia, and in most parts of the world it didn't exist until after World War II. The Fed/Bank of Japan (BOJ)/European Central Bank (ECB) becoming the forcing functions of the global economy via trillions in debt monetization in the past 24 months is somewhat new. These factors make people interact, changing them as a result and radically adapting their behavior. Big picture: Financial markets are not physics labs. They change too much.

The decisive issue is how radical the change is. If the change is sufficiently radical, then the hypothetical flows of bond dynamics do not converge in the average, and theorized laws of motion are meaningless. Nothing about the behavior of the system can be determined from them. This can be so because no discernible patterns about bond behavior can be gleaned, and initial conditions determine all. This also can be due to bonds being unique phenomena that depend on time, place, and culture.

One could argue that in finance change is so rapid that even a few years ago seems antiquated. If this is the case, then trading off 150 years of default rates actually can be more misleading than trading off bond yields and default rates since the last crash in 2008.

CASUAL EMPIRICISM

To apply these concepts to the historical data on default rates, I overlaid some historic events to the default rates. I reproduce the article's summary statistics in Figure 12.1

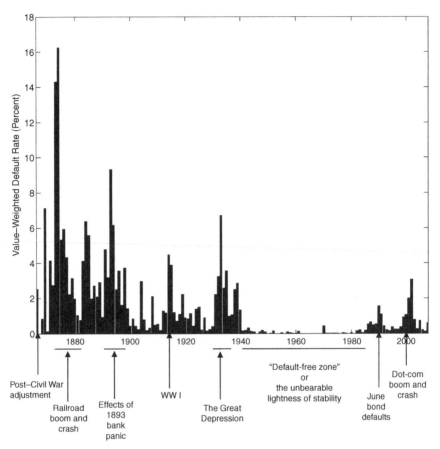

Figure 12.1 **Historical Default Patterns and Postwar Suppression of Default Rates.**

From the perspective of bond defaults, the Great Depression wasn't nearly as severe as prior crises associated with the railroad bubble or the bank crises of the late 1800s. In fact, by eyeballing, it looks like default rates in the Great Depression are simply mean reverting to the historical average preceding the Depression.

The most remarkable aspect of the chart is that from around 1942 to 1985, the United States entered a nearly default-free period. *Anybody who traded mean reversion to the average default rate of 1866 to 1941 would have been killed. To repeat: Would. Have. Been. Killed.* This lasted for 43 years. This behavior is why the 10-year Japanese government bond has the name the "Widowmaker."

The unbearable lowness of bond yields under "Japanification" is just another example of how long "untenable" things can go on. It doesn't make much sense given Japanese debt to gross domestic product (GDP) ratios, but it doesn't have to make sense. It is what it is.

THE UNBEARABLE LIGHTNESS OF STABILITY

Even within this interval of stability, there have been big moves in default rates—but not relative to defaults outside this interval of stability. They are "big" only when one looks at the closed time scale from 1942 to 1985. Outside that zone, default rates look historically low and as calm as the Pacific: This is a fractal dynamic.

It is unclear how massive the differences are in bond characteristics since 1866. Rating agencies may have started in the bond business only in the 1920s, but there is no reason to doubt that intelligent people discriminated among credit entities. There were clearly publications such as the *Commercial and Financial Chronicle* related to this, and probably more than a cottage industry in bond trading existed (including Goldman Sachs) going all the way back to 1866. Then again, perhaps high corporate yields made a generation of people untroubled by the high default rates of the nineteenth century. Investors will lend to even the riskiest credits at the right interest rate and off-par prices.

Starting in 1990, there's been resurgence in default rates. Although not on the chart, we saw another spike in default rates in 2008. In fact, 2009 high-yield default rates hit 13.7 percent. This time period has qualitatively different debt instruments, such as leveraged loans and synthetic positions, that can increase stress on default rates in a crisis. It would seem that because of these instruments, the notion of default rates is inferior to loss rates (a combination of default and recovery rates) in the current financial environment. Loss rates are a better metric than default rates alone for financial debt because the liabilities embedded in the synthetic instruments that dealer banks issue are higher on the capital structure. This alters the recovery rates of all but secured debt.

STABILITY SUCKS

There was one other factor going on in the default-free zone: the rise of central banking and deficit spending fiscal policies as a global ideology. Check out the quantiles the article reports to see the differences (Table 12.1).

Default rates went from 3 percent in the 1866–1899 interval to a little less than 1 percent after introducing an institutionalized lender of last resort in 1900–1945 and to less than 1/10 of 1 percent when you add activist monetary ideology and deficit-driven expansion into the mix after 1946. Why?

The simple reason is that such policies transfer risk held by debtors and creditors to taxpayers and savers. There is a debt resolution such that savers will eat a portion of the loss through devaluation. Facing default? Taxpayer bailouts, baby. This provides a low-risk environment that does have some societal benefits. Entrepreneurship and innovation are higher because risk taking is to some extent subsidized. Technology breakthroughs are more frequent. This contributes to big jumps in standards of living.

But there is a dark tradeoff. Transfering risk doesn't take it away. Rather, a share of risk is given to creditors to eat and is hidden in the footnotes of dealer balances sheets via counterparty exposures. Yet there are clues to find the aggregated risk if you know where to look. But the cost of stability is pathology.

Unloading fiscal costs onto future taxpayers and savers clearly suppress default rates and default volatility. But they create seriously nonlinear returns: For example, there may be a massive upside as a result of nuclear fusion research subsidies, but there can be an equally

Table 12.1 Default Distribution Quartiles from Three Time Intervals

	1866–1899	1900–1945	1946–2008
Minimum	0	0.107	0
25th percentile	1.976	0.347	0.009
Median	3.022	0.903	0.098
75th percentile	5.195	1.957	0.38
Maximum	16.255	6.725	3.071

Table 12.2 Default Distribution Moments from Three Time Intervals

Years	Mean	Standard Deviation	Skewness	Kurtosis
1866–1899	3.998	3.571	2.012	4.725
1900–1945	1.345	1.383	1.853	4.127
1946–2008	0.304	0.53	3.233	12.783

massive downside. What you get in exchange for control of fundamental laws of motion is asymmetry in outcomes and a much higher probability of extreme outcomes.

Complexity and interconnectivity within the financial system—crowded trades and herd behavior—create fundamental asymmetric instabilities. Asymmetry implies a false sense of security. The result can be massive concentrated positions in either paying or receiving on a swap because "an adverse unhedgeable move can never happen." Such positions are great when the good times roll, but under stress, performance collapses. It is clear that skewness and kurtosis in defaults have been much higher since 1946 (Table 12.2).

Over-the-counter (OTC) markets are a good example of how *well-understood risks that can be marked are transferred into unmarked balance-sheet risks* precisely because exposures of OTC swaps are available only in aggregate, are fragmentary, and there are no public data about specific counterparties. Brokers can bid and offer the same position to different counterparties at different prices. Dealers can mask a trade so that some counterparties can't see it. Prices are based on model-implied cash flows as much as actualized by a herd mentality that hits the bid because someone else just did.

There has always been some return asymmetry indicated by skewness in bonds. At par, a bond has limited upside and big downside risk in exchange for stability of coupon: There is limited price appreciation potential and much greater downside potential. Similarly, higher skew in default rates indicates asymmetric recovery expectations. But there is something else at work in the heightened asymmetric payoffs since 1946.

Fatter tails seen in default rates since 1946 imply higher probability of extreme events and a smaller probability mass. The implications are profound. For most American fixed-income history, prudence in the large was the real requirement for a fixed-income investor. You needed to be risk averse enough to handle the stress associated with greater default rates and volatility. Hedging was an unnecessary luxury because the risk of extreme swings in defaults had less impact relative to mean default rates. Since World War II, the probability of extreme events is much higher. Higher kurtosis implies that hedging against extreme outcomes is more important than before.

When a return distribution has these characteristics, sudden out-of-the-money price changes are more likely. This is so because tail-risk killing strategies incentivize leverage in an effort to maintain returns in increasingly crowded trades, raising the vulnerability of the financial system as a whole. Bond prices, implied volatilities, spreads, and defaults ultimately move in a dramatic way when leverage reverses.

CHAPTER 13

Product over Process: Balance Complexity with Liquidity

No, this chapter title is *not* "*Balance Complexity with Liquor.*" Instead, this chapter is about *liquidity.* The central problem for any *relative pricing* model is its inadequacy given systemic illiquidity because prices in all assets collapse simultaneously—and cash becomes king. Perhaps one shouldn't distinguish pricing models from valuation models, but at least valuation assumes some notion of fundamentals and aims at determining implied value, dubious as the effort is. Pricing models are relational, and illiquidity in such models can be disastrous.

People sometimes manage illiquidity by getting flat to the market: They take out shorts to cover the long losses. As declines persist, shorts keep lifting, and being flat to the market becomes cost-prohibitive. There is no substantive last-minute hedging when time horizons collapse.

Because asset returns have interdependencies and cluster, they are more complicated than conventional probability theory allows. Accommodation needs to be made for simple, straightforward approaches to the issue. One approach is to take price models with a pinch of salt. They work very well in a local context, but outside these local intervals, their implied prices have less value. Basis trades inexplicably behave "illogically," cointegrations lose their historicity, diversification makes thing worse, and so on. What matters in these situations is liquidity. *Other things may pass, but liquidity will always matter.*

It is true that reliance on exact definitions and axiomatic development of ideas through logical modeling is a recipe for clear thinking. However, when the assumptions that feed one's theory are inadequate, there is a space where abduction, experience, and luck trump deduction. This is true even of the most applied branch of measure theory—probability. Let's take a tour of the subject, blow some stuff up, and polish what survives the blast.

THE BASICS OF STOCHASTIC FINANCE

The core of probability theory is its limit theorems: the stronger and lesser laws of large numbers and the central limit theorems. They specify statistical regularity in large populations. The first proof of a law of large numbers was provided by Jacob Bernoulli in *Ars Conjectandi* (1713). Abraham de Moivre proved a first central limit formulation in *Approximatio ad summam terminorum binomii $(a + b)^n$ in seriem expansi* (1733). Gauss later proved that the limiting distribution of a set of independent, identically distributed (i.i.d.) random variables is the normal distribution. This is the classical central limit theorem, and because of Gauss's result, the normal is often referred to as the *Gaussian distribution*, although some argument occurs because of this attribution.

There are instances where extreme values occur in excess of what is indicated by the normal distribution, inducing heavy-tailed distributions such as the Pareto income distribution. These heavy-tailed distributions led Paul Levy to formulate a generalized stable density function in which the normal distribution is absorbed as a special case. For these instances, a generalized central limit theorem for stable distributions exists.

These limit theorems of probability theory describe convergence of large enough populations. Roughly stated, this means that if you combine a large number of random variables with mild restrictions, the outcome will be a convergence to a constant or a random variable with a well-defined distribution. The object of these advances in probability is generalization and refinement of this basic idea.

The unifying method of distilling stochastic processes into a unified mathematical subject is informed by measure theory, which, in turn, rests on rigorous notions of integration. We don't give adequate credit to the genius that crafted such rigorous notions—French mathematician Henri Lebesgue. It was Lebesgue who took the basic concepts of measurable analytic functions of Borel and crafted a unified conception of measure theory proper. The Lebesgue integral arguably was a part of the accomplishment. Of more importance was how measure theory cleaned up nearly a century of accumulated technical challenges to the fundamental theorem of calculus. It also set probability on a sure footing: Once a measure on a state space is established, integration of probabilities parallels the Lebesgue theory.

The thoroughly analytic sense of probability that we know today was possible only after Norbert Weiner defined random motion in terms of Lebesgue measure on the unit interval $[0, 1]$, thereafter called the *Weiner process*. The Weiner process $X(t, \omega)_t \geq 0$ is a strong Markov process. It is also a Gaussian process and a martingale.

The Weiner process is somewhat weird because every distinct t (the sample paths) of $X(t, \omega)$ is continuous but of unbounded variation on every compact time index, excepting sets of probability zero. Since Lebesgue's theorem states that functions of bounded variation have derivatives, the Weiner process is continuous but nowhere differentiable. This means that only the present matters, and all prophets are false. Knowledge of the past and present asset price is no better at predicting the future price of the asset than knowledge of only the present price. When there is no dependence of the past on the future, the Markov property holds.

The Gaussian property makes it possible to pick a sample path $t \to X(t, \omega)$ and see where it goes because all paths are continuous (on a compact space at least). If the index set T is $\mathbf{R}$, then X is *stationary* if the Gaussian property is preserved across translations $t \to t + h$. More generally, stationarity means that the underlying probabilistic structure is invariant under the one-parameter (the time index) unitary group $P(t)$: $X(t) \to X(t + h)$. A heuristic meaning for stationarity is that "This condition ensures that a system is in a steady state even as it continually undergoes random fluctuations."

These described features make normality and stationary assumptions desirable, but the assumption isn't particularly realistic. To address this unreality, people relax the assumption and specify different probability measures to contend with.

SOROSIAN REFLEXIVITY

Perhaps this "relax and respecify" technique is only a halfway approach that replaces one unrealistic assumption with another. In financial markets, the effects of illiquidity create counter examples for all assumptions. Another approach begins with the observation that life and natural processes make static engineering-type models radically inadequate. Life learns, adapts, and reacts in turbulent ways. In investing, people have one eye on future valuations and another eye on what others are doing. Sometimes people don't look at cash flows at all. Sometimes the only "other" they look at is the Federal Reserve; sometimes they don't concern themselves with Fed policy, creating extreme melt-ups and meltdowns.

These dynamics of fundamental and momentum trading imply something deeper than saying that probability laws are not preserved across time translations. It is not quite Bayesian thinking either. The Bayesian approach assumes a random variable θ with a given distribution π prior to observing x. Inference about the state of θ is made through the conditional density or posterior distribution $h(\theta|x)$. This density is given by Bayes' formula:

$$h(\theta \mid x) \propto f(x \mid \theta)g(\theta)$$

where the densities are derived with respect to Lebesgue measure.

There is merit in the notion of beliefs being updated by new data, which, in turn, then affect the posterior distribution, and a lot of ingenuity comes into play in finding combinations of prior and posterior distributions that interlock in a tractable way. But this ingenuity leads us to a common assumption that some relationship remains fixed regarding the prior and posterior distributions. Discarding this assumption leads to intractability, which is painful for the quantitative mind. But if it is the reality, so be it.

There is nothing empirical to support the notion that a probability distribution remains identical over time. Everyday examples of this abound: OTC derivatives evolve from unlisted contracts where even market makers have limited information regarding exposures to exchange-traded cleared contracts where participants can monitor member exposures, radical changes, and on and on. Financial markets constantly remake themselves because the premium on learning, adaptation, and creativity makes their evolution accelerate. This, in turn, makes the information content of past data quickly diminish.

This is formalized in the following way: A process X_1, X_2, . . . , X_n observed sequentially can be decomposed into subprocesses where each subprocess has different data-generating mechanisms. At random times, the process can switch from one mechanism (and a corresponding distribution) to another. On a short time scale, this is "risk-on, risk-off" regime switching. On different time scales, this is what George Soros calls "reflexivity."

PAINT IT BLACK

Another point. There is not much support for thinking that X_t and X_{t+1} are independent of each other. In fact, sequentially observed X_1, X_2, . . . , X_n are rarely independent of each other. Just as a parts failure in a factory machine creates the likelihord of other parts failing. Or a car fails when a piston rod is thrown. Or an algae bloom kills all life in a pond. Simply put, when the life of a system is only as long as the life of one of its components, tail estimation quickly can become a joke. The strength of dependence and the number of components in the structure determine how vulnerable the system is. *The complexity of a system—meaning the interactions of its components—eliminates independence in a statistical sense.*

People sometimes think of statistical independence in a loose "these things are unrelated and removed from each other" sense. This is not the rigorous notion of independence required to power probabilistic models. Noncorrelated time series are not sufficient to establish independence of time series because correlations can break any time. For example, CME stock correlated with China for most of last year. When the stock took a big hit, it started correlating with financials. Independence, in contrast, means that the $\Pr(A \text{ and } B \text{ and } C \ldots \text{ and } Z) = \Pr(A)\Pr(B)\Pr(C) \ldots \Pr(Z)$, a condition connected to the existence of suitable decomposition of probability measures.

Nonstationarity and a lack of independence can have apocalyptic effects on a stochastic model. To see this, recall the Weiner process $W(t, \omega)_t \geq 0$. The differential dW of this process has deep connections in mathematical finance via the Black-Scholes option-pricing formula. dW in this process is referred to as *white noise*. Indications of how it acquired that name are obvious in Figure 13.1, a simulation based on randomly generated numbers under an assumption of normality.

While the 17,000+ observations are (pseudo) random, it is clear that they fall within finite upper and lower bounds. For this reason, future values are predictable within some modulus of error.

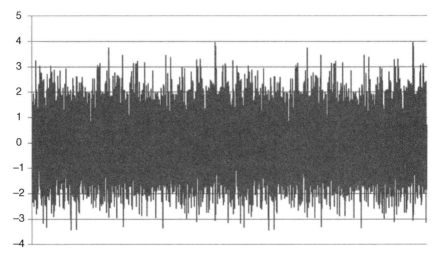

Figure 13.1 **White Noise Number Generation.**

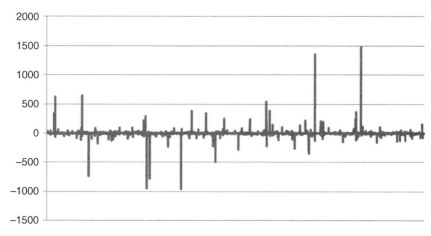

Figure 13.2 **Black Noise Number Generation.**

There is a whole rainbow of other colored noises, but the focus here is on black noise, the yin to the white noise yang. It is persistent and *non*stationary (Figure 13.2).

Across most of the interval, it is very much like white noise, but at times there are big jumps that cluster around each other. These extreme negative and positive jumps blow positions out of the water, financially speaking.

BALANCE COMPLEXITY WITH LIQUIDITY

Timing markets is futile, as is trying to outthink them (you can't), or relying on luck (while calling it prediction). Take risk to get reward, have a long enough time horizon to hold underwater positions comfortably, and most of all, keep some powder dry. Here's why. Going back to 1998, I calculated the average losses incurred during "crashes" on broad classes of assets (Table 13.1).

Table 13.1 Average Losses, (1998–2009)

Developed equities	−9.46%	*Emerging equities*	−26.63%
iBoxx HY	−2.63%	*iBoxx HG*	−2.02%
Sovereign bonds	1.00%	*U.S. T-bills*	0.80%

Table 13.2 Including the "Lehman Crisis"

Developed equities	−18.9%	Emerging equities	−27.4%
iBoxx HY	−7.4%	iBoxx HG	−6.4%
Sovereign bonds	−1.9%	U.S. T-bills	0.7%

I also looked specifically at the most recent crash, calling it the "Lehman crisis" (Table 13.2).

Nonstationarity creates opportunities for investors who maintain or have access to liquidity. These opportunities happen because of the ability to increase exposure to illiquid assets precisely when compensation for taking liquidity risk makes it most attractive. Examples using median loss estimates clarify the point, hopefully, in Table 13.3.

Even though $100 of net worth is reduced after a crash, an investor who has invested in some liquid low-risk, low-return assets has $20.20 to acquire additional risk exposure (Table 13.4). A more realistic portfolio contains leverage, proceeds, and contingent assets.

It isn't really adequate to consider leverage as a fixed margin call added at the end of the day, because different asset classes have higher haircuts than others. So there is an "Added Liquidity Problems" column (Table 13.5). Assets also typically generate cash flows, so a "Proceeds" column is added as well. These additions make for a more realistic understanding of liquidity. Liquidity beats getting flat to the

Table 13.3 Simple Portfolio

	Assets	Initial Position	After Losses (1998–2009)	Portfolio Liquidity
Equities	Developed equities	$ 30	89%	$26.7
	Emerging equities	$ 20	73%	$14.6
Fixed Income	iBoxx HY	$ 10	97%	$ 9.7
	iBoxx HG	$ 10	98%	$ 9.8
Cash-Like	Sovereign bonds	$ 10	101%	$10.1
	U.S. T-bills	$ 10	101%	$10.1
Illiquid	Structured notes	$ 10		$ 0
Gross Liquidity		$100		$81

Table 13.4 Levered Portfolio

	Assets	Initial Position	After Losses (1998–2009)	Portfolio Liquidity
Equities	Developed equities	$ 30	89%	$26.70
	Emerging equities	$ 20	73%	$14.6
Fixed Income	iBoxx HY	$ 10	97%	$ 9.70
	iBoxx HG	$ 10	98%	$ 9.80
Cash-Like	Sovereign bonds	$ 10	101%	$10.10
	U.S. T-bills	$ 10	101%	$10.10
Illiquid	Structured notes	$ 10		$ 0
Gross Liquidity		$100		$81.00
Less $10 cash needs for margin		−$ 10		$71.00

market because it does more than cancel out losses on a position: It enables additional risk exposure at better prices. You still take a whale of a hit, but in this case, liquidity keeps you from blowing up entirely.

Illiquid assets and term risk offer higher returns than lower-risk investments, but the concentrated illiquidity they carry will blow up your book in a crisis. Since crises are unpredictable, a balance between illiquid assets, cashable assets, and cashlike assets is wise. This has little to do with "diversify into uncorrelated assets" arguments. Correlation

Table 13.5 Portfolio with Leverage, Proceeds, and Complex Assets

	Initial Position	Portfolio Liquidity	Added Liquidity Problems	Proceeds	Adjusted Portfolio Liquidity
Equities	$ 50	$47.70	−$5.00	+$1	$43.70
Fixed income	$ 20	$14.6	−$3.00	+$2	$14.60
Illiquid	$ 10	0	0	0	$ 0
Derivatives (notional)	$ 10	0	−$5.00	0	$ 5
Cashlike assets					
Gross	$ 20	$20.20	+$2.00	+$0.5	$22.70
Less cash needs	−$ 10	−$10	−$20.00	0	−$30.00
Net	$ 10	$10	+$2.00	0	$12.00
Total value	$110	$72.30	−$16.00	$2.5	$55.55

and its generalizations are fleeting. But there will always be liquidity needs. When liquidity is needed, it is everything. Use what liquidity you have to staunch the bleeding or to take on more risk exposure when no one wants risk.

The core of a portfolio should be centered on exposure to returns that compensate you for risk. This includes fixed income, equities, and illiquid assets.

CHAPTER 14

High Yield and Market Makers

I missed a big part of the high-yield run-up. I even thought that there was an implosion imminent in the second quarter (Q2) of 2010. Boy, was I wrong.

- I underestimated the capacity for debt refinancing.
- I didn't appreciate the power of extreme monetary policy. I didn't research economists with useful firsthand knowledge.
- I missed some implications of market-maker derivative books. Over-the-counter (OTC) derivatives are not evil. They function mostly to control market makers' huge aggregate risk in an increasingly illiquid secondary market.

To begin, credit has some nice features. The price-to-hopefulness ratio common to equities is never a part of valuation. Few people have trouble parting with a bond when the price is right. This creates a fuzzy but ever-present upside limit. There is a downside bounded by the recovery rate. There are simple opening lines: Acquiring higher yield implies taking more risk by (1) lengthening term risk, (2) taking more credit risk, (3) moving down the capital structure, or (4) some combination. In the large, I avoided number 2.

Table 14.1 Mortality Rates by Original Rating—All Rated Corporate Bonds (1971–2007)

No. Yrs.	Cumulative Probability of Default in Years after Issuance									
	1	2	3	4	5	6	7	8	9	10
AAA	0	0	0	0	0.04%	0.06%	0.07%	0.07%	0.07%	0.07%
AA	0	0	0.29%	0.42%	0.44%	0.46%	0.46%	0.46%	0.51%	0.51%
A	0.01%	0.08%	0.10%	0.15%	0.20%	0.28%	0.33%	0.54%	0.62%	0.66%
BBB	0.31%	3.38%	4.63%	5.78%	6.44%	6.71%	6.93%	7.08%	7.19%	7.54%
BB	1.13%	3.49%	7.62%	9.69%	11.90%	13.01%	14.42%	15.36%	16.79%	19.63%
B	2.78%	9.22%	15.83%	22.93%	27.54%	30.65%	33.36%	34.93%	36.20%	36.80%
CCC	7.88%	21.98%	36.56%	43.96%	46.26%	51.37%	54.07%	56.58%	57.02%	59.02%

SOURCE: Standard & Poor's.

My summary view on high yield (HY) consisted of the following:

- *"Low policy rates don't have as much of an impact on speculative-grade debt as balance sheet concerns.*
- *Mortality rates for lower-rated debt are much higher than for investment-grade debt; the three-year mark is where defaults really start to bite.*
- *Three years ago (2007), 51 percent of HY issuance was rated B or below.*
- *Mortalities have been accelerated by economic factors, but cumulative default rates still will be high.*
- *Although a buy-and-hold strategy with a broad index of HY debt consistently outperforms the Treasury benchmark, trading strategies benefit from Treasury positioning."*

Take a look at Table 14.1 in regard to the mortality rates from 1971 and 2007.

"The three-year mortality rate for B-rated credit is 15.83 percent. The three-year mortality rate for CCC-rated credit is 36.56 percent. And 51 percent of 2007 issuance of HY debt is rated B– or below!"

Thesis: When a bond is rated less than B, three years into an issue, mortality rates really bite, and there is little excess return for the risk. This conclusion was a screw-up of a joke. I saw that negative growth and no inflation would make HY very risky because these factors reinforce the deleveraging theme. This was a plus for invest-ment grade names (HG) because they had room to delever. I consid-ered it unlikely that HY would be able to cut much leverage and avoid default. This may be right someday, but that doesn't justify the failure to see an opportunity. It led me to a default-rates estimate of 7 percent, which has way too high.

Reality: *U.S. HY default rates were less than 1 percent in 2010.*. HY hasn't seen tights implied by the low default rate, unlike HG. Low default, low growth, and low inflation make HY really attractive.

The central problem: Figuring out how default rates can be so low in the face of consumer-credit contraction, income decline, and wealth destruction.

WHAT'S HAPPENING

HY names adjusted quickly to financial stress, and CEOs took deci-sive action to improve their positions when opportunities arose. They had access to the bond market and used the spread compres-sion induced by quantitative easing (QE) to refinance existing debt (see Figure 14.1).

About two-thirds of all HY issuance was refinanced in 2009 and 2010. Share-issuance proceeds had similar allocations.

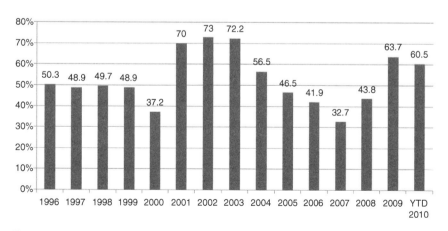

Figure 14.1 **Proceeds Used for Refinancing (%).**
Source: Bank of America.

POLICY BACKGROUND

It is also important to understand how monetary policy affects HY performance. A literature review from naughties (00s) concerning Japan helped me to decode the effects of monetary policy on the very low default rates. This was relevant because (1) deleveraging and retrenchment are decisive factors and (2) the Fed is using the Japanese policy approach. There are similarities with what happened then in Japan and what is happening now in the United States.

When problems arise, a central banker provides liquidity and mitigates financial intermediation lock-ups. In a real crisis, *the bank assumes chunks of credit risk for banks and corporations that can tap capital markets.* This implies spread compression for bonds but does not lead to increased bank lending to borrowers with no access to bond markets. Risk taking happens under very circumscribed conditions.

The spread compression made the Bank of Japan (BOJ) operate like a crutch to the Japanese financial system.[1] The BOJ succeeded in lowering risk premiums through all kinds of liquidity programs, but the declines didn't imply a sustainable solution to the credit crunch for small business because returns didn't accurately reflect credit risk. As a result, short-term funds avoided money-market mutual funds (MMMFs) and poured money into "riskless" assets such as Japanese government bonds (JGBs), U.S. Treasuries (USTs), and other government securities. The money eventually flowed into longer-term risk such as the 10-year JGB. Meanwhile, subsidies to cover shortage of funds in the money market were accomplished by more and longer BOJ liquidity operations. For example, *BOJ funding operations have terms of three to six months, and in some cases, even nine-month funds are offered.*[2]

This is what QE does anywhere it is applied: It crowds out money that recognizes risk and replaces it with reliance on the central bank. *"The QEP, which was partially directed toward alleviation of financial institutions' liquidity problems, has led to a decreased intermediation function by private banks in the money market and created a strong reliance on the BOJ's market operation".*[3] All the accommodation effectively warps an economy. Liquidity provision occurs at any sign of financial market instability, and the distinction between ordinary monetary and

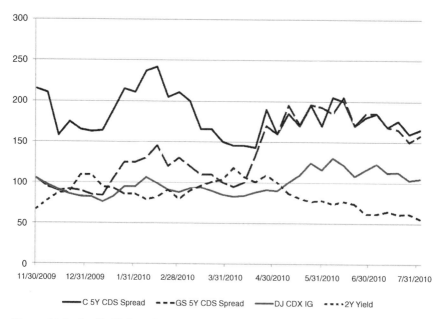

Figure 14.2 **Credit Risk and Spread Compression.**

extraordinary prudential policies gets lost. Fewer businesses can stand on their own two feet because so much organic growth is crowded out.

There is nothing especially Japanese about this. This is more about the effects of central planning. A picture view of the monetary effects during the QE period says it all (Figure 14.2).

- Rising and converging credit risk in tier 1 banks is reflected in the CDS spreads of Citibank and Goldman (intrasector correlation is high because of all the Fed support).
- Credit risk in the IG space is more subdued.
- Two-year bond yields began dropping like stones.

It seems that investors who formerly supported MMMFs are now pouring money into 2-year bonds. Term extension is going on too.

BANK RISK APPETITE STOPS AT BOND MARKETS

Companies without access to the capital markets get credit lines cut when their main banks experience financial problems. This is so because banks act to minimize material losses instead of taking credit risk and compensatory return. Since intermediation is busted, most small companies have few options if a bank won't roll their existing loans. This benefits bonds precisely because issuing names have more channels to acquire capital, and with all the cheap money floating around, HY becomes an easy reach for yield.

Not every business got a bailout in Japan. Sick Japanese banks were put on life support by the BOJ, and sick Japanese companies were put on life support by market makers. This was possible because of supercheap money and bank forebearance for on-book zombies instead of realized losses on market inventory. *"Due to capital limitations, banks have been reluctant to extend new loans to this class of borrower. In many cases, however, they continued to roll over existing loans without raising lending rates much. Lending rates to lower-rated borrowers have been well below those that cover expenses and default risks. Demanding higher lending rates would have made many borrowers insolvent, forcing banks to realize losses; banks, however, lacked capital for such action. As a result, high risk premiums have not been observed here either. The same reasoning explains the underdeveloped nature of the distressed asset market."*[4]

So ZIRP and unorthodox monetary policy in general make credit markets gravity-defying but leave companies that rely on loans in a difficult spot even when company balance sheets are not impaired. In Japan, a *". . . deterioration in balance-sheet conditions, especially in bank balance-sheet conditions, hampered the investment of smaller non-bond-issuing firms more severely than . . . larger bond-issuing firms."*[4] It is the deterioration of bank balance sheets that killed credit lines to companies that couldn't raise capital through the markets.

This has less to do with any perversity in the Japanese financial system and more to do with changing global conditions for market makers. Avoiding realized losses on paper inventory is imperative for market makers because secondary market liquidity isn't deep. If they can't move it, keeping the name alive with cheap credit makes sense.

Market makers are more than ever huge portfolio managers carrying gigantic aggregate risk. This explains the rise of prop trading more than anything, as well as the bulk of OTC derivatives. Nothing particularly evil is going on there. This didn't start yesterday; it's been a growing trend for years.

LESSONS

I'm going to talk about a specific debt grade here because estimating a common density for HY (BB to C) is inappropriate because of granularity. Check out the nonparametric density estimate for BBB bond yields from March 2009 (when the Fed officially became the whore of Babylon) to the present: The black dotted line is a normal-distribution reference curve, and the solid gray line is the estimate (Figure 14.3).

In broad brushstrokes, there are very short tails and an interquartile asymmetry indicative of a risk-on, risk-off mentality. Therefore, if you have a bond price close to par, the expectation for bond prices is little upside and big downside. These features are consistent with HY on a long enough time line. Implication: HY positions must rely on income for the real upside and effective hedging against downside risk, especially as changes in market-maker behavior make it hard to unwind without a bid-ask reaming.

Market structure changes seriously alter book performance. Central banks can't do everything, but I am continually amazed by the magic shows they put on. I am even more surprised at how tough times can strengthen a balance sheet. Bets against human ingenuity in a tight spot carry downside risk too.

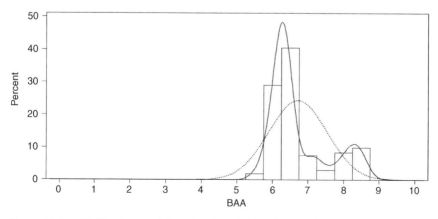

Figure 14.3 **BBB Yield Kernel Density, May 2009–September 2010.**

CHAPTER 15

Thinking Outside the Bubble: A Pairs Trade on the EU Experiment

Nothing tests the mettle of an idea like laying money down. It's where cool calculation stands in stark contrast to sunshine pumping. People can talk all they want about how great Greek bonds are. If they're *really* on board with the technocrats and think that the European Union (EU) is going to hold together as is, then long that 10-year Greek debt and short 10-year German Bunds. The trade shows the risks of the status quo more clearly than anything else.

The whole thing looks like picking up pennies in front of a steamroller, because buying cheap can be a fateful trap too. One needs faith that time will be on your side, and soon, and that the world's tail-risk killers will succeed. On one side of the tade are hubris-riddled bureaucrats with a deep line of taxpayer credit to distort reality. It's the force of history via out-of-sample mean reversion versus the hubris of humans. Who says investing doesn't have tragic plotlines?

TAIL-RISK KILLING AND THE BUBBLE WORLD: TREASURIES ARE NOT GREEK GOVERNMENT BONDS . . . YET

Central banker (and political stooge) socialization of financial system losses makes sovereign debt default concerns light up like a night in Vegas. So too is there much fear of the "Treasury bubble" popping. Treasury yields aren't the only thing people should be worried about: *Almost every asset has a bubble valuation now.* In many cases, the sovereign debt run-up is just a symptom of the problem, not the problem itself. The real problem is private-sector debt creation in reverse. The tail risks associated with this are why Bernanke is pushing the money machine to the limit. He's doing what he thinks will kill those tail risks. His perceived middle game is probably some Japanese variation—the tail is much worse.

Today we are conditioned to living in a bubble because of all the leverage. So forget about "quality" and "fundamentals" because they are so distorted the notions lack meaning. Nobody thinks a U.S. Treasury bond displays awesome fundamentals. This is not why you buy them. Treasuries are not a flight to quality at all. But when debt reduction is the prevailing wind, what really matters is liquidity. People sell quality assets because the higher mark allows them better loss cover. They ride out the storm in the most liquid instruments.

Pricing of risk is completely altered when living in a bubble. Supereasy monetary policy makes you desire what you should fear and fear what you should desire. Liquidity policies are designed to obscure insolvency and illiquidity up to the breaking point. Risk in a meltdown always looks like a "flight from the despised" bubble. In a bubble world, though, it is really a flight from leverage. Assets with little leverage possess valuations that offer more than commensurate return in exchange for the risk. Such bottomed-out assets (such as sugar no. 11 of May 2010) are uncommon. With gobs of cheap money lifting all boats, nothing stays despised for long. A buying cheap and selling dear strategy has a high success rate.

The bubble world has lasted long enough to blind people to the alternative valuations that lie outside it. But the bubble world we live in is not irreversible. It is actually pretty unique from a historical viewpoint. Bubbles pop. So it is wise to prepare for phase transitions, where nonstationarity makes the rules change as one goes, and liquidity becomes like a gasp of air in a vacuum. The macro themes of unsustainable systemic backstops pitted against organic deterioration of economic conditions are telling signs of a coming reality shift.

JOUSTING WINDMILLS: SOVEREIGN DEBT AS AN ASSET CLASS

Sovereign debt markets are a good asset class to position macro trades that play off these themes. When spreads rise, it is a moment of clarity when risk is weighed realistically. When spreads explode, it is the moment of panic at the top of the food chain.

Government securities are somewhat like a bond and somewhat like equity; credit-default swaps (CDS) have changed this little. Government bonds don't obey default probability formulas the same way as other debt. As with any debt instrument, there is an interest rate beyond which debt service becomes unsustainable. What makes them "equity-ish" is that recovery-rate assumptions are meaningless because bankruptcy is more than a little ambiguous.

Thus the root problem is that government credit risk is not easy to quantify: It is the good faith of people and leaders to sacrifice and honor their commitments. One country will find a way to pay service debt and another will not under similar conditions. For existential reasons, a country such as Latvia takes pains to keep the good graces of its creditors to the west. Latvians are scared of what history says about the people to the east. Greece provides another, opposite example.

Residual stuff such as history and culture surely plays some role. Cultures can be rooted in the idea of the state as a civil entity, where the state is merely the custodian of laws and does not seek to impose any preferred pattern of ends but merely facilitates individuals to pursue their own ends. Other cultures view the state as a business: Government is a manager of an enterprise that legislates standards that equalize people to some degree. These differences may matter in reflecting the scope of spending excesses but at the same time be irrelevant in predicting taxpayer willingness to default.

This is all running in the background before assessing credit risk even starts. Thus, metrics such as current account and external indebtedness and model outputs are mostly a confirmation of preconceived risk assessment. Measures such as tax-revenue forecasts and gross domestic product (GDP) projections are almost surely unrealistic. Macroeconomic data don't tame the noise in what underlies a cash-strapped nation's faith and credit.

MARKET-NEUTRAL METHODS: COINTEGRATION AND BURNING WITCHES

A way to express a spread bet on government securities is through a pairs trade. Pairs trading has a lot of different names depending on the assets used in construction. It is a market-neutral strategy (a short leg and a long leg) that depends on mean reversion. There are practical problems associated with any such pairs-trading construction, for example, demands for margin cover, reducing carry cost, and keeping equity capital on board before things have ripened. There also can be model failure or failure in trading-period selection. Still, market neutrality is a good way to manage liquidity, when waiting on mean reversion can be a killer. Using quantitative methods is a way to rigorously find solutions to the issue of waiting.

The rigor comes from statistical models developed from data in a training period and deployed in a trading period. These quantitative pairs trades have method problems too; the issue of training-period selection is decisive. The point of such a model is to determine cointegration between nonstationary variables. Cointegration specifies a predictable relation, be it causal or coincident, within the training period. This relationship then is traded outside of sample. Choosing an appropriate time period for robust cointegration is hard because the relationship is very sensitive on the sample data. Outside the sample, relationships can quickly break down. This problem is well understood by those who trade based on 60-, 100-, and 200-day moving averages. Selecting the appropriate time frame is guesswork in both contexts. Macro trades require correct *human judgment* about whether the model should incorporate data going back to, say, May 2009, 2000, or 1973. The risk of the trade is that the appropriate mean, much less mean reversion, is unclear.

COINTEGRATIONS BREAK

Everyone knows that correlations break. Cointegrations are no different. Even in low-leverage, high-frequency settings with small trading windows, it could be nothing more than randomness that makes pairs trading work. It may not matter which of the pairs is shorted because noise dominates at microsecond increments. Even if our mean estimate is sufficient because we choose all available information, there are other troubles. Consider a time series of Bible prices going all the way back to 1608. We have two pairs: prices in the struggling Jamestowne Settlement in Virginia and prices in Franz Buirmann's witch-barbecued Köln. In reality, the conditions between Jamestowne and Köln were so different that there was no way to trade a risk-free arbitrage in the market for Bibles. Or consider another example of Köln in 1430, when Bibles were hand-copied versus 1436 after the Guttenburg press was running; this is a classic bifurcation induced by technology.

Difficulties aside, pairs trading is also suited for macro trades exploiting a *qualitative* theme. As the world shifts from an easy liquidity, colored-by-noise framework to a liquidity-starved austerity, most models won't provide much advantage. The sample data are too limited to arrive at meaningful cointegrating vectors when the regime totally changes. Relying on such models is far too conditioned on contemporary history and not able to capture the jumps that things such as monetization or International Monetary Fund (IMF) bailouts generate. These policy interventions make *precision* effectively impossible, and neither assessment nor calculation does much good in defining proper action. What really matters in the described phase transition is good information, intuition, and an ability to be resourceful and stubborn. Confidence comes from being *broadly* right. This is the human edge: The games of Mikhail Tal and Alexei Shirov show how some have sharply higher intuitive power in the face of complexity when others buckle under ambiguity.

Bureaucracies seldom have such an edge. Appointees such as the central bankers and finance ministers don't have more coolness under fire or resourcefulness than the average person, and this is an investible thesis. In fact, because of the sheer scale of influence they exert, when panic strikes, central bankers and finance ministers frequently make things worse. They suppress present tail risk and in so doing create bigger future tail risks. One such qualitative theme is the limited intelligence and dubious quality of governance. This may be the macro theme Nassim Taleb has in mind when he talks about shorting Treasuries. There are sharper instruments than Treasury shorts to profit from stupid bureaucratic stubbornness.

THIS IS THE HOUSE THAT FUNK BUILT: EU INTEGRITY OR FRAGMENTATION

Belief in the EU staying intact is equivalent to govvie spread convergence. Collapse is equivalent to spread divergence. Anyone who shorts German Bunds and longs Greek debt as a mean reverting pairs trade is counting on two things: (1) Greek bond yields coming down or (2) German Bund yields blowing up. Although the first is a joke, a German commitment to the EU makes the second scenario likely. Germany's stable economy and solid macroeconomic data could crater. Its controlled fiscal deficit and efficient tax policies could buckle under commitments to other member nations. Its economy is the largest in Europe, but borrowing from the market will not be cheap going forward. Being on the hook for other nations' default-like situations will magnify Germany's credit risk.

Mean reversion is at work in shorting PIIGS (Portugal, Ireland, Italy, Greece, and Spain) too, but it is reversion to yields outside the sample period in Figure 15.1. This implies spread divergence, not compression. Throughout the decade, there is massive convergence of yields and a low implied risk premium. But there are deeper historical forces at work, expressed in the recent spread widening. Propping up the status quo won't continue indefinitely. Voter refusal to subsidize an artificial spread compression is where reality breaks with the last few years of performance.

Indeed, a trade on the spread explosion between Greek government bonds (GGBs) and German Bunds earlier this year was a masterstroke.

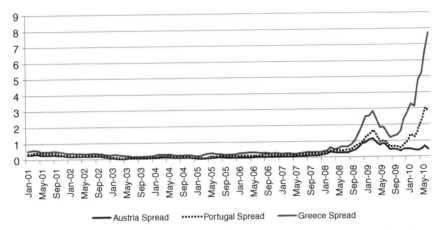

Figure 15.1 **Selected 10-Year Government Security Spread to German Bunds.**

Now risk assessment of Greek prospects is far more realistic than a few months ago, but there is little point in closing the trade. And Greek debt isn't the only instrument to take a view on EU integrity. Figure 15.1 shows some candidates for a spread trade on things going deeply wrong in Europe.

Each bond in Figure 15.1 carries its own psychoses. Portugal, too, has a long way to go before accomplishing what is needed to put its house or banking system in order. Rising Greek internal tensions and resistance to public-sector job cuts and strikes make it a time bomb. Internal stresses from Spain, Portugal, Ireland, and others reduce the extent of fiscal assistance even as Central European periphery problems poison the Austrian banking system.

A 10-year Portuguese bond spread of less than 3 percent over German Bunds is not reflective of 9 percent of Portuguese banking assets coming from the European Central Bank (ECB). It takes a real pile of crap to need the level of life support Greece has. It also tells you that someone in the EU is invested in making the center hold.

CHAPTER 16

Dropping Acid in Disneyland: Thoughts on the New Normal

Finance is behaving psychedelically because asset correlations increase market crashes and stresses. Looking at the tapestry of cash and synthetic assets sheds light on the boom and bust cycles of the vernacular "new normal." This characterization provides clues about the nature of its endgame and progress toward that end.

- Economic growth fueled by easy monetary policy leads to excessive investment in specific assets (bubbles), resulting in more extreme boom and bust cycles.
- Government policies to regulate the cycles lead to further crises that affect higher levels of capital structure.
- In particular, very steep yield curves result in a generalized carry trade.
- Equity valuations always get smashed in a crash. However, in the new normal, the top of the corporate capital structure is not as immune as it has been.
- The next to get smashed? Sovereign credit.

Table 16.1 Remembrance of Meltdowns Past

		Equities			Bonds			
	Date	MSCI All-World Index	MSCI Developed Markets	MSCI Emerging Markets	iBoxx High-Yield Premium	iBoxx IG Premium	Sovereign Bonds	U.S. T-bills
LTCM Stumblebum	Aug.1998	−14.20%	−13.50%	−29.30%	−2.20%	−1.50%	2.50%	0.90%
Tech bubble Screw job	Nov. 2000	−6.20%	−6.10%	−8.80%	−1.30%	−0.70%	2.00%	0.70%
September 11, 2001	Sep. 2001	−9.10%	−8.80%	−15.50%	−1.40%	−0.70%	0.80%	1.00%
Idiot quant crisis	Aug. 2007	−0.20%	0%	−2.10%	−0.80%	−0.90%	1.60%	0.70%
Lehman clusterfluke	Oct. 2008	−19.80%	−18.90%	−27.40%	−7.40%	−6.30%	−1.90%	0.70%
Average loss		−9.90%	−9.46%	−16.62%	−2.62%	−2.02%	1.00%	0.80%

Note: Gray cells indicate losses greater than average over the listed crashes.

The endgame? Either the U.S. government lives within its means, or U.S. T-bills get hammered. Then it's really bad.

The typical stuff you often read is that "averaging these losses out, optimal return is obtained with standard asset class allocation. . . ." The situation is quite different. Observe that the boom-bust cycles exhibit a tendency toward greater losses at the top of the capital structure. This is not just in corporate names. Even sovereign debt was marginally affected in the latest bust (see Table 16.1). You can see it written all over SovX quotes. (SovX is an index basket of quoted sovereign credit default swap spreads.) It will get worse until policymakers stop rewarding failure.

My conjecture is simple: More and more capital structure senior assets are synchronized to a measure of disruption in the subordinate capital structure: traded volatility index (VIX). This instability is the new normal until another new normal comes along.

FOCUS IN ON CAPITAL STRUCTURE EFFECTS IN 2008

A closer look at capital structure losses in the 2008 bust gives a feel for the cloth. That the S&P 500 Index vaporizes is typical in any crash. The new wrinkle we see now is in newer instruments like swaps.

Table16.2 The Year the Music Died, Selected Quotes

Milestone Insolvencies	Date	VIX	ATM 5-Year Volume	S&P 500	5-Year Swap Rate	CDX.IG Spread	iBoxx IG Bond Spread
	1/2/2008	12.0%	18.7%	1,417	5.06%	0.33%	0.14%
Bear Sterns	3/17/2008	32.2%	27.0%	1,277	3.17%	1.85%	4.64%
Merrill Lynch	8/29/2008	20.7%	25.4%	1,283	4.03%	1.43%	3.43%
Freddie, Fannie	9/8/2008	22.6%	25.2%	1,268	3.91%	1.38%	3.41%
Lehman	9/15/2008	31.7%	25.3%	1,193	3.69%	1.94%	5.04%
AIG failure	9/16/2008	30.3%	26.3%	1,214	3.45%	2.00%	5.07%
	12/31/2008	40.0%	35.3%	903	2.10%	2.14%	8.13%

The 5-year swap rate condenses interbank lending and Treasury yields into one measure of risk-adjusted demand for capital. The traded credit default swap index for the investment grade basket (CDX.IG) is an index of big liquid credit-default swap (CDS) names. There was a tremendous amount of stress on cash markets, shown by the IG bond index blowout and that the term structure of the Standard & Poor's (S&P) 500 Index volume was inverted for a good chunk of the fourth quarter (Q4) of 2009 (see Table 16.2).

THINKING SORT OF LINEARLY: PIECEWISE REGRESSION AND CORRELATION FUNCTIONS

Imagine a financial experiment across a spectrum. At one extreme are very solid senior credits; at the other extreme are residual securities, subordinate in terms of capital structure. Shocks to one extreme manifest in higher credit spreads to the "risk free" reference rate; the other extreme results in selling. I use daily bond spreads and the volatility index (VIX) quotes for this. The VIX is good for this purpose because it is traded and thus demonstrates extreme effects better. And yes . . . , I too am stunned, benumbed, and burned by the hateful chasm between ratings and reality. But ratings do provide meaningful categories for analysis.

The model:

$$(\text{Baa spreads})_t = \beta_0 + \beta_1(\text{AAA spreads})_t + \beta_2(\text{closing price of VIX})_t = \varepsilon_t$$

where t = daily quotes, and AAA, Baa spreads = ratings based on Moody's seasoned bonds, daily quotes.

Table 16.3 Regression: January 1990–December 1999

Variable	n	Parameter Estimate	t Value	Pr > |t|	R²
Intercept		−0.38698	−14.41	<0.0001	0.9804
VIX	2620	0.01144	24.48	<0.0001	
AAA spread	2625	1.12232	**354.96**	<0.0001	

Table 16.4   Regression: January 2000–December 2005

Variable	n	Parameter Estimate	t Value	Pr > |t|	R²
Intercept		1.20161	33.24	<0.0001	0.9546
VIX	1447	0.02261	26.24	<0.0001	
AAA spread	1435	0.88106	**134.28**	<0.0001	

From 1990 to 1999, the fit was near perfection (R^2), and Baa spreads were dominated by AAA spreads (t value) (see Table 16.3).

From 2000 to 2005, the model says essentially the same thing, although the overall fit is marginally diminished (Table 16.4).

From 2006 to April 2009, the situation is different. The overall fit now admits specification issues (it's still a real good fit), but more to the point, the VIX now has more explanatory power over Baa spreads than AAA spreads (bold t value) (Table 16.5).

In these regressions I lagged the VIX as well. There was no appreciable difference in fit of parameter estimates. This implies that either the relationship between the VIX and Baa spreads is simultaneous, or the effect in time is somewhat complex.

The correlation function is a way to determine how the relationship of the VIX and Baa spread evolves in time. The correlation function is a mapping that measures the correlation of changes in one time

Table 16.5   Regression: January 2006–April 2010

Variable	n	Parameter Estimate	t Value	Pr > |t|	R²
Intercept		2.28122	11.96	<0.0001	0.8183
VIX	1149	0.05061	66.36	<0.0001	
AAA spread	1137	0.62153	17.81	<0.0001	

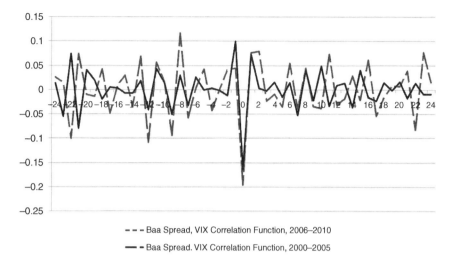

Figure 16.1   **Baa Spreads and Vix Correlation Function: Differenced Data.**

series with changes in another time series. Figure 16.1 takes a given Baa spread in time and measures the strength of correlation with the closing price of the VIX from 24 days before to 24 days after.

The closer a line is 0 on the horizontal axis, the less relationship there is between Baa spreads and the VIX. The more positive or negative the points become shows how positively or negatively correlated Baa spreads and the VIX are with each other when looking at Baa spreads on, say, January 1 and the VIX 24 days in the past and 24 days in the future.

Changes in the Baa spread are negatively correlated with the closing price of the VIX on the same day. However, Baa spread rises made the VIX more likely to rise than the next two days afterward. Note also that the correlation between Baa spreads and the VIX has more extreme positive and negative correlations in the 2006–2010 period.

CHAPTER 17

Synthetic Fixed Income and Rates—A Repo Puzzle: What Happened in July–August 2007?

The conventional wisdom about derivatives and other markets at the core of the financial system is that they are too complicated to understand without years of training and perspiration. Financiers want to keep it this way because it gives them an advantage.

The financial environment is actually pretty simple, and everyday experience has some clear analogues to its architecture. Start with people, businesses, and governments with financing needs. Depending on who they are, they can finance in a number of different ways. People typically take out loans from banks. Businesses can take out loans, issue bonds, and offer pieces of ownership (stocks). Governments issue debt. Dealer banks inventory these instruments and market them to others. These banks exist as middlemen, and investors have a choice to take what they offer or not. They bundle mortgage and commercial loans, among other things, and sell these securities to others. They inventory at wholesale rates bonds and stocks and sell them with a retail markup to entities that want the risk exposure. These dealers and some other large players in the financial system sometimes use this inventory as collateral to get different risk exposure for themselves. Such lending occurs in repurchase agreements. Repos, as they are called, are one of those structures that lie at the center of the financial system. It's like a securities loan with collateral.

This system works well most of the time. Dealers have the advantages of superior information and faster execution, so they can de-risk off faster than everyone else in a crisis, and their connection to central banks gives them the liquidity to scoop up the risk that retail dumps in the aftermath of a crisis. And then dealers start moving risk assets to retail as their appetite for it recovers. It's a cycle like evaporation and condensation.

LIQUIDITY

The key to this cycle is *liquidity*. Liquidity depends on dealer financing activity. As mentioned, the sell side of dealers facilitates widespread trading activity by lending securities held in custody to buy riskier positions. Hedge funds and other buy-side actors depend on these financing arrangements to finance their activities. This financing becomes increasingly complex as it involves multiple counterparties and multiple asset classes domiciled in multiple jurisdictions.

Both buy and sell side lending is secured by collateral in a repurchase agreement. In essence, these agreements are secured loans with posted collateral and a fixed interest rate (the repo rate) over a very short term (usually overnight, sometimes three months). The market is still huge, but the hedge fund and prop desk volumes have yet to recover since the 2008 crisis. This contraction in the repo market is an indication of the damage done to the financial system (Figure 17.1).

Many types of collateral are posted in the repo market, but it is easiest to repo T-bills. As a result, 3-month T-bill repo rates provide a benchmark for repo activity; other asset repo rates are defined by a spread over this rate. This rate and the resulting market changes determine "risk on" and "risk off" appetite and are among the most important market "fundamentals" when you live in a financial bubble.

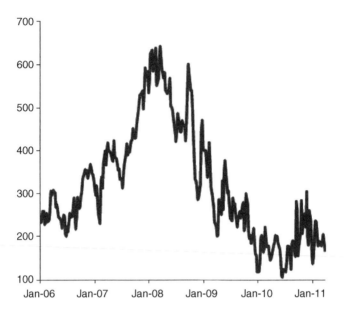

Figure 17.1 **Net Dealer Repo Leverage in $ Billions, 2006–2011.**
Source: BarCap.

The mechanism itself isn't so alien. The problem is that the repo market is large and exposures are opaque. Specific exposures, collateral composition, and market features are little understood outside the major clearing banks at the center of the system. So what are people naturally inclined to do? That's right, they theorize about it with limited data and don't sweat the small stuff.

In repo markets, the small stuff is crucial. Minute changes in rules and regulatory stance radically affect outcomes. When you sweat the small stuff, really weird events aren't so weird at all. It is easy to fall into a "big picture" trap at the expense of the details. Here's an example from the repo market.

PROBLEM IN THE REPO MARKET

The repo market for corporate bonds experienced a $6\sigma+$ delivery fail event (Figure 17.2). Delivery fails happen when parties in a repo transaction fail to deliver the needed collateral for the transaction.

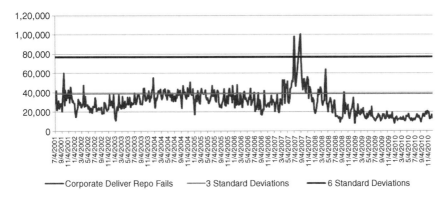

Figure 17.2   **Repo Delivery Fails: Corporate Bonds.**

A part of the puzzle is that this event was isolated to corporate bond deliveries. Mortgage-backed securities (MBS), Treasuries, and agencies saw no such spike in July–August of 2007 (Figure 17.3*a*, *b*).

The MBS securities market busted after the 2008 crash, and as a result, the haircuts on these securities are really volatile. (See Figure 17.3*b*).

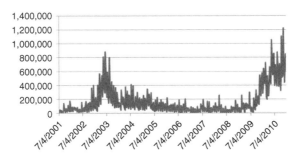

Figure 17.3*a*   **MBS Deliver Repo Fails.**

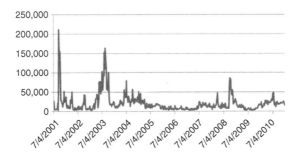

Figure 17.3*b*   **Agency Deliver Repo Fails.**

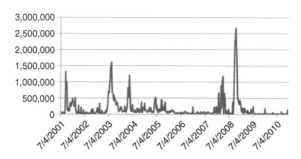

Figure 17.3*c* **Total Treasury Deliver Repo Fails.**

Agencies fared much better because they carry a U.S. government guarantee (see Figure 17.3*b*).

Treasuries are the premier de-risking asset, so when you see fails in the Treasury repo (Figure 17.3*c*), you know something really big is going down. The exact dates of these corporate bond delivery fail events were the weeks of July 4, 2007 (98,608), August 15, 2007 (80,505), August 22, 2007 (92,605), and August 29, 2007 (100,965).

It's a Thin Market

Corporate securities are not a big part of repo financing. Treasuries, followed by MBS, dominate the repo financing market (Table 17.1).

When supply is tight, then repo security delivery is naturally more difficult. When supply is thin in the first place, you have the potential for big spikes in failures. However, this doesn't explain what was essentially a unique event that occurred for 28 days within a 3,833-day period for corporate bond deliveries.

Table 17.1 Amount Outstanding as of December 29, 2010

Type of Financing	Overnight and Continuing	Term Agreements	Total
Securities out			
U.S. Treasury securities	1,126,113	667,486	1,793,599
Federal agency and government-sponsored enterprise securities	158,536	90,613	249,149
Mortgage-backed securities	409,897	322,737	732,634
Corporate securities	113,611	68,499	182,110

The Impact of Regulatory Change

Even small regulatory changes affect markets in huge ways, and such a change explains the spikes in repo fails. *The Securities and Exchange Commission (SEC) voted to remove the grandfather provision that allowed fails-to-deliver that existed before Regulation SHO to be exempt from Regulation SHO.* With the removal of the grandfathering position on naked shorting, investors scrambled to close out naked short positions before Regulation SHO kicked in. Formally, regulation SHO applies to short sales of equity securities. The term *equity security* is defined in Section 3(a)(11) of the Exchange Act and Rule 3a11-1 thereunder (17 CFR 240.3a11-1) which states that "a security convertible into an equity security is an equity security. Therefore, short sales of bonds that are convertible into equity would be subject to Regulation SHO. The staff will consider on a case-by-case basis securities, including structured products, to which the 'equity' status may not be clear."

There is nothing fancy involved in sweating the details. It's just hard work.

CHAPTER 18

Haircuts at the Core of Capitalism

Over-the-counter (OTC) derivative markets depend on financing, just like everything else because in this world there are precious few things actually owned. Most things contain a fraction of ownership and a chunk of borrowed capital that entitles a holder to its use. This relationship between credit and use rights *is* capitalism: There is no other way to view it. (So when you see banks being told to write off principal on underwater mortgages by regulators, know that capitalism at its essence is twisted into something grotesque.)

The same mechanics that apply to home mortgages—down payments, fixed repayment over a term, and canceling of use agreements through foreclosure—are straightforward analogues of interbank financing. When times are good, credit risk is lower (meaning that the likelihood of repayment is high), so creditors accept easier down-payment terms. This down payment in the interbank universe is called *collateral*. To adjust for credit risk (the likelihood of not getting paid back for credit extended), debtors must accept discounted value on their collateral. This is a *haircut*. When times are bad, haircuts are higher. Sometimes assets are no longer accepted as collateral—the haircut becomes 100 percent.

The data screams that developed-government securities in very bad times take small haircuts. In fact, the value of those securities appreciated and the haircut remained constant. Generally, the more risky the asset becomes, the greater the haircut. The haircuts on risk assets were extreme coming out of November 2008. This indicates that market valuations are unstable—fundamental value is difficult to establish. Don't be too quick to dump sovereign debt even though its "fundamentals" suck. The outlook and performance can change completely in a year or so.

Insights from really grim times show how the most loved assets can unravel and how the crappiest assets suddenly become the finest. Data from the dark days of the credit crunch indicate just what assets held the financial architecture together and what got flushed.

TAKE-AWAYS

- The extent of haircuts is a good measure of the extent of systemic financial collapse.
- Primary counterparties and hedge funds took only minuscule haircuts on G7 sovereign debt throughout the credit crisis.
- Postcrash, structured credit wasn't accepted as collateral. This implies that precrash valuations were way off.
- Collateral haircut rates were different for primary dealers and hedge funds.

The data are aggregated survey results from the Bank for International Settlements (BIS) Committee on the Financial System, with some accompanying open questions. Only point estimates are available; there is no indication of the dispersion of haircuts. Respondents represent dealers and hedge funds. More information on the survey and different policy recommendations to make margining practices "stable through the cycle" can be found at www.bis.org/publ/ cgfs36.pdf?noframes=1.

Stable through the cycle is shorthand for a way to control leverage ratios. However, the idea of controlling leverage could kill the repo market if a severe enough crisis hits and market-to-market (MTM) valuations say something different from what policymakers dictate.

In effect, leverage becomes a control lever. Is this really an idea worth entertaining?

RESULTS

The survey tells you something about real credit risk and asset pricing at the ground state. It also tells you something about different perceived counterparty risks in the transactions. What you see in Figure 18.1 is the difference in haircuts applied to prime dealers versus hedge funds in 2007 and 2009. There are two mechanisms at work. One is an increasing haircut in the type of collateral, based on its perceived riskiness. Note that short-term government securities from G7 countries maintained their minuscule haircut through the time of stress, whereas high-yield debt securities received a much higher haircut in 2009.

The other issue relates to different risk associated with counterparties posting collateral. Prime dealers always have had a smaller haircut applied to the securities they post as collateral. In 2009, those times of stress caused a 25 percent differential in haircuts between these dealers and hedge funds because of the higher counterparty risk associated with hedge funds.

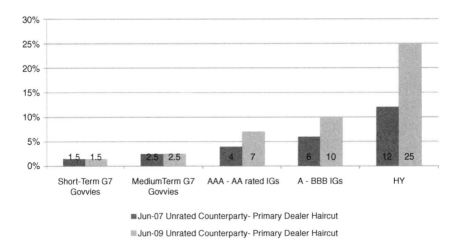

Figure 18.1 **Haircut Difference between Primary Dealers and Hedge Funds.**

OPEN QUESTION

The results show clear segmentation of haircut rates between primary dealers and hedge funds. Is this the result of the Fed Term Securities Lending Facility (TSLF)[1] program for primary dealers?

It doesn't seem like TSLF is the answer. Although there was some serious cash involved in this program (see Figure 18.2), schedule 2 collateral includes only collateral eligible for triparty repurchase agreements arranged by the Open Market Trading Desk (stated as investment-grade only), AAA/Aaa-rated private-label residential MBS, AAA/Aaa-rated commercial MBS, agency collateralized mortgage oblications (CMOs), and other AAA/Aaa-rated asset-backed securities (ABS). So TSLF doesn't explain the difference in high-yield haircuts. Counterparty profile and discount window reputation effects are more explanatory (see Figure 18.2).

ASSET CLASS VALUATION UNDER STRESS

The only collateral haircut that didn't increase from June 2007 to June 2009 was G7 government debt. This haircut stayed constant for both primary dealers and unrated counterparties (the vast majority of

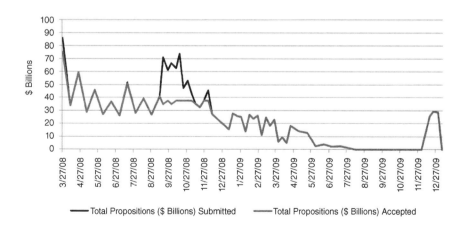

Figure 18.2   **TSLF Auctions, Schedule 2 Collateral.**
Source: Securities Industry and Financial Markets Association (SIFMA), Federal Reserve.

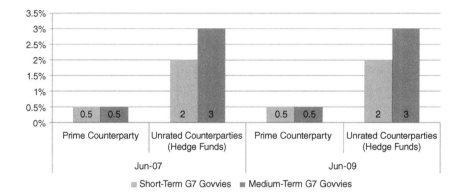

Figure 18.3   **Percent Haircut on Term Security Financing, Government Debt Collateral.**

these are hedge funds) through the crunch. *Never forget that government securities are the most liquid, and governments can and will raise taxes on the most creditworthy as needed.* It doesn't really matter who pays as long as it can be coughed up or it can be borrowed (see Figure 18.3).

Astronomers postulate that a black hole is at the center of the Milky Way, and its gravitational field is what holds everything together. If the financial system is anything like a galaxy, then government securities of G7 countries are at the center of the financial universe. Investors move into them in times of stress because they constitute low-risk investments with very cashlike qualities. This movement to the core is the essence of *de-risking.*

OPEN QUESTION

Are haircuts more influenced by MTM collateral performance or credit ratings?

It looks like collateral performance. I don't think that ratings agencies kept up with increasing haircut demands. Just looking at the extreme end of term security financing indicates that investment-grade (IG) haircuts increased by 10 percent in less than two years, and high-yield (HY) haircuts increased by 20 percent (Figure 18.4).

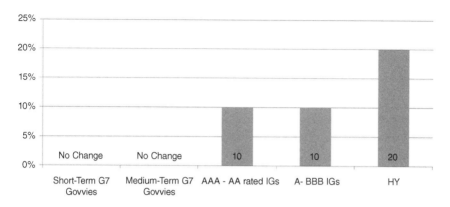

Figure 18.4   **Change in Hedge Fund Haircuts on Term Security Financing, 2007–2009.**

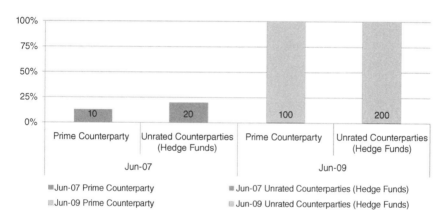

Figure 18.5   **Percent Haircut on Term Security Financing, AAA-Structured Paper Collateral.**

There's even more anecdotal support because the survey informs about pre- and postcrash valuations and rating-agency models. AAA-structured securitizations were not accepted as collateral by 2009 (Figure 18.5). It is clear that ratings meant nothing for asset class value in this case postcrash.

Prime counterparty haircuts for AAA–AA IG increased from 1 to 8 percent. The haircut approximately doubled for other cases (Figure 18.6).

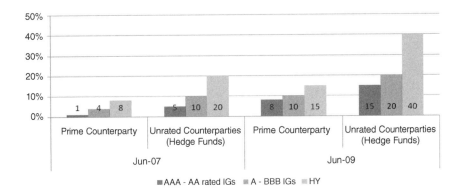

Figure 18.6 **Percent Haircut on Term Security Financing, Corporate Debt Collateral.**

Note the 40 percent haircut for HY in June 2009 compared with 20 percent in 2007, which is just astounding.

HAIRCUTS CONTROL LEVERAGE

Some draconian haircut rates emerged out of the crisis. The idea of smoothing these haircuts rates over a liquidity cycle is novel, like wagging the dog by its tail. Haircuts rise for a reason—call it due to bursts of clarity about fundamentals, panic, whatever. That haircuts rise is no more or less irrational than any other market action that goes on.

If you think through the effect of haircuts on leverage, you can see the natural mechanics of markets working here as they do everywhere. Think of the mortgage market. If a bank requires more down payment to release a home loan, the leverage is reduced on the loan. The down payment in the term financing described consists of collateral assets. The haircut controls the leverage of the financing.

Even though the monthly payment is lower, there are fewer people who can afford a home because they don't want to or can't lock up so much capital. The housing market operates such that the price of a home goes down when less leverage is embedded in the transaction. The same thing is going on in the repo market. The sheer size of the market situates it at the core of economic motion. When it glitches, everything feels it. This doesn't make risk reduction any easier.

RUMORS OF THE DOLLAR'S DEMISE ARE GREATLY EXAGGERATED

The International Swaps and Derivatives Association (ISDA) margin survey provides information about the OTC market, which differs from the repo market, but the same institutions dominate both. The OTC margin survey provides a take on fundamentals in the form of collateral and how things change. The data on OTC markets comes from the 2008 and 2009 ISDA Margin Surveys. Respondents included the 15 largest dealer banks in the world, hedge funds, insurance companies, and other banks.

Although the trend to greater OTC collateralization has been increasing for years, the Lehman bloodletting reinforced the need to reduce counterparty risk, get greater control of the funding cost of a trade, and better manage collateral. Collateralization is an integral part of the OTC derivatives market, and according to the ISDA, 70 percent of all OTC derivatives were collateralized by the end of 2009. Collateral is up to about 80 percent for all OTC contracts.

This is so because markets destabilized in 2008 as the collateral rate (i.e., the overnight rate) and the London Interbank Overnight Rate (LIBOR) diverged. In fact, the difference between the collateralized rate and LIBOR is a good measure of dealer counterparty risk. This LIBOR–overnight indexed swap (LIBOR-OIS) spread speaks of a nexus between the marginal buyers that actually drive asset prices more than anything else.

For the very same reason that U.S. Treasuries have a repo optionality that makes them valuable in a crisis, U.S. dollar (USD) cash collateral can be very costly to post in OTC markets. It has nothing to do with "quality"; It is nothing more or less than a flight to liquidity. This is pretty much the only fundamental that matters in a crisis. The rest is motion (β) and death (θ). Here are some details.

Received Collateral

- Among respondents, there was an 18.9 percent reduction in collateral received in derivative exposures compared with a *33 percent decline*[2] in gross market values of OTC contracts.
- Cash and government securities constitute about 92 percent of received collateral in both years. This is so because there

is no haircut on this collateral delivery. Cash is dominant because it avoids a number of complications associated with rehypothecation of government securities.

- The use of U.S. dollars as received collateral collapsed 32.6 percent compared with 2008, whereas the use of euros declined only 4 percent.
- The use of U.S. Treasuries as received collateral declined 46 percent. The use of European Union (EU) government paper increased by 8.7 percent. Received gilts as collateral increased 41.7 percent (see Tables 18.1 and 18.2).

Table 18.1 ISDA Margin Survey: Value of Collateral Received by Respondents

Collateral Type	Currency/Asset	Collateral Received 2009	Collateral Received 2008
Cash	USD	**484,130,000,000**	**718,507,000,000**
	EUR	**411,416,000,000**	**428,899,000,000**
	GBP	27,278,000,000	32,605,000,000
	JPY	27,396,000,000	25,799,000,000
	Other	16,455,000,000	8,800,000,000
Subtotal		**966,675,000,000**	**1,214,610,000,000**
Government securities	United States	**31,224,000,000**	**58,246,000,000**
	European Union	33,815,000,000	30,854,000,000
	United Kingdom	**10,693,000,000**	**6,233,000,000**
	Japan	24,540,000,000	25,210,000,000
	Other	16,455,000,000	10,316,000,000
Subtotal		**116,478,000,000**	**130,858,000,000**
Other assets	Government agencies	18,881,000,000	32,074,000,000
	Supranational bonds	2,425,000,000	3,173,000,000
	Covered bonds	913,000,000	1,297,000,000
	Corporate bonds	27,696,000,000	22,151,000,000
	Letters of credit	9,975,000,000	15,315,000,000
	Equities	25,123,000,000	19,269,000,000
	Metals and commodities	92,000,000	743,000,000
	Other	11,883,000,000	15,633,000,000
Subtotal		**96,988,000,000**	**109,655,000,000**
Total collateral		**1,180,140,000,000**	**1,455,124,000,000**

Table 18.2 ISDA Margin Survey: Value of Collateral Delivered by Respondents

Collateral Type	Currency/Asset	Collateral Delivered 2009	Collateral Delivered 2008
Cash	USD	**408,373,000,000**	**597,418,000,000**
	EUR	**305,068,000,000**	**311,267,000,000**
	GBP	34,332,000,000	39,266,000,000
	JPY	20,817,000,000	28,537,000,000
	Other	26,489,000,000	8,626,000,000
Subtotal		**795,080,000,000**	**985,114,000,000**
Government securities	United States	**43,438,000,000**	**73,540,000,000**
	European Union	55,586,000,000	64,689,000,000
	United Kingdom	17,831,000,000	17,473,000,000
	Japan	14,396,000,000	20,197,000,000
	Other	6,196,000,000	4,014,000,000
Subtotal		**137,449,000,000**	**179,913,000,000**
Other assets	Government agencies	9,661,000,000	13,298,000,000
	Supranational bonds	237,000,000	251,000,000
	Covered bonds	1,908,000,000	429,000,000
	Corporate bonds	9,152,000,000	6,455,000,000
	Letters of credit	1,238,000,000	200,000,000
	Equities	8,538,000,000	1,014,000,000
	Metals and commodities	0	0
	Other	6,473,000,000	7,178,000,000
Subtotal		**37,207,000,000**	**28,824,000,000**
Total collateral		**969,735,000,000**	**1,193,851,000,000**

Delivered Collateral

There are similarities for delivered collateral as well as differences.

- Among respondents, there was an 18.7 percent reduction in collateral received in derivative exposures compared with a *33 percent decline*[3] in gross market values of OTC contracts.
- Cash and government securities constitute about 97 percent of delivered collateral in both years. There is no haircut on this collateral delivery.

- The use of U.S. dollars as delivered collateral collapsed 31 percent compared eith 2008, whereas the use of euros declined only 2 percent.
- The use of U.S. Treasuries as delivered collateral declined 41 percent. The use of EU government paper declined by 14.1 percent. Gilts used as delivered collateral increased by 2 percent, as shown in Table 18.2.

In 2009, it appears that delivering counterparties didn't want to part with dollars. This is the essence of a "risk-off" posture. As conditions become favorable to risking, the use of the dollar increases. It is possible that more efficient collateral management could lessen the need for a vehicle currency.

Indeed, better cash and collateral management is another explanation for changes in dollar use in collateral composition. It isn't about the death of the dollar, just better management reducing the need for it as a facilitator of trade. Because of the lessened need for a vehicle currency, the differences in currency funding costs matter more. Have a look at Japanese yen (JPY; the de-risking currency du jour) and euro (EUR; a

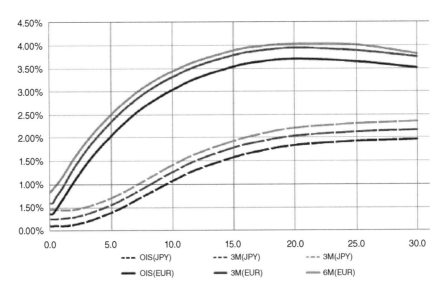

Figure 18.7 **Euro and Yen Funding Curves.**

risk currency) overnight, 3-month, and 6-month swap curves about the middle of March. This appears to be a long-term trend that contributes to dollar weakness (Figure 18.7).

Similarly, comparing 2008 with 2009, Treasures were used much less as collateral than other government securities. The quantitative easing (QE) program put the market on notice that there is a hard floor under Treasury prices in the case that the meltdown situation got worse.

CHAPTER 19

Some Rules of the Road for Risk Management: The First Three Axioms

isk management is about these words: *risk*, *volatility*, and *liquidity*. They get thrown around so much because the precise meaning of these words is truly hard to pin down. There are different grades or shades of meaning for each of these that are sometimes not recognized.

Here is an axiom system that outlines risk management in the abstract and characterizes the major players in the subject—risk, volatility, and liquidity. When math provides the most natural exposition, the axiom system is mathematical. At other times, a concept eludes adequate mathematical representation and is treated in a discursive way.

An *axiom* is a "self-evident truth." Axioms refer to observed regularities verified across a wide class of circumstances that are combined into systems to organize facts and which are necessary to make rational action possible. A good axiom system should be simple and natural, with easy-to-modify rules explicitly stated at the outset. Logical consequences flow from these premises, and it is easy to build on them.

It is not necessary that axioms be perfect or even completely accurate. What is important is their usefulness in establishing the explicit assumptions, how they make things work, and providing clues to what challenging an assumption means. This foundation, no matter how complicated the subject, attracts both artisans who built beautiful scaffolding and curious mavericks who are up to the task of challenging shaky foundations. Let's start by looking at the first three axioms for risk management.

AXIOM 1.0

There are five indecomposable ways to make money in financial markets:

- *Front running/insider trading*
- *Intermediation (brokering)*
- *Liquidity provision/risk transfer (insurance)*
- *Taking factor risk exposures (macro)*
- *Arbitrage (exploiting mispricing)*

More complex strategies are combinations of these five strategies. Combinations are expressed through financial instruments. Instruments proliferate across asset classes and reflect the complexity of the modern financial system, as shown in Figure 19.1.

AXIOM 2

All financial instruments exist to generate returns for at least one side of the trade. If they fail in this, they cease to exist.

It is not necessary that the market for a financial instrument be fair: The winning and losing sides of the trade do not need to cancel each other out over time. There can be newcomers and people who follow a herd instinct so much that losing behavior can persist for a long time on one side of a trade.

This is because not even the largest computers or the most intelligent minds can execute all computation problems. For example, the number of legally possible moves in chess is around 10^{44}, a number

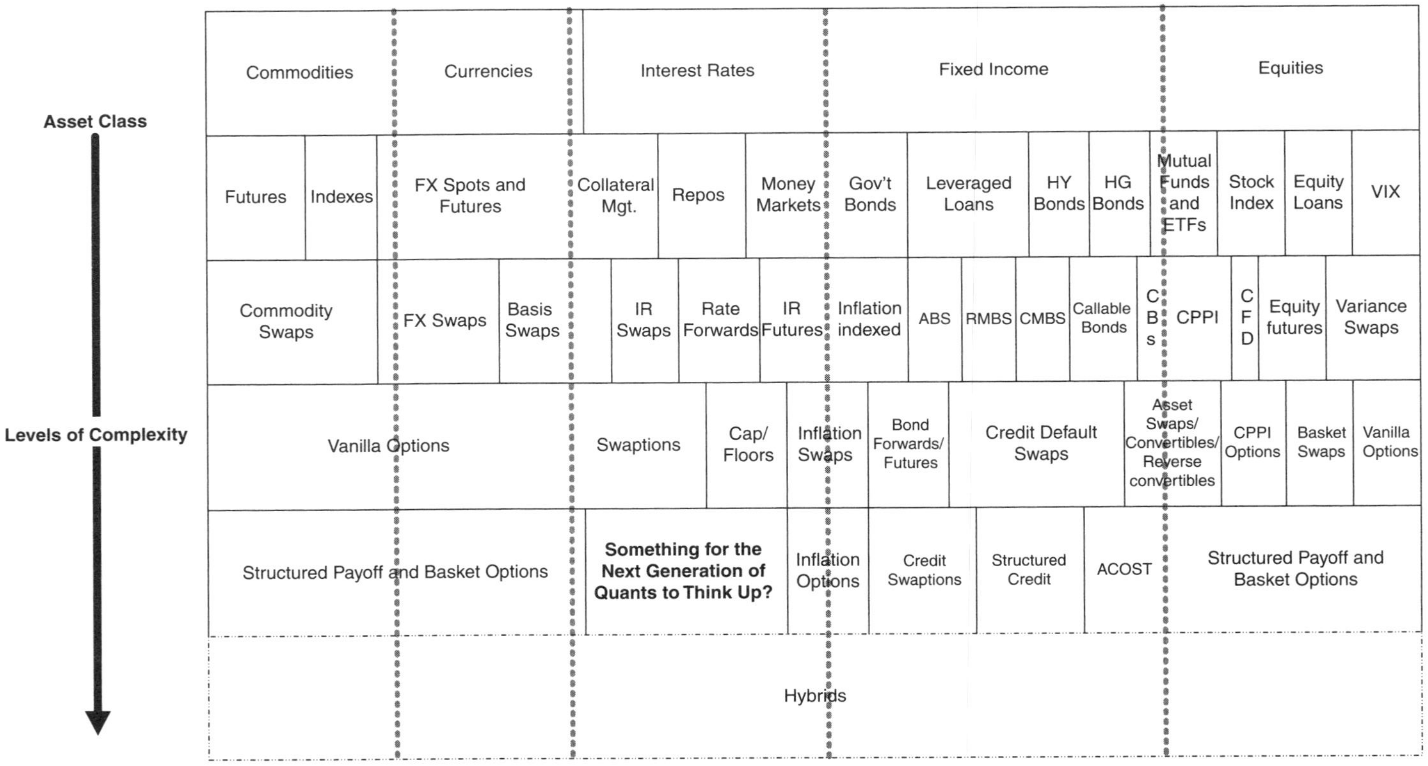

Figure 19.1 **Financial Instrument Taxonomy.**

larger than the theoretical number of molecules in the universe. It is not possible to process something of this magnitude.

To compensate for the intractable nature of these kinds of problems, the investor's subconscious impulse is to search for "good enough" actions given the objective of financial returns conditioned on recognized computational limitations of the investor. One strategy is to depend on expert opinion and follow provided trade ideas without acknowledging possibly conflicted interests. For example, an equity strategist may have a significant risk position combined with private knowledge that will impair the risky asset performance in the future. It is desirable only in a crisis for the firm the strategist represents to unwind risk in a one-off action as the firm discloses its expectations regarding the risk. Instead, the firm unwinds slowly, recommending the asset to retail investors, until the firm reaches a risk exposure suited to its outlook on the risk.

Other strategies follow rigid rules of investing consistent with "fundamental approaches." Such strategies ignore the possibility that rigid rules do not capture fair value adequately and thus the implied discount factor of an asset. For example, earnings before interest, taxes, depreciation, and amortization (EBITDA) is interpreted according to various accounting rules and procedures depending on the need of a business. A firm's debt level can be quite different from its total liabilities. For example, large pension contributions are often ignored in evaluating the fixed financial burdens on a company.

Financial instruments cease to exist when no one makes money on the trade. Investors become like amphibians in a drying pool, unaware that the habitat is overtaken by a spreading desert. Vitality is simple. Financial engineering will not die so long as it effectively serves the purpose of identifying what is cheap and what is rich. If it doesn't, it will die like a salamander in the desert.

AXIOM 3

Regardless of instrument and strategy, and discounting pure luck, successful prediction generally is impossible. Control methods based on prediction lead to unintended consequences.

The only reason people trade is because they think (with conviction) that the market is more wrong than they are about what is cheap and what is rich. This implies that they consider their predicted price as a better representation of value than prices reflected in markets.

Prediction implies theorization, human nature's way to make sense of the world. In this sense, a theory that "works" is one that accurately reflects some aspect of reality over a reasonable training period and over a wide enough class of situations. A working theory is not equivalent to perfection or even excellence: It is the stuff of creative imagination, a narrative craft or art form.

The wider the scope, the less theories work. The longer theories live, the greater is their fallibility. They diverge from reality with time and persist despite or in ignorance of the facts of a matter. Even when they obviously fail to reflect reality, they persist. This is so because of sunk costs incurred by experts and marginal returns to those experts that people follow as a strategy.

There is simply no way to escape prediction failure because there is no escaping outliers and tail events. An *outlier* is a value that a random variable attains that exceeds expected probabilistic thresholds—something that occurs outside of expectation. Tail events are related but more subtle. A *tail event* X_T from an arbitrary infinite random sequence $X_1, X_2, \ldots, X_n$ is an event that occurs or doesn't occur independent of how any finite number of random variables in the series behave.

Theorem 3.1 (Kolmogorov)

If X_T is a tail event, then $\Pr(X_T) = 0$ or 1.

A probability of 1 means that X_T will happen, and 0 means that X_T will never happen. The implication is that unanticipated things will happen or they won't. A difficult problem is determining which of these extreme values $\Pr(X_T)$ will attain. Even more difficult is determining the rate of convergence to 0 or 1.

The conclusion leads to ambiguities. One can live in California on a fault line and take out a small insurance policy that may never pay out, simply for peace of mind. Or one can move to Oklahoma and get killed by an F5 tornado. Unpredictability leads to horribly unsatisfying courses of action. Whether the Fed did nothing more than cover bank gambling losses via credit-default swaps (CDS) or whether the favorable settlement of CDS kept worse things from happening is the ultimate policy question of the age.

Below is a story that clarifies what I mean by both outliers and tail events, although there is some fuzziness here. Given subjective probabilities, one person's tail event is another person's outlier because one person may have superior information or more experience than another. For this purpose, though, the chika's performance is an outlier—an outlier that may be controlled subsequently after the casino loses millions and then sets up rules to deal with it, but an outlier nonetheless. The end scenarios are tail events with presumed $\Pr(T) = 1$.

Imagine a bunch of people playing blackjack in a casino. One woman consistently wins. It is found out that when she picks up a complementary drink, the server slips an ace into her hand, thus periodically giving her play a boost. Ultimately, her secret is discovered, and the casino installs security cameras so that it doesn't happen again. So next week, while the casino is bustling, the building catches on fire. Everyone runs out, except for a man who picks up a load of $10,000 chips remaining on the table. The casino then sets up identity-check rules as a precondition to cashing out so that it never happens again. A few months after repairing the fire damage, the San Andreas fault line snaps, and an earthquake destroys the casino. With the insurance money, the company rebuilds. A year later, nuclear war radiates the ground on which the casino is built, but strict decontamination protocols bring back the high rollers. Then, out of the blue, a kilometer-wide meteor hits Oregon, wiping out 50 percent of all terrestrial life. The casino becomes a habitat for irradiated roaches that begin to theorize about their origins. Eventually, the sun goes supernova, and the earth's crust turns into lava.

Prediction of future states of complex systems becomes exponentially more difficult with the elapse of time, attempts at control lead invariably to unintended consequences. Since a theory is only as good as its predictions, and predictions in general fail, the appropriate use of theory is opportunistically. One keeps a theory only as long as it works. When it fails, drop it.

On a long enough time line, the survival rate for everything drops to zero. In the meantime, civilization and what is good about living depend to a large extent on theorizing that things will remain roughly the same as yesterday. Aaron Brown quantified this in his "Personal Insignificance Principle"[1] (this article may be well worn, but it is fantastic).

His conclusions on how to live and operate are simple: Throw out the theory, attempt peaceful acceptance of how things are, and prepare for changes in how things are. Glimpses of this philosophy are common in Daoist yarns like the following.

> A farmer had a horse that ran away. The villagers all said, "That's too bad!" The farmer said, "How do you know?"
>
> The horse came back and brought with him a herd of wild stallions. The villagers all said, "That's great!" The famer said, "How do you know?"
>
> The famer's son was trying to tame the horses when one bucked him and broke his leg. The villagers all said, "That's too bad!" The farmer said, "How do you know?"
>
> The next week, soldiers came to the village to recruit all the young and able to die for the Emperor's cause. The farmer's son wasn't recruited. Harvest time came and went, but few of the boys ever returned to the village.

Outliers—good and bad—have to be accepted—not denied or censored, as theory-mongers commonly do in practice. Tail events in contrast are to be ignored. A meteorite hitting the planet that kills all life will either happen or it won't, and there is nothing comprehensible that influences it. Thus there's nothing to be done about it. So live for today, enjoy what you have, and prudently manage the outliers.

This is robust wisdom that endures millenaia, embodied in various texts such as Ecclesiastes and the *Dao Te Ching*. It implies taking up a bare-bones mentality that permits only minimal theory with limited scope. Everyone must be ready to trash-can even the most closely held faiths when they are obviously wrong. Anything else is dishonesty and pride that refuses to admit failure. Just as creativity is the greatest human strength, human pride is its greatest weakness.

Theorem 3.2: Nonconvergent Probability

The probabilistic counterpoint to tail events and outliers is *stationarity*. Stationarity implies that a process moves through time according to identical rules of behavior at every instant. It is true that random processes can appear stationary for a long time.

Take the simple example of a coin flip. Within a preconceived frame of reference, it follows the simplest probability model, the Bernoulli process. Assume that an equal probability is assigned to a head outcome and a tail outcome. Flipping of a coin assumes 50/50 chances, and if you flip a coin repeatedly enough, you will find that the outcomes converge to heads 50 percent of the time and tails 50 percent of the time. The implication is stationarity.

There are myriad things that can go wrong even in this simple probability model. You could lose the coin through a crack in the flooring. Or some tail event like the gravitational constant of the universe could shift, and coins could float upward into the nearest black hole. There is another, more practical problem: We assume only head and tail outcomes. The coin also could land on its side. Now the probability of a coin settling on its side on a flat surface is virtually zero, so we discount it when we flip the coin on a table. But a flat table isn't the only possible surface. Imagine flipping the same coin on a surface covered with spines a few millimeters apart. Landing on its side is in this case the most natural outcome for a coin of suitable thickness.

The Bernoulli process approximating a sequence of coin flips is a simple discrete probability model that falls flat on its face. Imagine how futile prediction is for settings where there are many possible outcomes and the probability laws have many interacting components. Interaction makes the basic notion of statistical independence break down. Stationarity isn't a viable approximation in these cases.

Further, the very attempt at controlling outcomes introduces complexities that have an adverse impact on the outcomes and prediction:

What seems bad becomes good in some cases. *Thus catastrophic changes are sometimes awesome for the lucky and sometimes the hard-working benefit, as in the following example.*

Magdalena and Krzystyna work at a factory bottling vodka circa 1987 Poland. They hate the system, and their pay is a joke.

Out of sheer defiance, Magdalena makes sure that every morning the machine is calibrated so that a bottle label is never applied straight. There's not even a random chance that one label will be aligned right. The foreman periodically realigns the labels but doesn't figure out that Magdalena is to blame.

Krzystyna is feeling like a G6 and doesn't want to work. She throws a piece of factory brick into the gears, causing multiple cascading failures in the production machinery. They both get a week's vacation with pay while repairs are made.

As a result, the plant goes out of business and is purchased by a Swedish concern that starts bottling Grey Goose. Magdalena gets a performance bonus, and Kryzstyna gets fired.

Theorem 3.3: Interaction Is an Agent of Chaos

Human beings innately interact with each other by building societies. Even nature abhors a vacuum and interacts in turbulent ways. Interaction invariably creates prediction and control problems, and breakdowns in predictability guarantee bad outcomes when you are heavily invested in a prediction. In the face of these natural undeniable forces, modern-day probability models often deny the problems by assuming stationarity and related concepts.

Think now about how complex financial markets work. Financial markets change so rapidly and data are so limited that even times before the latest crisis are of doubtful relevance. Small events can have huge implications that make control of possible events futile.

Static model building often requires an even stronger assumption than stationarity: It requires that $X_1, X_2, \ldots, X_n$ be independent and identically distributed. There is absolutely no reason to believe this to be true. Dynamic models require arbitrary updating equivalent to perfect foresight of future changes through the prism of past data. There is no perfect foresight.

CHAPTER 20

Some Rules of the Road for Risk Management: Axiom 4

Investing is taking risk in exchange for return. So understanding risk is a big part of the matter. This chapter delves into the concept of risk itself. Some risk can be thought of as a precise mathematical construction, as a residual that remains unexplained by a model, and as what is left unexplained when our best effort at representation fails. Not to get too Yoda on you, all of these aspects of risk lurk in the background of any investment.

AXIOM 4

To understand what is cheap and what is rich, you must understand risk. Risk premium is where the money is. After a meltdown, you really get compensated for the risk.

Corollary 4.0.1: When Assets Are Rich, You Are Not Rewarded as Much for Taking Risk

Risk can be measured and represented to some degree, but there are aspects of risk that escape measurement and representation. Risk falls into different categories.

Illusions of Control

The truth content of something contains a representation and a residual. Models and theories are representations. Risk is the residual. The truth content depends on the size and nature of the residual.

Risk can be classified, but these categories are not mutually exclusive. Risk can embody more than one classification. Models can define behavior well, or they can specify the nature of something in a very poor fashion. These categories lie on a continuum between certainty and a complete lack of knowledge.

It is true that time and human inquisitiveness unlock many mysteries, even the nature of things once considered insoluble. But there remains an insoluble core in all phenomena, however small.

Truth is something free of counterexample. This criterion unifies empirical science and logical mathematics. Both logic and empirical methods depend on counterexample-freeness to demonstrate *valid hypotheses* and *valid reasoning* connecting the hypotheses to the conclusion. Some things *are* true because they can be proved. However, some things are true, but no simple proof exists. What is true and theoretically provable may not actually be provable because the shortest possible proofs are too long for computation and comprehension. Some things are true only because everyone believes they are true: they are true for no real reason at all.

Certainty as Risk Sterilization

> My aim is to by the power of the written word to make you hear, to make you feel . . . before all, to make you see. That—and no more, and it is everything. If I succeed, you shall find there according to your deserts: encouragement, consolation, fear, charm—all you demand—and, perhaps, also that glimpse of truth for which you have forgotten to ask.
>
> —Joseph Conrad

Complete certainty is the extreme of all logical symmetry and no randomness. Certainty is *proven* by logical consistency embodied in mathematical proof and by the strength of agreement with observed reality. It is hopeless to argue that two plus two equals anything other than four in **Z**.[1] It was four ever since humans started counting on their fingers and will remain so long after the sun goes supernova. This is powerful reinforcement of certainty. No one alive has experienced anything outside this framework. That the sun rises day after day as it always has on nothing new is powerful reinforcement until time burns under unlaboring stars.

This kind of truth comes in two parts that complement each other. Important to certainty is the lack of any real-world counter-example, where two things plus two things do not equal four. Equally important is the logical demonstration that the abstractions known as *numbers* sum in a consistent way. It is true that a *four* can't be found in nature; instead, examples of four manifest.

Abstractions such as numbers lift valence outside of time and circumstance: The sum of two plus two is general and not a special case in most settings. However, notions of distance in some metric spaces and even constructed arithmetic rules violate the notion. The power of generalization makes conditions more precise, and changing standards of rigor alter the notion of deductive truth itself. As we shall see, it is not universally true that "mathematics rests on proof—and proof is eternal." Standards of rigor can change over time.

Once you take the notion of complete certainty out of the laboratory and put it in real life, it vaporizes. It survives only in precise and controlled conditions. It is like an ice peak that reflects sunlight with the indifference of a mirror until it melts. Reality requires the introduction of *risk*.

Risk as Doubt

Risk can exist within clearly defined rules of randomness. To grasp this type of uncertainty, think of card games or chess or *something with clearly defined, inviolable rules of operation*. Card games have probabilities associated with a given hand and the strategies possible given your hand. Chess does too, but it may become difficult to rationally compute the best course of action if the rules or permutations of the game become too complex.

For example, Gauss proved the fundamental theorem of algebra. Sort of. Twice. Both versions of his proofs were considered satisfactory *in his time*. But they both relied on an unproven statement Gauss said was "known from higher geometry" and that "seems to be sufficiently well demonstrated." The unproved statement was that if a branch of a real polynomial curve $F(x, y) = 0$ enters a plane region, it must leave it again. The gap remained in Gauss's final proof 50 years later. It was not filled until 1920.

This is really a glaring gap *by today's standards of proof*. This gap made this truly fundamental theorem uncertain. Thus even the titan Gauss submitted proofs with gaps. His acquaintance with uncertainty wasn't a bad thing. It most likely framed the first well-posed problem in algebraic geometry. The gap arguably was the beginning of algebraic geometry itself.

It is also overwhelmingly probable that very long and complicated proofs contain mistakes like the classification theorem of finite groups. Such mistakes are to a large degree self-correcting. If a proof is error-free after a couple of years, then the theorem ultimately falls into the category of complete certainty. However, the problem of those gaps remains.

A proof finds acceptance because there are no conceivable counter-examples. Independent proofs—proofs that approach the theorem from a different point of view and method—strengthen certainty. While concepts of proof and standards of rigor change, new proofs correcting inaccuracies lessen the impact. All the same, human mistakes and changes in knowledge require the introduction of *uncertainty*—ill-defined risk.

The Illusion of Safety: Reducible Risk

Simple calculus enables us to predict the trajectory of a fired cannonball—given the angle, the muzzle velocity, and the wind speed. However, the closer you look, the more factors need to be accounted for to control the margin of error. These small errors are insignificant in isolation, but in aggregate, they may contribute to significant firing inaccuracy.

Error can be reduced arbitrarily given sufficient time and enough resources. There always will be measurement errors that impart reservations to any prediction, but when risk is reducible, they can be controlled. The prediction (or agreement with reality) has a bound on inaccuracy. Effectively, the model is good enough to handle a robust number of cases, and there is a hard limit on the uncertainty regarding the underlying data-generating mechanism.

This type of uncertainty is pervasive in nearly all deductive models and can lead to model output that diverges from reality.

For example, one of the main unsolved problems in theoretical physics is the inconsistency between gravity and quantum mechanics. Closely related to this inconsistency is how to unify the various other forces with gravity and understand associated symmetry breaking. String theory offers a way to address this inconsistency.

String theory makes sense in terms of circumstantial evidence and predicts gravity. In fact, gravity is an unavoidable consequence of string theory. String theory also predicts space-time supersymmetry. However, it is difficult to connect string theory to reality. Supersymmetry is not an established empirical fact. There is an active search for verification of supersymmetry by way of high-energy supercolliders. There is no Higgs boson yet. Even without that boson, the study of the Big Bang continues, even though it may mix speculation and logic. Cosmologists and theoretical physicists encourage each other to refinements of speculation independent of observation.

As soon as you make more realistic characterizations, the bound on error unravels, and "everything" increasingly focuses on something that defies identification. Ill-defined but tractable risk is insufficient in these situations. Needed is recognition that at least some risk is intractable.

Partially Reducible Risk

> The belief in a supernatural source of evil is not necessary; men
> alone are quite capable of every wickedness.
> —Joseph Conrad, *Under Western Eyes*, 1911

Calculating the future value of a bond seems to be a simple exercise in math that depends on the compounding frequency of the bond. However, the upper bound of continuous compounding carries limited information because the introduction of default risk creates an ambiguous future value. It is not only the probability of outcome that matters. Equally important is the impact of imprecisely quantifiable default, no matter how small. There is always a chance (typically small and in large part unquantifiable) that a debtor will default, but the impact of a default is invariably huge to a creditor. Default can be predicted to some extent, but only with some inaccuracy.

This is why a default is represented by a discontinuous jump, a surprise event. There can be jumps in how things move (discontinuities), and future behavior can be so different that the past is no guide at all (nonstationarity). These categories of risk require an upper bound on how out of control events can become. This is best understood in terms of probability.

Consider a standard probability space (Ω, ϕ, P) where Ω is a state space (all attainable outcomes), ϕ_0 is the subalgebra (the filtration) generated by functions f_n, $n \leq 0$ (the past), and P is a probabilistic law. Assume a P measure-preserving transformation T on $\Omega \times \Omega$ and a stationary process, meaning a function f on Ω where $f(\omega_0) = f(T^t\omega)$.

Prediction consists of finding the conditional probability or expectation relative to the past and present—the information content of ϕ. Prediction is the estimation of $P(\cdot|\phi_0)$ and $E(\cdot|\phi_0)$ from past observations of a typical time-indexed function $[f_n(\omega), n \leq 0]$ of the stochastic process ω in Ω.

The core of prediction is uncovering the distribution of future observables or at least some scaling of states for their possible occurrence. Estimation is based on past observations of a time series, but in actual practice, we often have to predict the future values of a single time series X_n. In such cases, we usually regard the time series as being a typical time series of a random process, such that $X_n = f_n(\omega_0)$, ω_0 in Ω, and the predicted value of $E(X_n) = E(f_n|\phi_0)(\omega_0)$. Solvability and prediction depend on how well defined T is.

It is impossible in general to derive directly from the prediction theory of stochastic processes a prediction theory for general individual time series. Because $E(f_n|\phi_0)$ is an equivalence class of functions, any two of which can differ on the (variable) set of zero P measure, $E(f_n|\phi_0)$ (ω_0) is indefinite. Representing the equivalence class by one of its members is too arbitrary, except in special cases.

There is a well-defined way of determining $E(f_n|\phi_0)(\omega_0)$ only when

1. Ω is a topologic space and a function in the family $E(f_n|\phi_0)$ is continuous on Ω, or
2. Ω is a topologic space for which Radon-Nikodym derivatives are definable as limits of quotients of measures.

To recapitulate: Prediction depends on the stationarity of f_n. This is so because the stationarity condition is sufficient to ensure that X_n $= f_n(\omega_0)$, ω_0 in Ω, and $E(X_n) = E(f_n|\phi_0)(\omega_0)$. A bounded prediction on a stochastic process is possible if the governing probabilistic laws are invariant under time shifts.

The issue of probabilistic prediction reduces returns to whether any real-world process actually is stationary. It is not easy fo find stationarity. The real world works like a casino that may or may not be honest, and the rules of the house at least change without notice.

Irreducible Risk

> Introduce a little anarchy. Upset the established order, and everything becomes chaos. I'm an agent of chaos. Oh, and you know the thing about chaos? It's fair!
>
> —the Joker dude in *The Dark Knight*

In fact, the universe may be a casino where no one knows the rules and no one will ever know all the rules. The rules may change so often in degree and kind that there is no point in trying to figure out what is going to happen.

Physics always has played a dominant role in American science. But it faces serious trouble. The prevailing theory requires the existence of that Higgs boson, which has not yet been found. Searching for it requires investments in supercolliders around the globe, costing billions. Physicists have yet to decide even basic empirical questions such as whether protons decay and the absolute neutrino mass scale. But this irreducible uncertainty cannot be remedied by more data, better methods, or sharper thinking. It is not an issue of the unknown. The issue is *unknowableness*. In fact, physicists speculate a remote chance that the search for the Higgs boson could generate as a by-product a black hole of sufficient mass that it *would destroy the very fabric of the universe*.[2] This is cosmic game-changing.

The ideal is of an existent inviolable truth, much of it there for the taking. Over time, more and more things will be grasped. This is a foundation on which many thoughtful, beautiful, and ultimately fragile things find support. The triumph of Gödel is the disposal of this illusion via an *incompleteness theorem*.

Completeness in this sense means that one can logically prove whether a statement is correct or incorrect. The notion of completeness requires as a precondition for the notion of logical consistency. *Consistency* means that statements are contradiction-free: You can't prove a statement logically and at the same time prove the exact opposite of that statement logically. Best case, one puts consistency and completeness together to get the whole truth and nothing but the truth. The problem is that one cannot do this because Gödel showed that even the most basic logical systems are incomplete. There is no way by logical methods to decide whether some statements in just about any axiom system are true or false.

As an example, consider algebraic groups, objects equipped with generating laws such that two elements can be combined. An *Abelian group* satisfies the commutative law: *The order of adding elements does not affect the result.* The Abelian group G on the integers Z with addition as the operation can be decomposed into parts H and J, H being the subgroup and J being the factor group. The factor group is formed from G and H similar to dividing a number by another. G thus is the extension of H by J. Given H and J, there is always a trivial extension formed by placing H and J in a direct sum operation, where H becomes the group Z of integers. It turns out that this occurs if J is a direct sum of copies of Z. Such a group is called *free*. It is undecidable what requirements imposed on J will make J free.

Gregory Chaitin took Gödel's idea, recast it with the algorithmic information tools of Alan Turing, and established that such incompleteness is pervasive and nonpathologic. The implication is that some truths are not amenable to mathematical reasoning because randomness and arbitrariness lie at their center.

Some things you *can* know. Some things you *can't* know. Some things are true for a reason. Some things are true simply because they are. This implies profound and fundamental ignorance—and a great deal of risk.

But the search for truth still can go on once rigor and proof are understood as local criteria—relative, not absolute concepts. The search needs reservations and humility. *Realistically, the idea of knowledge should not be to determine all the truth in the world.* Knowledge has to be recast as a process or exploration and overcoming involving the following steps:

- Problem = running into a hard boundary.
- Trial = testing for weaknesses.
- Error = determining where the boundary is soft and where it is not.
- Speculation = guessing how to break through the boundary.
- Conjecture = a plan for breaking through to the other side.
- Proof = sufficient lack of counterexamples to say that you are on the other side.

Improvisation and creativity are necessary. There may be no place for Euclidian self-evident axioms, but a willingness to *assume* new principles and explore what follows from these alternations is the way forward. Good assumptions lead to organized knowledge. Truth depends on what you get, given the assumptions put in.

There is an order to the universe, but it is a partial order. Complete order is a pipe dream. While every system of axioms is incomplete, they aid in the search all the same. The structure itself is a necessary part of consistent thinking.

Atonal music jars at first by its lack of tonality. In time, the mind gets more used to it. It grasps patterns even as the sound remains unpleasant. It becomes less unpleasant, or unpleasant for understandable reasons. Without consistency, one comes face to face with real horror—inconsistent systems. Nobody wants an inconsistent world. This would mean that the universe is absurd.

The Void

> They wanted facts. Facts! They demanded facts from him, as if facts could explain anything.
>
> —Joseph Conrad, *Heart of Darkness*

Inconsistency implies that we can't figure out the rules because the rules contradict each other. In essence, there are no real rules. In effect, the universe cannot be seen as a casino: It is a madhouse. And one cannot know if the lunatics are running the asylum or not. There is no symmetry, and all is randomness. Anything reasonable that comes from this type of world is a product of pure good luck.

As much as we need it for our sanity, consistency is an *assumption*. A single, precise counterexample can be deadly. Few can grasp this kind of risk, and few other than poets and artists explore it. But it is there, always lurking under the surface. When we attempt to conceptualize it, it collapses under the weight of analytic method and then resurfaces as something else. It is what ancient sages called the Void.

Our understanding here obtains more from literature than from anything else: Joseph Conrad, Samuel Beckett, the Theater of the Absurd.

> In this world—as I have known it—we are made to suffer without the shadow of a reason, or a cause or a guilt.
>
> There is no morality, no knowledge and no hope; there is only the consciousness of ourselves which drives us about a world that . . . is always but a vain and floating appearance. . . .

A moment, a twinkling of an eye and nothing remains—but a clot of mud, of cold mud, of dead mud cast into black space, rolling around an extinguished sun. Nothing. Neither thought, nor sound, nor soul. Nothing.

—Joseph Conrad

This category called the Void is touched on in some religious thought and its condensates. There is not much more to say about this type of risk.

CHAPTER 21

Some Rules of the Road for Risk Management: Axiom 5

A tradable way that financial risk manifests itself is in volatility. Precisely because it is a tradable asset across different asset classes, it is worth a close look. Here we look at a derivation of the statistical properties of volatility in a general probability context and how its tradable nature gives it some interesting properties.

AXIOM 5: THERE IS A STRONG RELATIONSHIP BETWEEN VOLATILITY AND RISK

Definition: The Volatility of a Time Series Is the Square Root of Its Variance

Michel Fliess, Cedric Join, and Frederic Hatt characterized volatility in a probabilistic way in February 2011 in a preprint paper titled "Volatility Made Observable at Last."[1] The characterization employs the nonstandard measure theory construction of Loeb. The authors did not include an actual probability space construction, integration, or measure in their exposition. Assuming that the risk measure is partially reducible, it is possible to construct their volatility identity from a basic probabilistic standpoint.

The basic idea of Loeb measure supposes Ω as an infinite set constructed in a nonstandard space that satisfies all the formal properties of finite sets. Suppose that n is a normalized counting measure on Ω such that $\omega(A) = |A|/|\omega|$ for all subsets A of Ω. Any finite element r of the nonstandard real number s is infinitely close to a unique standard real number, denoted r°. $\nu(A)$ is a nonstandard real number between 0 and 1 and hence is finite. Let $\mu(A) = {}^\circ\nu(A)$. Thus μ is a finitely additive measure in the ordinary standard sense; its domain $\mathbf{A}$, the union of all internal subsets of Ω, is an algebra. This ensures a unique extension of μ to a countably additive measure on the σ algebra generated by A. The completion of this extension, $\underline{v}$, is called the *Loeb measure generated by* $\mathbf{A}$. Although this is a nonstandard construction, it is a countably additive probability measure in the usual sense.

Because (Ω, v) behaves just like an ordinary discrete set with a counting measure, integration is just summation. $(\Omega, \underline{v})$ is a probability space in the usual standard sense, and there is a link between integration (measure) and stochastic processes in this setting. The Lebesgue measure is derived with an infinite element n of the nonstandard natural numbers, and $\Omega = \{0, 1/n, \ldots, (n-1)/n, 1\}$. Let $h:\Omega \to [0, 1]$ be defined by $h(x) = {}^\circ x$. A set B in $[0, 1]$ is Lebesgue measureable if and only if $h^{-1}(B)$ is $\underline{v}$ measurable, in which case $v[h^{-1}(B)]$ is the Lebesgue measure of B.

This provides the foundation for Fliess, Join, and Hatt's work. They consider the interval $[0, 1]$ as time and nonstandard real numbers as infinitesimal sample ζ such that $\zeta = \{0 = t_0 < t_1 < \ldots < t_n = 1\}$, where $t_{i+1} - t_i$, $0 \leq i < v$, is arbitrarily small. A time series $X(t)$ is a function $X: \zeta \to \mathbf{R}$.

Since Lebesgue measure in this setting is a summation, the measure over any interval $[a, b]$, $a \leq b$, is its length $b - a$. The integral of the time series $X(t)$ over $[a, b]$ is equivalent to the sum

$$\int_{[c,d]} X \, dm = \sum_{t \in [d, d]} X(t) m(t)$$

X is Lebesgue integrable if and only if it is almost continuous and satisfies an integrability condition called *S-integrability*.

The Cartier-Perrin theorem then states that if $X: \zeta \to \mathbf{R}$ is an S-integrable time series, then the following decomposition

$$X(t) = E(X)(t) + X_{\text{fluctuation}}(t)$$

holds when the mean or average $E(X)(t)$ is Lebesgue integrable, $X_{\text{fluctuation}}(t)$ is quickly fluctuating, and the decomposition is unique up to an arbitrarily small tolerance. Note how this identity corresponds to the familiar "model + residual" way of thinking.

This result establishes that basic rules of variance and covariance apply to time series defined in this way. Two S-integrable time series $X(t)$ and $Y(t)$ are such that their squares and the squares of $E(X)(t)$ and $E(Y)(t)$ are also S-integrable. Then the products $X(t)Y(t)$, $E(x)(t)E(Y)(t)$, $E(X)(t)Y_{\text{fluctuation}}(t)$, $X_{\text{fluctuation}}(t)E(Y)(t)$, and $X_{\text{fluctuation}}(t)Y_{\text{fluctuation}}(t)$ are also S-integrable.

Thus variance, covariance, and volatility are

$$\text{var}(X)(t) = E\{X - E(X)^2\}(t)$$
$$\approx E(X^2)(t) - [E(X)(t)]^2$$

$$\text{cov}(XY)(t) = E\{[X - E(X)][Y - E(Y)]\}(t)$$
$$\approx E(XY)(t) - E(X)(t) \times E(Y)(t)$$
$$\text{vol}(X)(t) = \sqrt{\text{var}(X)(t)}$$

Higher volatility [$\text{vol}(X)(t)$] over a given interval implies that asset price changes are larger or more frequent than those of another subsample. Too little volatility and investors do not get paid to take risk. Too much and asset prices collapse. Volatility assesses returns from risk taking or the likelihood of policy intervention and investor uncertainty in general.

Collapsed market volatility depresses the return on taking risk. Return seekers raise leverage when volatility is low and reduce leverage when volatility is high. Lower α is earned when volatility rises unexpectedly. This is so because many investors are structurally long in risky assets. They recover only when volatility starts falling again.

Volatility has two components: actual price action defined by adjusted deviations from the mean and the implied uncertainty about future price action. Thus historical price volatility is an important driver of active investment returns and uncertainty about future prices is the main driver of risk premia in the market (the higher internal rate of return) on risky assets that compensates risk-averse investors for this uncertainty.

Increased uncertainty leads to higher volatility, which increases risk premia, the premium needed to compensate for risk exposure. Uncertainty about future prices shows up in the prices of options through the implied volatility of the future prices of the underlying assets. Asset prices change when either expectation of future cash flows change, uncertainty around them changes, or the rate of cash-flow discounting changes. Prices become more volatile as the number of reasons for investors to alter their views increases. Such changes stem from news flow or unexpected events.

Identity: Volatility = Surprises × Vulnerability

Volatility is the product of unexpected news flow and the vulnerability of markets to fear. Sensitivity is the degree to which news flow causes a change in portfolios, which, in turn, will be driven by leverage, risk capital, and funding costs. Fear can be generated by many sources; some major ones are shown in Figure 21.1.

The most connected nodes on the graph are attributed to government policy. This implies that monetary and fiscal policy is the most important determinant of vulnerability. Policymakers and central banks in particular generate a lot of volatility in currency and other markets. Activist policies are meant to foster growth, but are ineffective and inflationary.

Central banks and government can act to suppress tail risk, big extreme moves. They cannot provide increases in economic growth. Policy regimes shift over time in response to perceived tail risks. The shift to more activist-oriented policies—the new normal—will lead to

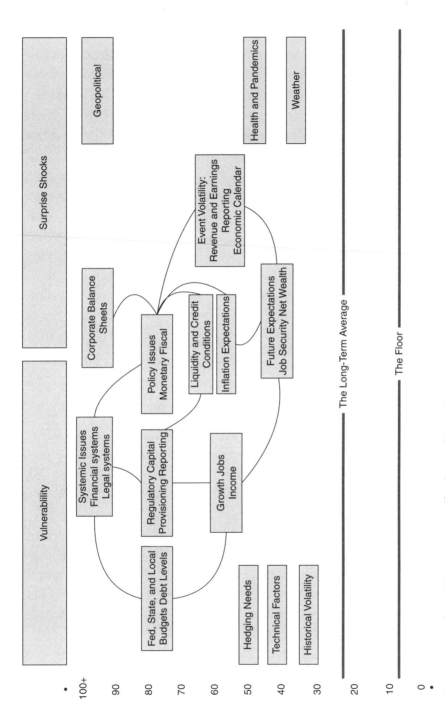

Figure 21.1 **Vulnerability, Surprise Shocks, and Fear Factors.**

higher volatility than seen in recent history. In the end, the policy will be effective in its aim of inflation, ineffective in its aim of growth, and destructive in its impact on incomes and wealth.

Volatilities Vary by Asset Class

Equity and commodity volatility typically jump in response to surprise shocks, whereas bond and foreign-exchange (FX) volatilities are less vulnerable to shocks.

This is because risky assets must generate sufficient excess yield over cash and carry over funding costs or they are sold. Since bonds and Eurodollar rates have fixed returns, managing carry is easier, reflected in their lower volatility. When government bonds trade close to the London Interbank Overnight Rate (LIBOR) flat, owing to a high supply of government debt, swap spread volatility becomes very low. Thus there is a positive correlation between swap spread levels and volatility. Credit markets with low spreads have lower spread volatility. In general, when asset prices drive yields or spreads close to the natural barrier of zero or negative carry, volatility falls. This is because the probability distribution of the market's expectation gets more skewed as yields approach this natural barrier.

Volatility can spike to the upside because of market structures like the prevalence of stop losses relative to stop profits. Directionality of volatility is driven by the breach of value at risk (VaR) limits and the dissipation of risk capital during bear markets, which makes forced selling more likely in stressed markets. A negative shock tends to hit many individual names simultaneously, causing an increase in correlation. As implied correlation rises, if amplifies the impact of volatility.

Volatility can also affect asset prices significantly through its impact on the risk-premium component of asset yields. In fair-value models, volatility and risk account for a significant component of asset yield or internal rates of return. Momentum strategies generally work better when volatility is high.

The reason why the volatility index (VIX) is more amplified than credit-default swap (CDS) spreads is that CDSs sell credit risk, and equity sells more risk factor. Credit risk is only one of the risks embedded in VIX pricing.

Most active financial managers seek to outperform by being long riskier, higher-yielding assets based on an implicit belief that the embedded risk premia are, on average, too high. When volatility rises suddenly from a low level, losses result as the risk premium at which they bought falls short of the risk delivered. Thus returns are poor when volatility rises quickly and in excess of what is priced into risk premium and implied volatility. As price gets lifted, yield declines. Leverage keeps returns constant as yields decline.

CHAPTER 22

Some Rules of the Road for Risk Management: Axiom 6

Just as risk is intimately connected to volatility, volatility is connected to leverage and liquidity. It is best to view liquidity as multifaceted and capture its essential facets based on different points of view. Hang on at the end; the excursion argument presented is an illustration from potential theory of how our reliance on statistical independence is a dead end when it meets a dose of realism.

AXIOM 6

There is a strong connection between leverage and volatility.

Leverage and volatility are negatively correlated because high volatility leads to reduced leverage and low volatility forces investors to leverage up. Leverage does not lead volatility—it lags.

Leverage introduces a new instability when funding pressures force unwinds. Positions and leverage are important drivers of market vulnerability, and excessive leverage leads to market instability, losses to smaller investors, and systemic risks.

Leverage makes markets more sensitive to shocks when a news event that goes against the dominant position of active investors requires them to exit, raising volatility as it creates a logjam as everyone sells at the same time. If leverage redistributes risk toward those most able and willing to carry risk, then this should improve the market's ability to handle adverse circumstances and thus reduce market volatility, because risky assets are held with a strong hand. This risk redistribution has a price via crowded trades. By concentrating risk in fewer hands, there is less diversification of risk and investment losses across market participants. If the market turns down 25 percent in a nonleveraged market, the five investors in it lose 25 percent each of their capital. Leverage makes the losses greater.

Liquidity Definitions

In a leveraged market, investors are required to maintain margin, necessitating a forced sale of assets in hostile market conditions. This pushes prices down further, exacerbating market volatility. It also leads to liquidity breakdowns. Liquidity is crucial. It is relatively easy to understand by experience, but it can be difficult to define.

Definition 6.1: Liquidity Is Stationarity; Nonstationarity is Illiquidity; Illiquidity Means That You Don't Know What an Asset Is Worth

An illiquid market does not allow price discovery, and one does not know how much an asset is worth. With trading or in a liquid market, one does within a fluctuating interval called the *bid-ask spread*. Price is inherently dynamic.

This dynamic requires one to account for the size of the trades being made. Small investors take prices as given. They enter a market, trade in the volume they choose, and leave without disturbing the market price outside of "microscopic" fluctuations. Large investors are price makers. The sizes of the trades they need to make shift market prices, and they necessarily lack the anonymity of the small trader, and this can be seriously damaging, to them, especially when a trader is forced to trade through publicaly visible weakness.

Liquidity is the expectation in markets, and equity has the everyday movement of heavily traded stocks under normal market conditions. Here, continuous price evolution (modeled by Brownian noise) may be suitable for many purposes, as in the Black-Scholes model, a benchmark model of mathematical option pricing. However, even here, the model does not withstand close scrutiny, particularly over short time intervals. The Black-Scholes model assumes that tails are much thinner than those actually encountered.

The price movements jitter because large numbers of small movements are taking place rapidly. This behavior can be better captured with a Levy measure that has infinite mass in the neighborhood of the origin (it is finite elsewhere)—and thus produces infinitely many jumps in finite time. The jumps in a Levy process are very natural for modeling purposes in finance.

By contrast, the independent-increments assumption is less easy to defend. It is perfectly reasonable (at least as a first approximation) to treat tomorrow's price-sensitive information as independent of yesterday's, under normal market conditions. It is not reasonable during a sustained financial crisis. Very basic modeling assumptions thus break down precisely when one needs them the most—during a crisis.

Much of finance is concerned with how prices are determined. One takes prices of an underlying asset as given, and the focus is on pricing and hedging (and so on) of things derived from the underlying. For a good number of assets—structured credit and hybrids—model breakdown implies profound ignorance about the price of an asset. It can well be that the market for them ceases to exist, and there is no adequate way to determine the price at all.

Thin markets are more prone to melt-ups and meltdowns.

The bid-ask spread determines the ease of getting in and out of a position.

Definition 6.2: Liquidity Means That Return to One Period of Time T_i's Price-Sensitive Information Is Statistically Independent of the Next Period of Time (T_{i+1})

The properties of return distributions depend on the length of the return interval. For a monthly interval, the return over a month is the sum of returns over the days of the month, and if these are taken as statistically independent (at least approximately), one has a Gaussian return distribution. This is true only when the return is the sum of a sizable number of approximately independent random variables, and the central limit theory applies when the returns are Gaussian, and one is comfortable with the Black-Scholes-Merton model.

At the other extreme, there are small intervals such as high-frequency data (tick data, with the interval in minutes, seconds, or microsecond). For reasons involving scaling, the return distributions in such cases have heavy tails that decrease like a power or like a regularly varying function. This is in stark contrast to the ultrathin tails in the Gaussian case with a large interval. As one might expect, for intermediate intervals—daily returns, say—one obtains intermediate tail decay typically, although it depends on the context. These are semiheavy tails in which the log density decays linearly rather than quadratically in the Gaussian case or logarithmically in the Pareto case.

As long as conditions are liquid, the interval effects do not differ appreciably, and market strategies that exploit stationary behavior like mean reversion work. However, illiquid conditions are synonymous with tail events where the difference in intervals matters.

Liquidity means that tail behavior has little importance; illiquidity means that it has huge importance.

Definition 6.3: Liquidity Is the Interval between Discontinuous Jumps in Asset Prices; Illiquidity Is a Jump Discontinuity in Asset Prices

Financial modeling often relies on the assumption of continuous-time trading. This is necessary because of reliance on stochastic integration of risk-neutral models. Such models do allow for concise and powerful representation of continuous-time trading strategies given the tractability of Ito's formula and stochastic calculus in general. Illiquidity makes such models unrealistic.

It is like assuming that there will always be a willing buyer or seller. Bids are not available at any time and may arrive randomly, and prices are observable based on past arrival times and do not reflect current conditions. Optionality on the underlying means that trading activity is low far from delivery and higher near delivery.

Trading occurs over a finite horizon at random times conditioned on price quotes. These bid and ask quotes are not available at any time but are more frequent near delivery and during a trading-period horizon. The stochastic calculus approach requires assuming that observed prices come from an unobserved continuous-time process that is independent of arrival times. This is a bad assumption.

Brownian motion (and so geometric Brownian motion) is continuous and provides a model in which prices evolve continuously. In broad outline, prices move continuously, but not under the influence of major economic shocks. In fine detail and during shocks, prices jump. This is partly so because prices are measured in terms of money, and money is quantized. More important, it is so because prices are determined through trading—price is the level at which markets clear or supply balances demand.

As long as there is liquidity, there is a reasonable presumption of stationarity. And if $X_1, X_2, \ldots, X_n$ are normal, stationary obtains, and the correlation coefficient r_j of X_i and X_{i+j} satisfies $r_j \log j \to 0$ as $j \to$ infinity, then the distribution of the extremes is the same as if they came from an independent, identically distributed (i.i.d.) sequence of normal variables.[1] This means that if you have measurements from an i.i.d. normal distribution and you're only worried about the univariate case, the average approaches normality not only in the center of the distribution but also in the tail subinterval.

However, if a firm buys assets with borrowed money, then illiquidity can create discontinuities in which a firm owes more money than it has. Default then follows. If this occurs on a large, correlated scale, it can cause additional creditors to default. Even when there is no default, the leverage creates instabilities.

The higher the leverage ratio of asset value to cash down payment means that a buyer at this threshold (where losses exceed cash) α times leverage experiences a loss of α percent for every 1 percent drop in asset prices. On top of this, the investor's liquidity needs are $\$[(1 - \alpha)/\alpha]$ of cash for every $\$1$ drop in asset price. There is no extra liquidity need when $\alpha = 1$ (no leverage). This effect of leverage on losses is nonlinear, as seen in Figure 22.1, where greater leverage implies a stronger impact on net asset value.

The feedback from falling asset prices to margin calls transforms buyers into sellers and can become self-sustaining as the sellers

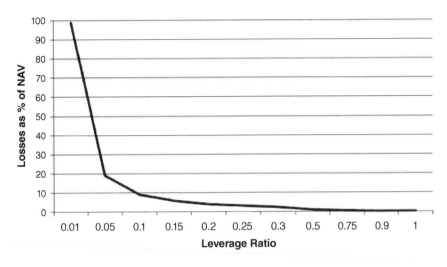

Figure 22.1 **Leverage Effects on Funding Needs.**

pressure prices more, leading to a cascading transformation of buyers into sellers. When there is no leverage, there is no feedback: The greater the leverage, the greater is the feedback pressure. Note that small leverage generates little impact on losses.

When leverage is below the threshold, then in a local sense, the effect of leverage is positive in that it makes sense to buy the dip. As a result, volatility is reduced. At the point where systemic leverage is at the threshold, negative feedback amplifies volatility.

A security is liquid when VaR works like it should; conversely, VaR doesn't work well when a security is illiquid.

When appropriate leverage is determined by similar value-at-risk (VaR) methodologies for marginal buyers and their books are sufficiently correlated, then prices become unstable owing to margin needs. Basing leverage ratios on relative volatility can be equally destabilizing because marginal buyers deleverage simultaneously. Instabilities that begin in relatively small ways that appear containable easily spill over into wider classes of asset markets.

These effects lead to extreme outcome distributions—fat tails. The implication is that too much leverage leads to too little leverage.

Illiquidity Means That Probabilistic Independence Breaks Down

In essence, Brownian motion is the trajectory of a particle moving at random in some state space. The model assumes that the future evolution of the process depends on the past only through the present state of the process. More precisely, assume the following (the strong Markov property): For a large class of random times T (called *stopping times*), any deterministic time t is a stopping time, as are such times as the first time the process encounters a fixed set.

Given this property, our best prediction of the future trajectory $Y(t) = X(T + t)$, $t \geq 0$, even given knowledge of the entire past [$X(s)$, $s \leq T$], depends only on the present state $X(T)$. Moreover, the probabilities inducing this prediction are those the original process would give if it starts off in state $X(T)$ at time 0. We call X a *Markov process*. Among Markov processes moving continuously in $\mathbf{R}^n$, one is singled out as canonical: Brownian motion is, up to a normalization transformation, the unique such process whose random fluctuations are homogeneous and isotropic in space.

These properties forge a link between analysis and probabilistic finance. A function $h(s)$ is harmonic if its average value over any sphere equals its value at the sphere's center. In probabilistic terms, $f(x)$ is the average value of f at the first place a Brownian motion encounters the border B, where the motion starts at x, and B is any sphere centered at x. There are simple interpretations of the classic notions of harmonic measure and regular boundary points. The former is simply that the law of the strpping time hits the boundary D of D depends on the initial point of the motion. The latter are points, starting from which the motion hits D immediately.

Brownian motion can be used to study the boundary values of functions h that are positive and harmonic on a domain D. If D is the unit disk, Fatou's theorem states that h has a limit along any curve that approaches a boundary point of D in a nontangential manner. For arbitrary domains, the geometric Euclidean boundary is inadequate; it must be replaced by the potential-theoretic Martin boundary. For Lipschitz domains, the two coincide. There, *almost every* refers to harmonic measure.

To go further, one needs to tie down the location at which the Brownian motion first leaves D. Doob accomplished this, introducing the notion of an h-transform. First, we modify the Brownian motion, killing it on leaving D. On first doing so, the particle evaporates, instantly jumping to some added "cemetery" state, from which it never returns.

Let H be positive and harmonic. An h-transform is a new stochastic process whose trajectories resemble those of killed Brownian motion, except that for small balls B centered at x in D, the law of the first exit from B starting at x is $h(x)^{-1}h(y)\sigma(dy)$, σ being normalized surface area on B. Thus the h-transform is driven toward places where h is large. If a subset A of D has positive harmonic measure, let h have a boundary value of 1 on A and 0 elsewhere. Then an h-transform is forced to leave D through A. There is another way of producing a process with this property: Use conditional probability, and "condition" the killed Brownian motion to leave D through A. The two turn out to be the same.

Despite the fact that $A = \{y\}$ has harmonic measure 0 and so is almost surely missed by killed Brownian motion, we still think of an h-transform as a Brownian motion "conditioned to leave D at y." The Martin boundary then acquires a probabilistic interpretation as a parameterization of the different ways Brownian motion can be conditioned to leave D. The potential-theoretic notion of a function f having a minimal-fine limit 1 at y turns out to be equivalent to $f[X(t)]$ approaching 1 almost surely as $X(T)$ approaches D, where X is a transform of the minimal harmonic function with pole at y.

A function that is positive and harmonic in D is minimal if it is not a sum of two other such functions (unless, of course, the summands are multiples of the original function). This is the key technical concept that powers the theory: A set U being minimal-thin at y can be taken to mean that for some initial point x, X has positive probability of missing U on its journey out to D.

Now suppose that a price process $X(t)$ is a Markov process with a price a. Call the trajectory of X between successive visits to price a an excursion of X away from a. If, with probability 1, X visits a repeatedly but only at a discrete set of times, then there is a first, second, and third number of excursions. The Markov property implies that they are all independent of each other.

In this case, there are standard methods for extracting information about the process from the common law H of these excursions. H is the law of a "typical" excursion, and if Λ is a set of possible trajectories, then $kH(\Lambda)$ is the average number of excursions, among the first k, that follow trajectories from Λ.

When applied to Brownian motion in **R**, regardless of the price a, the set of times t such that $X(t) = a$ almost surely have the topologic structure of a Cantor set—each excursion has another arbitrarily close to it. Thus there is no way of labeling the excursions as "first," "second," and so on, and one cannot single out a "typical excursion." For example, although the chosen excursion is underway at some fixed time t, its selection predisposes the excursion to be unusually long.

To circumvent this problem, Kiyoshi Ito's work devises the concept of local time at a. Brownian motion $\{s: s \le t, X(s) = a\}$ has the Lebesgue measure zero for each fixed t, yet there is a deterministic function g such that if this set is nonempty, then its g-Hausdorff measure $L(t)$ is almost finite and nonzero. $L(t)$ gives a local time at a, a way to keep time if it "ticks" when X is at a. The excursions turn out to come homogeneously and independently when we keep time in this way.

This is no longer a law of a "typical" excursion. Instead, it is the expected number of excursions that follow a trajectory from Λ that come during a fixed interval of local time.

Ito[2] showed that the number of such excursions coming in disjoint intervals of local time will be independent of each other and that the expected number coming in an interval $[s, t]$ will be $(t - s)$ $H(\Lambda)$ for some measure H. Since infinitely many excursions may come in every open interval of local time, H may be an infinite measure. Nonetheless, it is connected to the conventional notion of H. The first excursion of duration longer than d has a law expressed using H. It will be H restricted to the set Λ_δ of excursions lasting at least time δ but multiplied by a constant that gets small as $\delta \to 0$, as they come increasingly rapidly.

Maisonneuve[3] generalized Ito's decomposition, treating excursions away from more general sets M. An excursion is the trajectory followed by the process during a maximal interval during which the process doesn't visit M. For Brownian motion in $\mathbf{R}^n$ and M the complement of a domain D, one can define a local time on M and use it as a clock with which to time the starts of excursions into D. Thus, in a very general class of settings, *the excursions no longer will have the independence property* described earlier because they are tied together by the initial and final positions of the Brownian motion during the excursion.

CONCLUSION

Risk management begins with risk assessment and understanding the tools available to manage risk. It permits anticipating risk and mitigating its effects. But not all risks can be ascertained. These axioms are a starting point that captures essential aspects in a probabilistic way. Volatility is a measure of the uncertain risks that erupt to the surface in times of stress, and it is reducible to the second moment of a time series plus some residual element derived from trading. Liquidity is a state of markets such that expectation is stable, and prediction is possible.

No one is all-seeing when it comes to risk and volatility. No one is a master of liquidity. Axioms or not, putting liquidity into practice is easier said than done.

CHAPTER 23

The Fed Is a Two-Faced Mutant Pig

The problem with risk is that we manage it with what we know best, even when events outside our experience happen. For this reason, investors work under the assumption that the future is not appreciably different from the past. When radically different conditions arise, all bets are off. The Federal Reserve manages risk with what it knows best—easy liquidity. This will create a greater problem than it resolves.

THE PROBLEM IS INSOLVENCY, NOT ILLIQUIDITY

Insolvency is the real tail risk now, not illiquidity.

The Policy Premise

The prices for bank assets became "artificially" depressed by banks and other investors trying to unload their holdings in an illiquid market. As a result, they no longer reflect their true hold-to-maturity value. By purchasing or insuring a large quantity of bank assets, the government (the Fed) can restore liquidity to credit markets and restore banks.

The Policy Error

The "credit crunch" wasn't about liquidity at all. It *is* about solvency. Insolvency can't be fixed by short-term subsidies. You need liability reduction, asset appreciation, or a greater long-term equity cushion.

Long-term subsidies, such as the Fed holding who-knows-what to maturity, are like Soviet Communism. Short-term subsidies transfer credit risk, and they leverage parasitic behavior. Positive valuations assigned by shareholders to equities arise solely from anticipation of value transfer from firm debt holders or resource transfers from U.S. taxpayers. Debt holders get a piece of this action too if governments overpay for "toxic" assets backing up their claims. *Everybody* receives more than fair value for their investments.

So everybody's happy, right? Umm, no.

The Policy Victims: Everyone Is Happy Except Taxpayers and Currency Longs

Government resources that support markets by insuring assets against further loss amount to providing an insurance policy at a premium way below what is fair for the risks that U.S. taxpayers bear. *The Fed is just a retrocessionaire with a massive book of correlated tail risks.* Others will be on the stick when they breach treaty.

With All the Slosh, No One Knows the Extent of the Insolvency Problem Anymore

The Fed has put a bid under possibly worthless assets. Allowing the secondary market to price assets without the Fed bid would be the best way to assess the insolvency problem. The test condition is that if asset prices revert back to their "crash" valuations, then those prices imply that some major U.S. banks are now legitimately insolvent. Bank assets are fairly priced at valuations that sum to less than bank liabilities.

For Some Assets, the Crash Valuation Was Right

Securitization will revive in time because it is an excellent idea. But the current reboot focuses on supporting the status quo—lack of transparency, reliance on flawed (understatement of the century) rating-agency designations, and mispricing of underlying cash flows. It is ridiculous to think that the market is going to resume with uneconomic valuations without continued government guarantees.

MARKET CRASHES AS MOMENTS OF CLARITY

Market crashes provide clarification about the overall valuation.

The *World* Isn't Sure What to Make of Risk Anymore Because of the Massive Distortions

Two years ago, the whole world was going up in flames. What passes for risk these days is a sterilized construct bounded by government insurance cover on the downside. You know—the Greenspan put.

Stalling Market Crashes Isn't a Desirable End in Itself

Crashes aren't any more irrational than any other trading action. Crashes are just sudden moments of clarity that bring investors to new "fundamental" valuations. Greenspan puts and Bernanke variations don't short-circuit price discovery indefinitely; they just make transitions to different valuations even more violent for more and more bag holders.

Investors Get Painful, Periodic Lessons in Risk to Enhance Survivability

Risk is so much more real and interesting and wild and painful than the formulaic constructions people imagine it to be. Grossly unsuccessful mutations such as central planning don't last long in this world. Nature cleans up after herself.

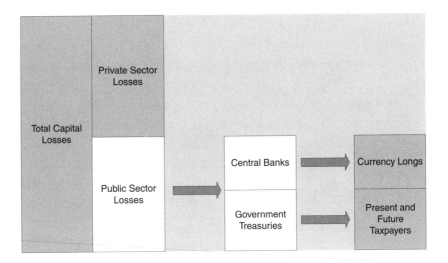

Figure 23.1 **Channels of Socializing Losses.**

The Fed is fast gestating into a mutation like a five-legged puppy, a medically deformed kitten, or a two-faced mutant pig. The gene code needed to express it? Simply sustain institutions unfit for survival, and by implication, penalize those most fit to survive. Figure 23.1 shows how this works.

First, governments dilute capital loss by backstopping losses; then the two instruments of modern economies, central banks and Treasuries, transfer the losses to present and future taxpayers while at the same time capital holders get their base eroded over time through currency devaluation.

CROWDED TRADES ARE INBREEDING

Crowded trades have undesirable results.

The Greenspan Put Reinforces Behavior Unsuited for Survival, Failure after Failure

You can see this in the negative skews of some strategies in the hedge-fund space. Skewed hedge-fund returns broken out by Credit

Table 23.1 Hedge Strategy Return Skews, January 1994–April 2008

CS/Tremont Hedge Fund Index	Sector Weight	Skewness
Convertible arbitrage	1.90%	−1.59
Fixed-income arbitrage	4.70%	−3.35
Multistrategy	10.40%	−1.06
Event driven	24.40%	−3.27
Emerging markets	8.50%	−0.79
Global macro	13.80%	0.05
Managed futures	4.00%	0.02
Long-short equity	26.40%	0.19
Equity market neutral	5.30%	0.34
Dedicated short bias	0.60%	0.83

Source: Malliaris and Yan; www.haas.berkeley.edu/groups/finance/Nickel11.pdf.

Suisse-Tremont subindices from 1994 to the crisis are reported in Table 23.1. The skew was calculated based on the monthly returns of each subindex.

In a general sense, skew is a measure of how much more volatility goes up when there is a significant downswing in prices compared with a similar swing to higher prices. The negative skew in this context is just a measure of a crowded trade and the herding of managers into taking the same trade. Thus, if the trade reverses, a negative skew is a measure of how much risk appetite would vaporize as prices drop.

See that some of the trading strategies listed in the table—statistical arbitrage, convergence trades, risk arbitrage—that hedge funds employ have serious negative skew. To see what this means, imagine that a trader tracks over time the credit spreads of a portfolio of bonds. When a bond's spread widens, the trader buys the bond. The trader waits for the spread to return to its historical levels, sells the bond, and pockets a profit. It works like a charm, except occasionally the spread continues to widen, and the trader is left holding a distressed bond and blows up.

When a bond's spread widens, this usually means something has happened to cause investors concern about the issuer. Most of the time, those concerns aren't realized, and the spread returns to its past levels. Occasionally, the concerns prove all too valid, and the spread blows out. In this sense, statistical arbitrage is like selling far out-of-the-money options. It makes consistent money but occasionally realizes a dramatic loss. It is a negatively skewed trading strategy. In the fixed-income setting, the skew can be viewed as an indicator of a jump to default risk or extreme rating-migration risk forcing a position rout.

LEVERAGE MAGNIFIES DISTORTION

There are ways to hedge negatively skewed returns, such as buying index protection, but there are limits to just how much you can do.

You Can't Escape Leverage in Financial Markets, No Matter How Hard You Try

A given investor may not leverage assets directly, but the investor is exposed to the self-amplifying effects of leverage and fat tails through other market investors. Market volatility is due more than anything to dumped positions due to massive leverage.

Leverage Increases the Nonlinearity Embedded in All Financial Markets

This makes the entire financial architecture much more sensitive to extreme risk. Equity is especially exposed to the nonlinear effects of leverage. Why? Business law gives shareholders the right to any residual profits. Bankruptcy law represents the company's exercise of its right to keep shareholders' money to pay off higher-priority liabilities (e.g., debt holders, suppliers, employees, plaintiffs in lawsuits, etc.). This makes stocks subject to extreme losses. Thus, when a debt-laden company experiences a default event, it may be forced into default with a 100 percent loss of shareholders' investments.

FORGET BEING YOUR OWN CENTRAL BANKER: BE YOUR OWN INSURER

Risk can't be entirely eliminated.

The Elapse of Time Makes Prediction Errors Grow Exponentially

Looking at a morning sky full of dark clouds and thunder makes it pretty clear that it will rain that morning, but it says nothing about the weather a week from now. Even those *obvious* morning forecasts aren't always right.

Prediction errors grow in part because what you do influences the prediction. Sooner or later your hard drive will crash or you will screw some measurement up that influences your prediction. Further, these unavoidable errors ensure that there will never be enough observations or simulation times to backtest to an arbitrary tolerance. Sooner or later certain unexpected patterns emerge and blow you up.

Don't Count on Elected Stooges to Reduce Your Risk

The stooges are working to reduce *their perceived* downside risk. It is your responsibility to manage your risk. Figure 23.2 presents a rough schema to conceptualize some risk categories, with hedge ideas.

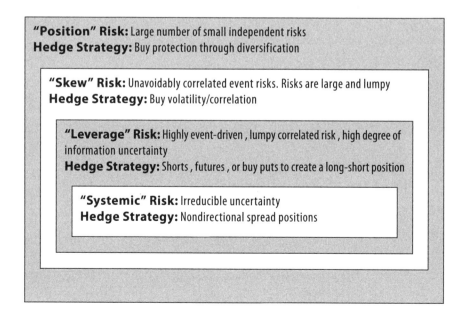

"Position" Risk: Large number of small independent risks
Hedge Strategy: Buy protection through diversification

"Skew" Risk: Unavoidably correlated event risks. Risks are large and lumpy
Hedge Strategy: Buy volatility/correlation

"Leverage" Risk: Highly event-driven, lumpy correlated risk, high degree of information uncertainty
Hedge Strategy: Shorts, futures, or buy puts to create a long-short position

"Systemic" Risk: Irreducible uncertainty
Hedge Strategy: Nondirectional spread positions

Figure 23.2 **Onion risk management.**

FED: PART COMPANY WITH IVY LEAGUE AND GO TO CHI-TOWN

Policy strategy needs to get away from economic theory and adopt market-based approaches.

Professors Bearing Doob-Meyer Decompositions Are Not the Only Way Forward

Although the honest, unpretentious, thoroughly decent Philip Protter[1] is the best guy in the world from whom to get this expertise, there are plenty of reinsurance actuary consultants with hands-on experience in making tail-risk collection a successful business model.

The Banking System Doesn't Manage Its Risks the Way the Insurance Industry Does Because Its Incentives Preclude It

Insurance hedging is capital-intensive, and return on assets (ROA) is much more volatile. The financial system can't handle this in its present form. Securitization is a way to handle this. If the Fed is afraid to take the bid off bank assets because of life-support concerns, try floating a CAT-like (catastrophe) bond on the Fed balance sheet's most toxic assets risks, and see what market action ensues. At least there will be some measure of risk pricing.

The skeptic can say: "So the Fed is like AIG overdosing on Viagra and cocaine. They have a printing press, so who cares? Taxpayers won't know what hit them."

This Is Too Short-Sighted a View Because Everything Eventually Breaks Down

The best trading system doesn't make you the first to dump crashing securities. Correlations break at the worst possible time. Assumptions are violated: "Sorry, those stochastic processes weren't stationary after all." Printing presses can't print fast enough, or they spit out product of such poor quality that no one can use it. When the breakdown does happen, order dissolves into chaos. Transferring risk doesn't make risk go away.

CHAPTER 24

What Lurks Behind
Your Trading Station

One of the most common words in the financial lingo is *risking*—the other is *de-risking*. The basic idea is that assets funded by being short dollars (borrowing dollars) generate returns that match the risk, but when funding and margin costs reduce the return, investors *de-risk*. Everyone sells at the same time, causing risk asset prices to crash. Since liquidity is most of what has driven up risk since early 2009, this risk-on, risk-off mentality works very much like a coin flip.

You can model a sequence of binary outcomes with a Bernoulli process that assigns a fixed probability to one of two possible outcomes and another probability to the other possible outcome. It is like modeling a coin flip. One actually can derive the Black-Scholes pricing formula using a history of coin flip–like processes called a *random walk*, a process that moves in defined "steps" through time. The assumption you need is that the central limit theorem holds.

The story of mathematical finance usually begins with Brownian motion or some variation. I'm going to start with an everyday coin and present Brownian motion in a way that fits the mathematical finance framework. This machinery finds fullest application in finance via risk-neutral probability models, a way to determine "fundamental value" from a probabilistic point of view, particularly used in derivative markets such as options, swaps, and futures.

You can find a detailed exposition of the modern theory of stochastic finance in a textbook. What you find in this chapter is an assessment of this theory from a basic starting point of flipping a coin. There are plenty of practical violations to the theory: There is front-running and bending the rules, and there can be situations where there is profit with no risk. There are fundamental problems, related to human behavior in financial markets, but they illuminate how expectations are formed.

Much financial work involves assessing outcomes depending on future states, and there are really two different kinds of probability at work in finance doing this. One reflects the limitations of reality when perfect prediction is impossible. The other reflects mathematical probability that estimates the unknown future based on well-known rules of chance. The former type of model is described as *risk-neutral*. The latter is *classical probability*.

Both models are based on *probability measures*—well-behaved mappings from state to state. One type of probability stems from looking at probability of default in a corporate bond using ratios based on historical data—*classic* probability. The other type stems from the implied probability of default based on probabilities backed out of current prices of credit-default swaps (CDS). This type of probability informs risk-neutral models. These two measures of default typically are very different from each other owing to the look-back nature of history and forward-looking nature of expectations. Neither measure is wrong until the future is realized—they are just different.

The classic measure looks solely at what history says about the future. Risk-neutral models express the future but refer only to the present for its realization, displaying a snapshot of current conditions, which do, of course, change. Everything relevant about the past is compressed into the present and then projected onto the future with risk-neutral models.

Both approaches provide a stripped-down version of reality where markets conform to mathematically established probabilities and asset markets are well behaved, abstract, and subject to control. Risk-neutral models have a desirable feature: If you assume that everyone plays by the rules (nobody cheats or steals) and everyone acts rationally all the time (no arbitrage opportunities), then you can apply some technical machinery called Girsonov's formula and the Radom-Nikodym theorem. This machinery implies a unique probability measure that converges to the present value of discounted future cash flows. This is to say, under very stylized conditions, asset fundamentals equal value.

Probability is not necessary for markets to work: The markets have done just fine without it in the past. The pricing of assets ultimately reduces to a simple search—a buyer and a seller of an asset finding each other in the marketplace. Long before they knew about stochastic processes, Japanese traders were pricing rice futures as early as the seventeenth century. Even before this, futures contracts probably existed in various parts of the world. Clearly, the concept of *optionality* existed as soon as there were second-generation assets with contingent claims (such as equities).

However, modern buyers and sellers of futures rely much more on probability as a system to complement/supplement buyer and seller search. It is conceived as the initial starting point for valuation, part of a larger effort to make risk precise and objective—sellable. In 1973, using a similar menu of assumptions, Fisher Black and Myron Scholes produced a set of equations that provided strict quantification of the prices of options where the underlying asset's volatility is implied. These equations enabled analysts to standardize the pricing of derivatives. This is only the starting point for pricing. Dealers dangle these starting bids in the market just as fishermen do. They alter the price to make it more attractive to buyers, raise the ask, and play head games such as "The demand I'm seeing tells me you should jump on this now. You may not see it tomorrow."

COINS AT THE READY

When you flip a coin, physical laws determine which side the coin will land on, but the coin flip is random anyway because the outcome of a head or tail is not predictable when the coin rotates in the air enough times before it lands. Random-number generators work the same way: They generate numbers by deterministic rules of machine code. The complexity of the governing rules makes it appropriate to consider the generated numbers as random.

True randomness occurs when a sequence of outcomes is independent of previous outcomes—the probability of an outcome is not influenced by previous outcomes. A coin fits this characterization because it has no memory of past flips, and there is no divine order that guarantees the number of heads or tails will even out as the number of flips grows large. It is equally plausible if you flip a coin 10 times that you will get one of these sequences of heads and tails: HHHHHHHHHH, TTTTTTTTTT, and HTHTHTHTHT, even if HHHHHHHH and TTTTTTTT don't look random at all.

The process of tossing a coin generates a process called a *random walk*. Start at the origin (0, 0), and flip in the coin $1, 2, \ldots, n$ times. If the coin flip x comes up heads, then add $+1$ at time t. If tails, then add -1 at time t. In general, therefore, you get a process that just, well, meanders around in no general direction. To explain this more formally, let $m =$ the number of flips. There are $2m$ possible functions (these are all possible sequences of heads and tails), called *paths*, and they are all equally likely to occur. Let S_m denote these paths. Obviously, $-m \le S_m \le m$, although for m very large, $S_m = \pm m$ is very unlikely.

A fundamental result in probability theory; the central limit theorem states that as $m \to \infty$, $S_m/\sqrt{m}$ has the probability distribution of a normal random variable with mean 0 and variance 1. Therefore, in generalizing this process so that the jumps occur at $x = k/n$, for some large integer n and all k in the positive integers including 0, we essentially must take the jump size to be $1/\sqrt{n}$ if we do not want the resulting processes to be either immediately unbounded or identically zero as n goes to infinity. For each n, denote the generalized process by X_n.

We can take $\lim_{n \to \infty} X_n$ so that it is a collection of paths that are continuous on $\mathbf{R}+$. This limit process is Brownian motion, which we denote by $B = \{B_t(\omega), \omega \in \Omega, t \in \mathbf{R}+\}$, where Ω is a probability space and B is a collection of random functions. Before one flips a coin the first time, $B_0 = 0$, and given the properties of a coin flip, B has stationary independent increments. By *stationary*, I mean all increments of the same length have the same probability distribution. Even though the process is continuous in the limit, the randomness of the outcomes makes it visually jagged at nearly every point. In fact, Brownian motion as a measure-theoretic construction is nondifferentiable. The existence of such a large collection of continuous nondifferentiable functions seemed quite remarkable when Wiener first showed this in 1923.

Wiener's construction replaces the coin with a more general mechanism. As first principles, he begins with a function wandering about in a general way, following probabilistic rules. This function is situated in sets that are measurable: They have desirable properties regarding generalizations of analytic tools such as derivatives and integrals. For a measurable set $A \in \mathbf{R}^1$, consider $\mu_t(A) := \int_{0 \to t} I_{\{B(s) A\}} ds$ the amount of time the Brownian motion path, starting from 0, spends in A up to time t. For fixed t, $\mu_t(A)$ is absolutely continuous with respect to the Lebesgue measure. We denote its Radon-Nikodym derivative by l_t^x. This is a random variable because it depends on the paths in B. One forms the stochastic process from the collection of random variables $l := \{l_t^x, (x, t) \in \mathbf{R}^1 \times \mathbf{R}+\}$. This can be done in such a way that l is continuous on $\mathbf{R}^1 \times \mathbf{R}+$, or "jointly continuous." This stochastic process l is called the *local times of Brownian motion.*

Kolmogorov showed how these measure-theoretic concepts are a natural fit for probability. He normalized a measure space Ω with the restriction $\mu(\Omega) = 1$, where the points ω of Ω are like coin flip outcomes, but more general in the state space of all possible events. He set E as a measurable subset of Ω, then $\mu(E)$ as the probability that the occurring ω is in the set E. The space Ω and the measure μ are given and assumed to be fixed once and for all.

Probability theory in this setting becomes the study of the measurable functions f defined on Ω. If f is a real-valued function, then the probability that f takes on a value in the Borel set $B \subset \mathbf{R}$ is $\mu[f^{-1}(B)]$, meaning that these measurable functions are completely determined by the measure α on the real line $F \to \mu[f^{-1}(B)]$. It is a probability measure when $\alpha([\infty. -\infty]) = 1$ and is called a *distribution of f.* $\int_\Omega f(x) d\mu(x) = \int_{(\infty, -\infty)} x d\alpha(x)$ is the expected value $\mathbf{E}(f)$ when it exists. $\int_\Omega [f(x) - \mathbf{E}(f)]^2 d\alpha(x) = \int_{(\infty, -\infty)} [x - \mathbf{E}(x)]^2 d\alpha(x)$ is the variance of f. The function f has an expectation and finite variance if and only if $f \subset L^2(\Omega, \mu)$. When this is the case in one random variable, everything can be expressed in terms of the measure α.

This measure-theory setting makes it straightforward to move from a discrete flipping of coins to continuous actions so that random variables parameterize on t on the real line instead of a sequence indexed by an integer i. This continuous process is called a *Weiner process;* it uses sample functions instead of sample sequences, and the measure μ in Ω reconstitutes a measure in the space of all sample functions.

The switch to a continuous setting makes it convenient to formulate a Weiner process as evolving according to a general second-order elliptic differential equation:

$$L = \frac{1}{2} \sum_{i,j=1}^{d} a_{ij}\,(x)\frac{\partial^2}{x_i\,x_j} + \sum_{i=1}^{d} b_i(x)\frac{\partial}{x_i} + V(x)$$

where a_{ij}, b_i, and V have some boundedness properties (they are Lipschitz functions) in $\mathbf{R}^d$. This partial differentiation is how Black-Scholes is formulated.

The class of solutions of $Lu = 0$ on a bounded set $D \subset \mathbf{R}^d$ is designated $C_L(D)$. The probabilistic solution of $C_L(D)$ requires the construction of a measure P on the path space $\Omega = \{\omega \in C([0, \infty), \mathbf{R}^d) : \omega(0) = 0\}$ representing the trajectories of particles undergoing Brownian motion. The function $W : [0, \infty) \times W \to Rd$ defined by $Wt(w) = w(t)$ has the distributional property that under P the random variables $W_{t1}, W_{t2} - W_{t1}, \ldots, W_{tn} - W_{tn-1}$ are independent and Gaussian with mean zero and variances $t_1, t_2 - t_1, \ldots, t_n - t_{n-1}$. P gives mass 1 to paths that are nowhere differentiable.

The next step in deriving a Black-Scholes is a representation of the diffusion naturally associated with the operator $L_0 = L - V$. The association between the diffusion X and operator L_0 is captured by the requirement that as $b \to 0$,

$$E\left[X_{t+b}^i - X_t^i \mid \sigma(W_s : s \le t)\right] = b_i(X_t)b + o(b) \qquad 1 \le i \le d$$

$$E\left[(X_{t+b}^i - (X_t^i)(X_{t+b}^j - X_t^j)] \mid \sigma(W_s : s \le t)\right] = a_{ij}(X_t)b + o(b) \qquad 1 \le i, j \le d$$

where E is integrated with respect to P, and the conditional expected value $E[\cdot(\sigma(W_s) : s \leq t)]$ is integrated with respect to the σ-field $\sigma(W_s : s \leq t)$. In this context, X solves the differential equation

$$dX_t(x) = \sigma[X_t(x)]dW_t + b[X_t(x)]dt$$

where σ is any square root of a, and $\sigma \, \sigma^* = a$.

The challenge is that with P probability, W has no derivative in the conventional sense. Stochastic integrals provide a unique solution to the differential equation given a regularity condition (the Lipschitz condition) on σ and b.

When an underlying asset S follows a geometric Brownian motion in discrete time, it becomes

$$dS = \mu S \Delta t + \sigma S \Delta W$$

dS is analogous to the differential equation $dX_t(x)$. Solving this differential equation provides a way to calculate the price of options on the asset S. Much of modern financial theory extends this probabalistic construction to different distributions and contexts, but the basic conclusion is that asset moves resemble a random process that can be understood and predicted. It leads to the closely connected concept of risk-neutral models.

RISK-NEUTRAL MODELS

Consider a $100 investment that has a payout structure with a 50 percent chance of losing $50 and a 50 percent chance of a $150 return. Some investors may take a small position equivalent to buying a lottery ticket, but the 2:1 possibility of losing $50 of the initial capital will make very few people take the trade. If you look at the investment over time, you have an average payout of $100, meaning that there is little chance that repeated trades of this kind will net you a gain or a loss. Statistically, there is really no reason to consider the investment at all because there is no compensation for the risk.

The trade becomes increasingly attractive as the initial investment is adjusted down. Let's say that the required initial capital becomes $90. This changes the 50 percent loss/50 percent gain chances to 40 percent loss/60 percent gain chances. The initial investment amount related to the perceived risk embodied in the trade, and the difference between the expected value ($100) and the discounted need to entice investors ($90) is called the *risk premium*.

The risk premium affects the payout probabilities on the investment, and in this sense, prices are expected values. This is nice because expectation is a linear operator. The probability measure that adjusts for the risk is called the *risk-neutral measure*.

Risk-neutral measures work well when the premium doesn't vary much investor to investor and there are only small transactions costs to buying and selling an investment position. A good indication of uniform premium is if the difference in the bid-ask spread is narrow. When the bid-ask spread widens, this indicates that the variation of risk premium across investors increases and also indicates a deterioration of liquidity in the market. Both indications closely intertwine with each other.

Wider spreads are indicative of a risk measure under change. The change could be a minor tweak of distribution parameters, or it could mean something more daunting—that the distribution we assume to hold in a general way doesn't. Think about it this way. If there were uniform expectations about prices and prospects for assets, no one would trade. Trading implies that you think that the "market"—the views on the future reflected in prices—is wrong and your view is right. Views on future outcomes for a portfolio or views on how the market moves are not probabilities based on expected values of observed frequencies. Such views are based on a subjective degree of belief in part multidimensional, intuitive, and emotive.

Risk-neutral measures are free of contradiction and incorporate some first principles of risk that fit observed reality. They permit extreme precision. However, the measures can approximate risk poorly, particularly when one depends on them for clarity the most.

The central problem posed for these measures is the valuation of uncertain future cash flows. The first step is to calculate the net present value of the future cash flows. One then estimates the expected values of the future cash flows for all periods of the investment term and discounts these cash flows to the present period using a discount factor. The estimate involves a spread applied to Treasury bond rates for fixed cash-flows or applied to some other reference rate like LIBOR for floating cash flows. The spread between the assumed rate and the reference rate compensates for the credit riskiness, but there is no way to fully quantify the degree of uncertainty that reflects the spread. The best policy is to find an asset with similar cash flows that trades liquid and applies the risk-neutral premium to this valuation that reflects investor preferences.

Investment Example

Risk-neutral measures play a central role in credit default swaps. Consider a default swap that pays out when a triggering event happens within a year. The payout is S, paid out at the end of the year. If the triggering event doesn't happen within the year, there is no payout, and the contract ends.

The payment P needed for an investor to take the trade is

$$P = S/(S + i) \times Q$$

where Q is the probability of the trigger event happening within the year, and i is the reference interest rate. This P is the discounted expected value of the investment at the end of the year. Typically, the probabilities implied by the quoted Q are much higher than the "true" probability of the trigger happening during the year.

The difference in payment implied by the implied probability versus the true probability is the risk premium. To see this, imagine that there is a known true likelihood for the event, and i is the precise return an investor could achieve when investing the payment.

For trigger events, there is no way to know a true probability of the event. The art/smarts/luck involved is getting Q right.

In many cases in finance, the probability measure is given, from known quoted CDS spreads (prices loosely speaking) and assumed recovery rates. Thus default probabilities are implied from the inputs. Consider a one-year upfront (payments made at the outset) CDS contract.

S: CDS spread payment
Q: default probability
R: recovery rate

The protection buyer expects to pay S, and the expected payoff is $(1 - R)Q$.

When two parties enter a CDS trade, S is set so that the value of the swap transaction is zero:

$$S = (1 - R)Q \leftrightarrow S/(1 - R) = Q$$

This means that Q is the probability needed to generate enough risk to cause the trade to happen, making it a risk-neutral probability. "Risk-neutral" implies a premium needed to entice buyers and sellers to take the trade, not the true probability of an event occurrence. It serves as a benchmark of valuation that imparts less weight to favorable events compared with what is reflected in the historical probability P and imparts more weight to unfavorable events compared with what is reflected in true probability P.

Historical probability measures P are seldom known in their entirety. Instead the measure is derived from a subsample. As a result, P is deficient in some contexts. Risk-neutral probabilities are, in contrast, implied by a financial model. All probabilities depend on unobservable future events, not past frequencies or models, and as such are impossible to predict with accuracy.

It is possible that risk-neutral probabilities are not unique given certain conditions on its probability space. If risk-neutral measures are not unique, it implies that arbitrage opportunities exist in a persistent way. This is possible given high transactions costs (such as investments that require a minimum of millions in capital lockup) or very costly search for opportunities.

Bookies use something like risk-neutral measures, although the probabilities (the odds they give) are altered for the express purpose of evening out the money on both sides of the bet. When a bookie has $10,000 on Ohio State and $10,000 on Florida, he or she profits off the commission he or she charges with no downside risk regardless who wins or loses. It is up to the gamblers to predict which team wins. In the same way, investors have to predict what investments will be successful while the dealer moves inventory with a mark-up.

ILLUSIONS AND ARBITRAGE

Sophisticated risk-neutral measures are defined as a martingale or some generalization of it, like a semimartingale. However, for the model to work adequately, the semimartingale representation must completely characterize the price process of an asset X_t such that there is no arbitrage. Arbitrage is an event such that one makes a profit without taking any risk.

The arbitrage-free assumption is necessary and not a convenience. The notion of risk neutrality depends on the assumption because it is equivalent to the existence of a probability measure P for which all expected rates of return are equal to the risk-free rate. This unique measure P is how prices are derived. This may seem to be a technical device, but the practical impact is huge. If there is no arbitrage, then the price of any security is the P-expected sum of its future discounted cash flows. If arbitrage opportunities do persist, then most conventional financial models don't work as they should. Persistent and large arbitrage opportunities destroy the predictive content of the probability model.

Consider an example where a stock follows a Weiner process X, r is the risk-free rate, and $\mathbf{E}(P)$ is the expectation with respect to the measure P. The price of a call on X at time T and strike K at T_0 is $\mathbf{E}(P)[e^{-rT} \max(X_T - K, 0)]$. A front-running-free, arbitrage-free, liquid, reasonably informed market would permit straightforward pricing. One simply assumes a distribution for the fundamental variables, estimates parameters using available information and priors, and uses the backtest outputs to simulate future prices, price securities with the model, and trade at will.

This risk-neutral probability measure = no arbitrage construction is the foundation of quantitative finance. This assumption makes the following statements equivalent:

1. All expected rates of return are valued fundamentally.
2. Risk-neutral valuation is the sum of an asset's future discounted cash flows.
3. Any security can be decomposed into continuously tradable replicating portfolios, and by trading the replicating portfolios continuously, you can choose any probability measure you want.

This model also sheds light on mispricing of assets. The residual of the risk-neutral price less the observed price is a "bubble." The size of an asset bubble is

$$B = S_t - RN_t$$

where B = bubble
S_t = market price at time t
RN_t = risk-neutral implied fundamental price

Philip Protter provides a typology of these bubbles. He observed that if B is a local martingale, then the bubble is like fiat money—a medium of exchange. It has no intrinsic value and becomes almost (or fully) worthless. This has been observed in a variety of hyperinflations throughout history. Hyperinflation of a fiat money is an example of a phenomenal bubble, but bubbles can be much more common and benign than this. Bubbles can be inflated in a variety of ways and pricked by something as simple as noting short interest in size.

These commonplace bubbles are a big problem because when they burst, illiquidity and arbitrage *both* can pop bubbles and deflate risk-neutral implied pricing because of the effect on cash flows. In a quick risk-off move, risk-neutral prices can collapse, but market prices can drop even more. *Bubbles can become negative* in this case.

Bubble convergence to zero is how relative pricing works. But aberrant meltdowns are where the real money is, meaning that when a bubble is negative, long is truly a low-risk position. Mean reversion here implies that bubbles don't stay negative, and they don't when a tail risk killer is at the printing press.

CHAPTER 25

The Limits of (Statistical) Independence

Everything we know is based on observable phenomena subject to chance variation. This is how probability works: Observe some data, assign some distributions, and derive rules that govern the behavior of chance. The workhorse idea that makes this more than arbitrary guessing is the limit-theorem notion. Limit theorems highlight how given observed frequencies converge to probability distributions that embody clearly defined rules for prediction.

The convergence imposes a useful regularity when the number of possible outcomes is fixed and bounded measureable sets are the framework. Namely, given an independent sequence of random variables with finite mean and variance, as the sample size tends to infinity, the statistical properties of the sample converge to the normal distribution. This statement of the theorem is stated broadly so as to focus on the essential point. You need a reality that is fixed, not an evolving work in progress. You need a sequence that has extremely limited dependence relationships. Further, even if we assume independence, the speed of convergence can create significant problems unless you actually can get to infinity from here—which you can't, outside of the mind's eye.

So a central limitation of modern financial theory is to characterize probability distributions given observed frequencies without the assumptions necessary for limit theorems. There are some things we can know about a sequence in this context without these assumptions.

PROBABILITY DECOMPOSITIONS

State this context in the following way: If a family of distributions F possesses a certain property P, then under some conditions, it is true that a distribution has the property P only if it is a member of F. This matters because if a statistical procedure is valid only when property P holds and this property characterizes the family F, then certain methods are valid only when the underlying distribution is a member of the family F. Simply put, what does a "mound shaped" sampling distribution say about the family F? This problem provides some bounds on what we actually can know without an unknown distribution.

Here is a brief history of some results on the problem. In 1923, George Polya[1] proved that

- If X and Y are independent random variables with the same distribution F,
  Then F has a finite second moment (the variance is bounded).
- If there exist positive constants a, b so that $aX + bY$ also has the same distribution as F,
  Then F is a normal distribution with zero mean.

Notable progress was made by Macinkiewicz[2]: If $\{X_n\}$ is a sequence of independent random variables all having the same distribution F having finite moments of all positive orders and there exist two linear forms $\Sigma a_n X_n$ and $\Sigma b_n X_n$ whose distributions are identical, then F is normal.

Linnick[3] did some amazing work in this area, building on the work of Paul Levy[4] (Mandelbrot's mentor). His starting point is that the law L_t of a random variable X_t is described by its distribution F_t or by its characteristic function f_t. The set of all laws is metrized by the Levy metric $d(F_1, F_2)$. If $X = X_1 + X_2$ is the sum of independent random variables X_1 and X_2, then its law is described by the convolution, or composition, $F = F_1 \times F_2$ or by the product $f = f_1 \times f_2$. The law

$L = L_1 - L_2$ is decomposable or factorizable into components L_1 and L_2 if L_1 or L_2 is not degenerate.

Levy himself produced indecomposable nondegenerate laws. On the other hand, there are infinitely decomposable laws $L = L_n{}^n$ for every integer $n > 0$. This is true if and only if $f = e^\psi$ with $\psi = (\alpha, \Psi)$ given by

$$y(t) = i\alpha t + \int_{-\infty}^{+\infty} b(x, t)d\Psi(x)$$

where α is a real number, ψ is a nondecreasing function of bounded variation, and

$$b(x, t) = \left(e^{ixt} - 1 - \frac{ixt}{1 + x^2}\right)\frac{1 + x^2}{x^2}\left(= -\frac{t^2}{2} \quad \text{at } x = 0 \text{ by continuity}\right)$$

P. Levy stated without proof that normal laws are decomposable into normal components only. In 1935, he deduced normal decomposition "stability": If a law is approximately normal, so are its components, *approximately* being defined in terms of the Levy metric. In 1936, Cramer[5] proved the Levy conjecture. In 1937, Raikov[6] proved a similar decomposition for Poisson-type laws into Poisson-type components only. Both proofs used the Hadamard factorization theorem for entire functions.

Linnik combined these results: If a law is composed of a normal law and a Poisson-type law, so are all its components. Normal decomposition stability was extended to all decompositions by Linnik (1960) and in so doing put us all on the threshold of a unified theory of characterization laws.

The fundamental characterization theorem states that every law can be represented as a condition of at most two laws, one law consisting of a countable number of indecomposable ones and the other one, the I_0 law, having no indecomposable components. This decomposition is not necessarily unique.

For example, the uniform distribution on $[-1, +1]$ with $f(t) =$ (sin t)/t has a set of distinct decompositions (into indecomposable components) of the power of the continuum.

An example of an I_0 law is that the geometric distribution with $f(t) = (1 - p)/(1 - pe^{it})$, $0 < p < 1$, is infinitely decomposable, but its components are indecomposable. Every infinitely decomposable law is composed of a countable number of I_0 laws. Indecomposable laws are the set of all indecomposable laws dense in the complete metric space of all laws. The set of all purely discontinuous indecomposable laws is dense in this space.

For example, let the spectrum $S(F)$ of a law be the set of all points of increase of its distribution function F. Call a set A on the real line R *decomposable* if $A = B + C$, where B and C each have at least two points; otherwise, A is "indecomposable." For every two distinct pairs (x, y) and (x', y') of points of A, $x - y \gtrless x' - y'$, then A is indecomposable.

In decomposition theory, random variables and vectors figure only in terms of their laws. While the problem stated may be probabilistic, the technique deployed to answer it is pure functional analysis. The basic idea is that there is an arithmetic possible that can be used to reduce probability laws into basic components.

The normal distribution holds a privileged place in this theory because of the nice analytic properties it has. But there's really no other justification for all the attention it gets given the limitations of the central limit theorem.

TWO THEOREMS ON PARTIAL SUMS

These decomposition properties provide the machinery necessary to establish probability distribution from empirical data, called in the vernacular *partial sums*. Since infinite sequences aren't observed in reality, one cannot assume any given distribution family or even any properties of random behavior based on theorems that rely on infinity.

In this case, the distribution function can be characterized from the partial sums if the process is independent, identically distributed (i.i.d.), and if the observation error is small with probability 1. When the error terms are negligible, the empirical distribution functions $F_n(x)$ based on the first n terms of the sample will tend to $F(x)$. Practically speaking, this means that if the histogram resembles the underlying true distribution so much that you can identify what it is, then limit theorems take care of the rest.

It is more meaningful to consider a more general setting where nothing is assumed about the errors. Let a sequence of i.i.d. random variables $\xi_1, \xi_2, \ldots$ with an unknown distribution $F(x)$ be given. Denote the partial sums $\Sigma_l = 1$ to $k\xi_l$ by r_k, $k = 1, 2, \ldots$. We observe a sequence $r_k + \varepsilon_k$, $k = 1, 2, \ldots$, where ε_k is some error term. The error is bounded by a function $f(k)$, that is, $\lim \sup \varepsilon_k / f(k) \leq 1$ with probability 1, but we know nothing more about it. Can we recognize the unknown function $F(x)$?

Theorem (Bartfai, 1966[7])

Let F be the class of distribution functions with an absolutely continuous density function of bounded variation. Let $r_1, r_2, \ldots$ be the partial sums of i.i.d. random variables with a distribution f in F. Then the unknown distribution F can be recognized from the sequence $[r_k]$, $k = 1, 2, \ldots$ with probability 1.

Note how limited we really are in knowing anything about the distribution:

1. The random process must be independent and identically distributed.
2. The unknown distribution must be absolutely continuous.
3. The unknown distribution must be of bounded variation.
4. The existence of a moment generating function is assumed.

Halasz and Major found that replacing assumptions about the moment-generating function with the condition $F(-x) + [1 - F(x)] < C_1 e^{-u(x)}$, $x \geq 0$, C_1 a positive constant, ensures, in general, the information contained in the partial sums is insufficient in general to recover the unknown distribution function.

Theorem (Halasz and Major[8])

For any $u(x)$ for which $\int u(x)/x^2 \, dx$ is bounded, there is a distribution $F(x)$ such that $F(x)$ cannot be recognized even if $f(k) = C$, whatever the positive constant C is.

The implications here are profound: Without major assumptions, there are serious problems in identifying probability dynamics in the general case. Further, even in simple cases, an existence proof is quite separate from knowing how much data are needed to ensure that your estimate converges to a known distribution. Further, there is a basic assumption of an independent, identically distributed (i.i.d.) random series. This—not an assumption of normality—is the basic problem of probability models. There is no particular support for this assumption at all aside from being essential for probability modeling.

BACK TO THE COINS: RISK-ON, RISK-OFF AND THE PRIMORDIAL SOUP KITCHEN

One such departure is large, complex adaptive systems. These systems are a collection of possible states the system can attain, just like the conventional probability space, and a mapping that describes the possible attainment of these states, just like a probability measure. The states can be very small or very large in number (typically given a matrix representation).

In the schematics below, the states are the round buttons and the lines with arrows describe how these kinds of systems work, first using the simplest probability model and working toward the more complex.

Case 1: Risk-On, Risk-Off

A simple example of emergence is the familiar coin flip. Call the two recurring states A (risk-on) and B (risk-off). A can either emit 0 and remain in state A or it can emit 1 and go to state B. State B always emits 1 and goes to state A. If you assign the probability of a state emitting 1 or 0 at 50/50, then the transition matrices for states A and B are

$$T^{(0)} \begin{bmatrix} 0.5 & 0 \\ 0 & 0 \end{bmatrix} \quad \text{and} \quad T^{(1)} = \begin{bmatrix} 0 & 0.5 \\ 1.0 & 0 \end{bmatrix}$$

The process can be visualized as shown in Figure 25.1.

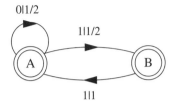

Figure 25.1 **Risk-On, Risk-Off Process.**

Case 2: Primordial Soup Kitchen Squared

Now consider that there are more states and more complex rules that determine risk preference evolution, such as moving from flipping a coin to rolling the dice to more complex settings that form a network of random decision making. Emergence of multiple states of risk with multiple attainment rules for each state of risk is diagrammed in Figure 25.2. In this case, risk oscillates among three states. Call them greed, fear, and malaise. In Figure 25.2 T is a transition from state to state and each subscript denotes a different transition rule.

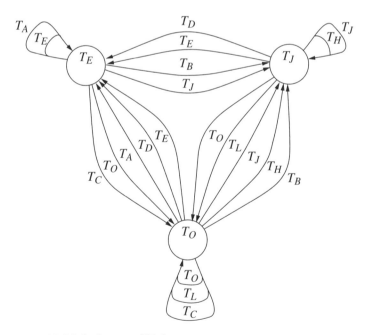

Figure 25.2 **Multiple States of Risk.**

Case 3: Emergence of Complex Structure

It is easy to extend the concept to even more complex multicomponent structures. The basic mechanism to model is very simple, but risk aversion becomes computationally huge (see Figure 25.3).

This complexity, generated by incrementally increasing the components within a mechanism, implies emergence.[9] States of risk aversion can be expanded recursively to an arbitrarily large size.

Even these types of emergent models are not without problems, though. Estimating the transition probabilities from state to state is not reliable when the data-generating mechanism undergoes phase transitions. Further, in a fundamental sense, even though there are very simple rules that govern how risk preference evolves, as these rule aggregate

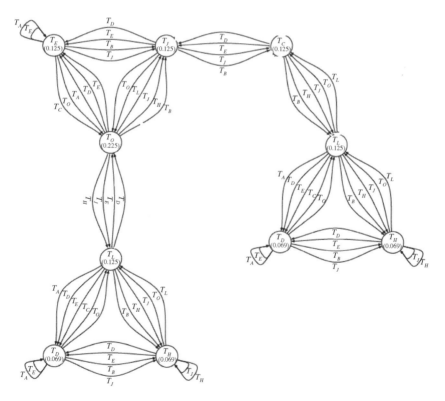

Figure 25.3 **Risk-Aversion Complexity.**

over wide classes of agents, they become intractable. The rules also may be inherently uncertain because they are too hard to quantify.

Quantum States and Risk-On, Risk-Off

Decisions often exhibit dependence relationships that are not based on explicit interactions, such as the emergent model of risk. Interactions can be indeterminate, meaning that there are no clear rules that govern the transition from one state of risk to another.

Quantum mechanics is a good place to get a handle on this idea because indeterminism is a fundamental and irreducible property of how modular systems interact with the environment and lead to systemic fluctuations and random noise. This quantum indeterminism amplifies to random noise at higher levels of aggregation. Since this randomness is irreducible, it provides a beginning iteration for spontaneous switching from one risk state to another.

Quantum mechanics is more general than conventional intuition and allows a quantum coin to have more possible states for the same two-sided coin with which we started. Imagine the same two states of the world, risk-on and risk-off, and the quantum habitat is the plane described by two axes formed by these states.

The state of a closed quantum system is wholly described by a unit $n \times 1$ matrix of complex numbers. Consider a coin that can either be heads or tails. This implies that there are two degrees of freedom ($n = 2$). A risk-on corresponds to a quantum state:

$$\begin{bmatrix} (1, 0) \\ (0, 0) \end{bmatrix}$$

Risk-off corresponds to

$$\begin{bmatrix} (0, 0) \\ (1, 0) \end{bmatrix}$$

Now, if the switching from one state to the other is unobserved and uninfluenced (like the box that held Schrödinger's cat), it would behave like a quantum process. So the operation risk-on plus risk-off is permissible. Risk-on and risk-off can coincide at the same time. This phenomenon is called *superposition* and transitions are represented as follows:

$$\left[\begin{array}{c} \left(\dfrac{1}{\sqrt{2}}, 0 \right) \\[2ex] \left(\dfrac{1}{\sqrt{2}}, 0 \right) \end{array} \right]$$

EVOLUTION

Quantum states in closed physical systems evolve according to a transition matrix of superpositions. So a closed physical system in state V will evolve into a new state W over time by the operation $W = UV$, where U is a matrix of complex numbers. Since V is an $n \times 1$ matrix, U must be $n \times n$ (to permit matrix multiplication). Evolution under U takes an allowed quantum state into an allowed quantum state.

MEASUREMENT

Quantum measurement is a probabilistic process where the state probabilities sum to 1. When a physical system in state

$$V = \begin{pmatrix} V_{11} \\ \vdots \\ V_{n1} \end{pmatrix}$$

is measured, it yields outcome I with probability $p_i = |V_{i1}|^2$.

When outcome i occurs, the system is left in the state

$$W = \begin{bmatrix} (0, 0) \\ \vdots \\ (1, 0) \\ \vdots \\ (0, 0) \end{bmatrix} \leftarrow i\text{th position}$$

Given a risk-on plus risk-off state,

$$\begin{bmatrix} \left(\dfrac{1}{\sqrt{2}}, 0\right) \\ \left(\dfrac{1}{\sqrt{2}}, 0\right) \end{bmatrix}$$

when you measure it, you will know that outcome 1 occurs with probability

$$p_1 =: \left|\dfrac{1}{\sqrt{2}}\right|^2 = \dfrac{1}{2}$$

so the quantum system will be left in state

$$\begin{bmatrix} (1, 0) \\ (0, 0) \end{bmatrix}$$

The key intuition here is that the state of the system gets changed given measurement. In essence, the coin in state risk-on plus risk-off is asked to choose between risk-on and risk-off. The choice is random, but once it is made, it remains consistent with the choice: Its new state is either risk-on or risk-off—a state that is both risk-on and risk-off collapses on measurement to either risk-on or risk-off. Before measurement, though, the system behaves experimentally like risk-on *and* risk-off.

QUANTUM MULTISTATE ALGEBRAS

The mathematician Yuri Manin showed how quantum processes can evolve into more complex structures.[10] He did this by replacing the typical outcomes of risk-on and risk-off $\{x', y'\}$ with the space of *quantum vector outcomes* $\{x, y\}$. Thus one has pairs of formal variables x, y satisfying the commutative rule $xy = qxy$, where q is a parameter. The underlying structures (the endomorphisms) of this space are 2×2 matrices acting on the outcomes by left multiplication of the matrices

$$\begin{pmatrix} a & b \\ c & d \end{pmatrix}$$

with entries a, b, c, and d satisfying the commutative relations

$$ca = qac$$
$$db = qbd$$
$$ad - da = q^{-1}cb - qbc$$

The 2×2 matrices that together with their transposes satisfy the preceding relations are by definition 2×2 quantum matrices as described in this chapter. The quantum group $GL_q(2)$ of endomorphisms of the quantum space of quantum vector outcomes $[x, y]$ is by definition the algebra $M_q(2)[D^{-1}]$, where $M_q(2)$ is the algebra generated by the entries of quantum 2×2 matrices and

$$D = ad - q^{-1}bc$$

is the quantum determinant.

NEW VISTAS BEYOND CONVENTIONAL ASSUMPTIONS

In mathematics, there is nothing so highly prized as a beautiful counterexample to a rigid theory. Counterexamples are the way of logical progress. Incorporating them into the grand scheme of things is honesty and the best antidote to easy-to-explain oversimplifications of how the world really works. Quantum coins and complex adaptive systems are a start.

There are clear alternatives to assuming normality without support. Dependence relationships a bound in real-world problems. There is a lot of work to be accomplished in crafting solutions, but we are moving in that direction.

CHAPTER 26

Risk and Regulation

Regulation is an instrument of government control. Sometimes it is benign, in the form of coordination. Coordination is necessary. Without coordination, streetlights are meaningless and getting to work every day would look like a war zone of crashed car pileups. Sometimes regulation is not benign. Either way, people accept this kind of regulation even if it is a form of coercion. At the extremes of regulatory order there are horrific things, such as tens of thousands of perfectly choreographed North Koreans, each with an identical iron grimace of forced joy, celebrating the dictator who is their puppet master. At the extreme of disorder, there is the equally horrific Cambodian mob that literally rips two government officials apart and eats their livers.

The type of regulation experienced is a reflection of collective views on human nature. The idealistic view that all human beings need to achieve their greatest potential in education leads to a laissez-faire attitude. However, the belief that humankind is to be mistrusted and is, in the large, irreparably ignorant leads to central planning and totalitarian control. James Madison famously said, "If all men were angels, we wouldn't need a government." This practical, middle ground fosters institutions capable of dealing with human variations that make us sometimes a little lower than angels and sometimes nothing better than devils.

Regulation in all cases implies hierarchy. There is an innate urge to herd for safety in times of danger and weakness and a corresponding urge to challenge authority in times of strength. This behavior is as relevant for big-horn sheep as it is for nation-states. But just like the probability models we've discussed, hierarchical models are stable until trust or illusions or both break down. The illusion is that regulators have control over what goes on, and they act not in their own best interests but rather in the best interests of the greater good.

Everyone figures out eventually that regulators are easily corrupted, often incompetent, and commonly are disadvantaged by having no real experience over the domain of which they are in charge. Financial institutions and governments are not typically populated by either angels or demons. They are part of a larger, complex interacting system of society, and this influences them in subtle and overt ways. But no exertion of control goes on without unintended consequences.

A better regulator is Mother Nature, or the Dao, or God's divine reminders that humans are just puppets in a play and will never have it all figured out. Take your pick on what you wish to call it, *but the best regulator of behavior is pain*. Pain makes all parts of the system self-regulating. This is the radical, frightening, obvious solution that will never happen because it would put regulators and their retinue of flunkies out of work and governments out of many spheres of activity. It doesn't rely on human nature's angelic goodness or a totalitarian eradication of greed from the human psyche.

It's simple, really. Set clear rules going forward, written into law. Then let nature torch those unfit for survival, put the beat down on the unlucky, and pick off the weakest of the herd. Once the herd gets thinned out, it becomes more adaptable and fit for survival. Nature's predatory attacks will subside. *In short, let the buyer beware of seller motives and the seller beware if he or she wants anyone to buy what he or she peddles the next time.*

Let banks decide their capital ratio when they don't get essentially free money at the Fed discount window and can't get their bad bets settled at par courtesy of Maiden Lane *ad nauseum*. This will ensure that it actually means something to be insolvent. Insolvency without recourse to one's counterparties and creditors means no paycheck, no business, and no salvation by discount window. Instead, you get angry creditors who come after you. Just as no mother ever chose anyone over her only child, someone who chose senior secured bank debt literally will destroy a management team if he or she gets torched by them.

The problem is that central bankers, the wayward shepherds of the global system, won't stand out of the way until the consequences of failure are so enormous that market discipline risks social and political stability. They have created a vomitorium. And it keeps getting worse.

ENTER THE VOMITORIUM

Before the financial crisis of 2008, the essential tool used by developed nations' central banks was the short-term interest rate. The Fed funds or the overnight rate defined the policy landscape. With short-term interest rates near zero, currencies play a larger role in international adjustment than ever before. Beware: Currency debasement, which is effectively raiding national stores of wealth, now acts as the shock absorber in the global economy.

Currency control was a policy tool for emerging nations for decades before the crisis. Exchange rates were suppressed by running a current accounts surplus and then investing the surplus in dollar-denominated assets. Now every central bank is in on the con. These conflicting aims create tensions between developed and emerging nations. Floating exchange rates imply that currencies never exist simply to facilitate trade. The Bank of Japan (BOJ) has intervened in currency markets for over a decade to offset upward pressure on the yen. Brazil uses tax policy to deter capital flows. Now the policy of the United States actively promotes currency devaluation. The ultimate outcome of these conflicting central banks' policies is unclear, but they signal what Brazil's central banker has called a "currency war."[1]

The U.S. effort to devalue is hamstrung by the policy of its largest trading partner, China. China's pegging of the yuan to the dollar raises employment, exports, and undeniably higher Chinese standards of living overall. But this continued support for the dollar provided by countries with current accounts surpluses enabled a massive Chinese credit binge of epic proportions. It also has widened the gap between the rich and the poor on multiple scales.[2] The low yuan may stimulate employment creation, but it doesn't stimulate wealth creation. Currency depreciation that results in inflation lowers the standard of living for the poorest more than it does for the richest because the poor typically have few choices when it comes to storing their wealth. The rich have more options that mitigate the impact of inflation. In this sense, central banks not only permit but also encourage theft on a breathtaking scale. This is tail risk killing.

There are yet deeper acts of depravity. Note that banks and governments have a cozy symbiotic relationship with tail-risk killers. Governments seldom retire debt. Unless they have to, they roll debt. Prime dealers are an essential tool for rolling these securities. There is a point, however, when rolling debt becomes expensive. And at this point, prime dealers have governments in a tough spot, and they both know it. So central banks lower nominal policy rates to ease government funding pressure. This liquidity bids up risk assets booked in a network of bank counterparty exposures that are difficult to assess with balance sheets. Then, when liquidity pressures reach another breaking point, risking collapses and volatility explodes.

Credit and rate derivatives came into existence because of a natural and organic need to hedge against rate and credit risks that tail-risk killers suppress until the final breaking point. Then these derivative instruments—a symptom of the problem—are singled out as the cause. And then the "more regulation will fix everything" sideshows begin. You get institution changes such as central clearing, in contrast to over-the-counter (OTC) clearing. You get Basel III capital requirements. Both look like great ideas on the surface, yet they create just another sieve through which to find loopholes and design exceptions to the new rules.

And so, despite reforms and new prudential measures, the financial system remains effectively as unregulated as ever by government regulators. It is too large, too virtual, and too complex for industry oversight boards to police. Also, the income potential in the financial industry makes it uneconomic to be a regulator. People with competent expertise in, say, credit desk aren't regulators. Such experience, combined with the rewards, gravitates them to trading and possibly some part-time academic role. Second, the real return to competence for a regulator does not come from the salary. It comes from not making waves and taking side payments even when a train wreck is coming. Third, banks are quite capable of hiding lurking horrors from someone who has no incentive to uncover the real issues. Auditors get paid whether they do a decent job or not.

Seriously, the idea of some Federal Reserve regulator coming into Goldman Sachs and counseling about risk management makes me laugh as I type.

Even assuming regulatory noncluelessness, high ethical standards, and real incentives to disclose violations of regulations, it is difficult to police the financial system because just like any growing thing, it evolves in ways that avoid regulation. It is not concentrated in any particular nation-state or subject to any transnational regulatory body; there are havens where anyone can escape clumsy efforts at "shoring things up." It is difficult to track activities because balance sheets can be interpreted and reinterpreted as the need arises. They are designed such that it is not always possible to determine identifiable exposures. A famous example of this fantastic silliness: Rumor on the street was that the controller of Lehman Brothers estimated its net worth using a back-of-the-napkin calculation. It was as good as anyone else's guess. The financial world is the most virtual institution around. The footprint of mathematical equations implemented through global Internet connectivity can move international financial markets in seconds. It is everywhere and nowhere at once.

The current pattern needs new regulators to regulate existing regulators, and on top of that, the new regulators need regulators, on and on in an ever-spiraling clusterfluke. Seriously, Greek bank regulators have no business even opening their mouths given the credit risk reflected by their credit-default swap (CDS) spreads.

CLOSE-UP ON A SAD SACK

Speak of which, the sovereign debt situation in the European periphery ("Club Med") is a classic example of regulators oblivious to reality. Greek insolvency is nothing new. And only because regulators

Table 26.1 Some European Sovereign Debt Episodes

	Adjustment Period	Baseline Primary Balance (% GDP)	Ending Primary Balance (% GDP)	Primary Balance Adjustment	Adjustment per Year
Germany (1975–1989)	15	−4.2	2.7	6.9	0.5
Netherlands (1990–2000)	11	0.5	5.6	5.1	0.5
France (1993–2001)	9	−3.1	1.5	4.6	0.5
Spain (1982–1989)	8	−6.3	−0.3	6	0.8
Portugal (1978–1984)	7	−5.2	0.3	5.5	0.8
Italy (1985–1997)	13	−4	6.6	10.6	0.8
Belgium (1981–1990)	10	−7.4	4.9	12.3	1.2
United Kingdom (1993–1999)	7	−4.9	3.8	8.7	1.2
Ireland (1981–1989)	9	−6.3	5.1	11.4	1.3
Italy (1975–1977)	3	−7.9	−3.9	4	1.3
Greece (1989–1994)	6	−5.5	4.2	9.7	1.6
Finland (1993–2000)	8	−2.6	9.7	13.6	1.7
Sweden (1993–1998)	6	−5.5	5.8	11.3	1.9
Greece (2010–??)	??	−7.9	??	??	??

Source: BarCap.

disconnected behavior from consequences is the situation so unprecedented and catastrophic now. The flash point in early 2010 sheds a lot of light on the issue of moral hazard and how fragile the ability to hedge moral hazard really is.

First, compare Greece with a number of other European crisis modes in Table 26.1.

These crises show that fiscal adjustment is a slow process. It doesn't matter what country or how disparate the circumstances. It takes time and shared sacrifice to muddle through this kind of pain. Greece has been through so many plans and resolutions that it is impossible to reasonably estimate the ends to which policymakers will go, much less how the current debt crisis will unfold.

Table 26.2 Greek Bond Outstanding Debt Profile

Year of Issue	T-Bills Issued (Million Euros)	Bonds Issued (Million Euros)	Bond Maturity (Years)	Percent Floating
2009	14,560	60,589	**7.25**	18.30%
2008	1,788	35,736	**6.66**	15.67%
2007	1,364	46,527	**18.5**	0.60%
2006	1,804	24,562	**7.11**	11.11%
2005	2,072	40,416	**13.4**	14.56%
2004	2,273	32,526	**7.81**	13.37%
2003	1,702	33,004	**9.94**	1.00%
2002	1,471	31,713	**10.36**	2.21%
2001	1,178	10,041	**8.21**	4.86%

We know that there are massive roll needs based on Greek debt profile and coming maturities (see Table 26.2).

Even worse, future roll shows mounting stress until 2015, as shown in Figure 26.1.

CDS are a way to synthetically hedge the credit risks on government debt that didn't exist (in a meaningful way) during past European fiscal crises. They also present a new wrinkle that isn't properly appreciated. On one side, it is argued that without these

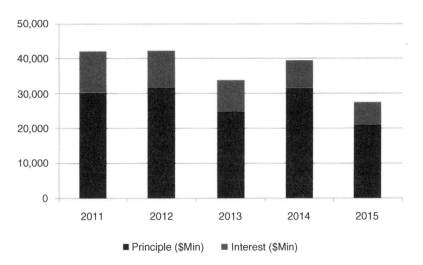

■ Principle ($Min)   ■ Interest ($Min)

Figure 26.1 **Greece's Mounting Stress.**

instruments, the only alternative is wholesale unwinding of positions, leaving the Greek debt situation even worse. On the other side, it is argued that the correlation risks and leverage associated with CDS reduce them to hedges that do not function as well as theorized Of course, there is no straight answer from politicians and lapdog regulators. They have to blame someone other than themselves for the mess they find themselves in, so their opinion is that the real fault lies with those buying CDS protection on their Greek bond holdings.

It is fundamentally legitimate for investors to use CDS and their information content for any purpose so long as it is their own capital on the line, and taxpayers and currency longs are not on the hook for a decade or more of moral hazard. No one, certainly not some Mount Olympus wannabe, should be proclaiming how and what mere mortals can do with their money while hypocritically aiding their cronies. This is how totalitarians think and do. In a free world, a person's wisdom and authority are as good as anyone else's until proven otherwise in the market jungle.

CDS aren't the problem. The root-cause problem is the coddling that CDS selling counterparties receive in the background, with the buyers cursed as demon seed from the political soapbox. If you make people pay for their mistakes, they will have respect for the pain caused. Capital ratios demanded by solvency needs—not the dictates of idiots—will become meaningful, leverage will be controlled, correlation risk will be respected, and faith in models and assumptions will receive some healthy skepticism.

Not only do CDS act as hedges that protect against default on an underlying bond, but the spread quotes also contain actionable information on credit risk of a given name and maturity at a point in time. Think of the information content of this spread as representing the prevailing view of market participants who have money on the line. There is information in looking at CDS spreads at different maturities. The collection of these points is the CDS term structure, which corresponds to the yield curve of bonds. It gives a view of how a potential default scenario will unfold over time—when it is most likely to occur, if it does. As the shape of this term structure shifts, an investor

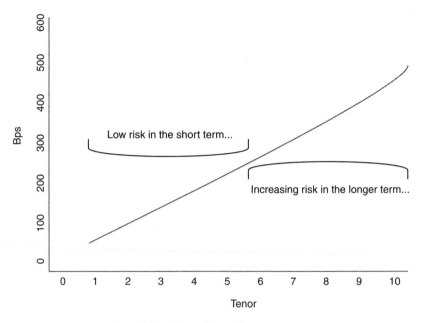

Figure 26.2 **Increasing Risk as Term Extends.**

can see where the credit risk is concentrated. Some examples help to explain this.

Steep = healthy behavior in a name (Figure 26.2)

Flat = costly in the near term (Figure 26.3)

The kink is where the pressure point is in terms of credit risk (Figure 26.4).

It works just like more familiar yield curves. The problem is that these curve trades are extremely illiquid. People looking for protection typically demand some measure of liquidity, and that liquidity typically resides in the five-year maturity. Any term other than five years typically is for traders with big money or big positions at a specific maturity.

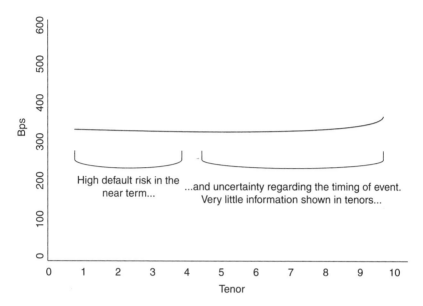

Figure 26.3 **Default Risk Flat Over Term Structure.**

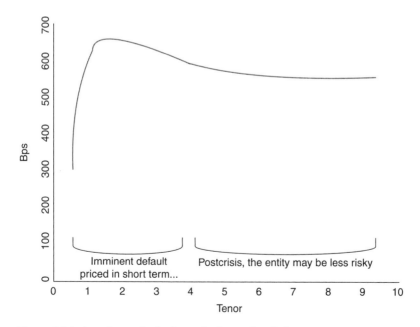

Figure 26.4 **Imminent Default at the Inversion Point.**

Since there is a rough equivalence (ignoring some factors until later) between being long an underlying bond and short a CDS contract, a common measure of assessing risk compares the bond yield to the CDS spread. The difference between the CDS spread and the bond yield is called the *basis*. Big discrepancies in this basis signal mispricing of risk.

APPLYING CDS TO THE GREEK FLASH POINT: JANUARY 2010

Rumors of a Greek default have been in the headlines since January 2010, so let's go back to the beginning. There's no wonder that this is a big deal: A default of any European Union (EU) sovereign paper would lead to a cascade of risk-asset liquidations conceivably similar to what was experienced when Lehman Brothers failed. CDS can shed a lot of light on the situation. The CDS spread is the premium paid by a buyer in exchange for becoming restored in the event of a default. See how the most liquid CDS contract, the five-year maturity, prices this protection (Figure 26.5) up to June 2011.

The term structure provides a lot of clarity to the turmoil going on in Greece. There is more information to be gleaned from Greek cash-bond yields because steepness, flatness, and inversions of the yield curve imply divergences in risk perceptions between bond buyers and CDS sellers, implying a lack of clarity regarding credit-risk pricing.

The divergence midcurve to the long end of cash bonds and CDS term structure shows really serious and worsening inversion in

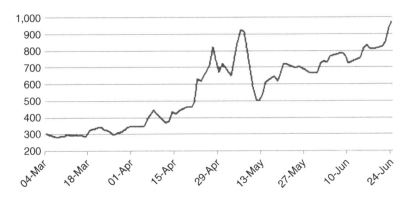

Figure 26.5 **Greek 5-Year CDS Quote.**

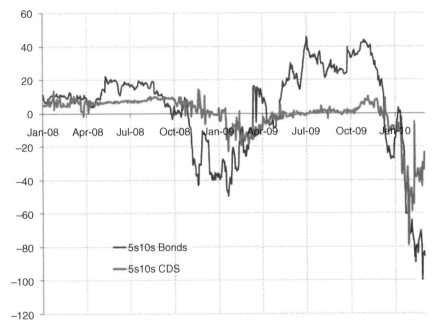

Figure 26.6 **Greek Bond and CDS Spreads (5s and 10s).**
Source: Credit Derivatives Research.

cash bonds, whereas the 5- and 10-year CDS curve steepened after January 2010 (Figure 26.6). This "curve basis" on Greek sovereign debt shows that the breakdown seen in 2008 isn't unique. It is the interplay of synthetic to cash when markets go illiquid. It isn't anticipated by theory, and theory only absorbs it after the fact. Finance typically unfolds in this unpredictable fashion.

So you have an unanticipated event that blows desks up. There is fear in the air and a lot of blood on the floor. All the necessary ingredients exist to instill the silly idea that somehow regulators can better anticipate and deal with these types of cognitive breakdowns before traders begin feeling pain. Worse, since regulators find it desirable to preserve the status quo, they mitigate the consequences so that no one really learns the hard lessons of incompetence and ill luck.

What grand illusions thus are made, usually ending in tears. Investors need to get used to it. Regulators need to get a new job. Let markets discipline the unworthy and the unlucky, and everything else will take care of itself.

CHAPTER 27

The Bond-CDS Basis and a Fixed-Income Conjecture

I wrote in a previous chapter: ". . . [C]redit has some nice features. The price-to-hopefulness ratio is never a part of valuation. Few people have trouble parting with a bond when the price is right. There is a fuzzy but ever-present upside limit. There is a downside bounded by the recovery rate. There are simple opening lines: Acquiring higher yield implies taking more risk by (1) lengthening term risk, (2) taking more credit risk, (3) moving *down* the capital structure, or (4) some combination" (italics added).

This is a pretty provincial view of fixed-income trading, kind of like chess before Nimzovich. The key concept in modern stochastic fixed-income strategy is the rethink it requires regarding capital structure. *Synthetic instruments have greater seniority than senior bonds*, or at the least, they introduce a nonlinearity in capital structure. The synthetic instruments to which I refer are credit-default swaps (CDS).

Understanding that CDS are a way to step up the capital structure allows them to be absorbed into fixed-income trading in a natural way. At the same time, they open up some terrific opening lines. One can basis trade based on the whether a CDS is priced rich (or not) against an underlying bond. One can trade dispersion by selecting name(s) that outperform an index basket or by selecting a CDS that outperforms another CDS. There is curve trading of same-name CDS at different maturities. I'm not going to go further, but the capital arbitrage strategies can extend beyond the strictly fixed-income space. That "sell volatility index (VIX), buy CDS" arbitrage is an example.

The focus here is on the first opening line: *basis trading.* All this hypermodern thinking leads me to a conjecture about the peculiar behavior of the cash-CDS basis in a crisis. I've had some helpful comments and thoughts from some ego-free people about the subject. Special thanks to an anonymous buddy of mine regarding his thoughts on basis trading.

Here's the point: There is a theoretical equivalence between buying a bond and selling a CDS. Let me sketch this out in outline. A CDS is equal to buying a bond and swapping its cash flow to floating. When the price is right, buying a CDS on a name with the same maturity is a risk-free portfolio (given certain assumptions). Given this, we can reconstruct a corporate bond (and define a CDS) in the following way:

Long corporate bond = risk-free rate + swap counterparty risk premium + default event risk premium + (actual recovery rate − assumed recovery rate) + liquidity risk premium = short CDS

The fact that basis traders exist and make money on the convergence reinforces the equivalence. But this equivalence often doesn't hold up in a crisis. Observation makes it clear that CDS and bonds are not equivalent no matter the theoretical arguments. Based on everything I've said so far, why would this be?

I asked some colleagues about this: *Why should buying cash or selling synthetic instruments fare differently in the face of large absolute moves?*

Here is a good answer I got from that anonymous buddy:

One word: liquidity. If you buy a bond, you need some funding, that is, bind liquidity until maturity. Yes, you say you can get out anytime before; just sell the bond and go away. But if things turn sour, people will sit on their cash like Scrooge McDuck, and nobody will buy your bond. Thus the price drops, and the bond-CDS basis skyrockets. For CDS, you have to post collateral, but that can be anything your collateral agreement allows.

I respect this answer, and I know there is truth in it. From a practical standpoint, not all risks, especially not liquid risks, can be hedged. Because of this, one has to deal with those risk premia that have gone haywire. But this answer seems more like blaming the problem on a technical glitch. For banks and financial institutions, however, this isn't the whole story. There is another factor to consider.

This factor is the behavior of the cash-CDS basis in a crisis of confidence: Investors move up the capital structure. How this really affects settlement is in dispute regarding net present value (NPV) when trading for an unwind.

CONJECTURE

My conjecture is that for dealer-banks with short CDS exposure, there is a huge difference between a CDS contract and a bond in settlement: In bankruptcy, derivatives are settled first, so they have effective seniority over cash instruments unless those cash instruments are secured.

After Lehman, London Interbank Overnight Rate (LIBOR) funding shot up. Such spikes in funding costs conceivably could cause a cascade of defaults, and derivatives houses potentially could seize collateral and unwind trades on a scale not seen before. It was necessary for investors to react to this contingency.

Investors could see what happened to Lehman's unsecured creditors. They got screwed because derivatives are settled before cash creditors can exercise collateral. If you as an investor know this and can't get *secured* senior debt on a money-center bank, then a CDS contract is at least as good an instrument, if not a better way (because of capital lockup issues), to get exposure.

CHAPTER 28

Fear Is Where the Power Is: The Politics of Credit-Default Swaps

November 2008: The situation was dire. But was it ever really an apocalypse? Everyone was conditioned to think that without government intervention, a waking hellscape of crappiness awaited. And it continues. Over and over we are told of being just a step away from U.S. government default if someone dares fiscal sensibility. Or some variation of a bank implosion, or everyone going into foreclosure immediately, or some other equally horrible catastrophe. These outcomes are debatable, and they deserve to be debated. Everything that happens in the future is debatable.

What is not debatable is that we continue to be threatened with imminent doom if politicos don't get what they want. I'm not a believer in global conspiracy theories, much less a perpetual ruling class, but I am a believer that democracies are absolutely awash with propaganda, veiled threats, and fear mongering.

Why? Fear is where the power is.

Anybody who knew what was going on in November 2008 was afraid. But living in a state of fear—being afraid of the future simply because it is unknown—is exhausting and self-defeating. The only way to defeat such fear is to make it known, to see the beast in the clarity of thinking. A willingness to communicate and engage is the step forward. No matter how big, ugly, or evil it is, one *can* stand up to the future and prepare for it.

It's time to break the spell of fear that makes this whole planet reek like week-old gym socks. We must be unafraid to communicate, be open and receptive to ideas, and weigh them on their merits. This doesn't mean "find some guru and accept his or her crap ideology at face value." No one is totally, unambiguously right. Ideas may be challenging and unpleasant, but the ones based on facts don't wither under scrutiny. Here goes.

CAN A COMPANY BE "SHORTED TO DEATH?"

I've heard many reasonable, intelligent people say that AIG was *shorted to death* by Goldman Sachs, among others. On the face of it, it sure looks like it. After all, Goldman Sachs took out protection on AIG exactly when it was most vulnerable. It profited from the demise of the largest insurance firm in the world.

The question is not *if* Goldman Sachs did it. The question is *why*.

The reason why Goldman Sachs did it is because AIG was the insurer of a large chunk of the equity tranche securitizations Goldman Sachs held. Those securities were risky, and Goldman Sachs bought protection on them in the case of default. This protection was desirable not just as default protection. The price of protection goes up in times of stress, meaning profit, so it was a way to manage daily marks.

So Goldman knew there was a housing bubble that would pop and that it would lose when it did because of these securities on book. Goldman also knew that AIG insured more than just its paper. In fact, AIG was the biggest insurer for these types of securities. Before the crisis even started, AIG was having trouble posting needed collateral to cover its losses associated with the securitizations for which Goldman (and others) paid insurance. If this trouble in posting collateral became a bankruptcy, then Goldman effectively would have been paying insurance premiums for nothing because AIG wouldn't be around to pay out. Goldman Sachs was at risk of not being around if AIG didn't receive coverage on the protection Goldman bought.

So Goldman Sachs bought credit-default swaps (CDS) on AIG as a company. This action at least would make it possible to recover a portion of its losses in the event that AIG went under. This is the naked shorting that has been talked about so much. It isn't really naked at all because it was insurance on the insurer of Goldman's book assets. This was a good business decision. It didn't bankrupt AIG because the swap counterparties got AIG paid out if AIG went under. *What bankrupted AIG were bad business decisions by AIG.* Goldman had to mitigate risk exposure, which it did.

So did "shorting AIG" actually bankrupt AIG? No. AIG didn't pay out CDS on its default; another CDS counterparty would pay out. Could the situation be repeated for other companies? It is true that a blowout CDS curve can affect a company's funding costs, and this is especially bad for financial companies. But insurance policy holders such as Goldman Sachs aren't to blame for the spread blowouts. *A company that makes bad business decisions that takes it to bankruptcy is to blame for spread blowouts.*

And this isn't a Goldman Sachs issue. Just about everybody with securitizations on book who knew what was going on did the same thing. In a sense, Goldman Sachs gets singled out because it wasn't a sucker holding the bag. Why should anyone weep for some sucker such as AIG or some Wall Street firm that didn't insure its book? Nobody weeps when the hammer comes down on retail investors ever.

Am I saying that the Federal Reserve should have settled all the CDS contracts with no haircut? No. All the bailouts and effectively free money were not the right thing to do. Free money and political cronyism are separate issues. It may or may not be an issue of Goldman corrupting "Uncle Stupid" and the Fed to screw taxpayers and others for years to come. I don't know, but I remain open to evidence to know either way.

THE OPPOSITE OF THE BLACK SWAN: DID MARGINING MITIGATE THE APOCALYPSE?

CDS were designed to manage credit risk: One leg gets a payout given a triggering event, and the other leg receives a premium up to that event—sort of like an insurance premium, although CDS are used often to take a speculative view on the credit risk of an entity. Either way, to do this, there has to be a buyer and a seller. Market makers are pretty much flat credit risk. Prop desks, hedge funds, and institutional books buy protection. Net sellers are the monoclines and insurers—beat-up companies such as AIG.

CDS are transacted in terms of notional amounts, but that notional amount isn't paid at the outset. It is funded, meaning it is paid in some series of installments, like a financing loan, typically at close to the London Interbank Overnight Rate (LIBOR). Because they are financed in this way, and because the price of a CDS fluctuates based on supply and demand for credit risk, the market value of a CDS position is monitored mostly on a daily basis. To cover adverse swings in price, the party affected by losses must post collateral.

So we come to times of crisis. What do you think happens to CDS in these times? That's right, the spreads blow out, and more collateral has to be posted. More collateral is very beneficial for dealing with a crisis because a chunk of the crisis is paid for daily *as spreads widen, before the default actually happens.* This means that the losses were less sudden and more manageable than they would have been otherwise. Losses accumulated on a daily basis instead of all at once. CDS helped because the problem was insolvency, and CDS procedurally expedited the insolvency process.

The problem was inordinate concentration of risk, meaning that one side of the risk was taken on by too few parties, or equivalently, the parties that paid in the event of default didn't charge enough premium (because more premium reduces risk).

HAS NOTHING BEEN LEARNED?

Well, the question of whether anything has been learned is an open one that is in some ways a legal issue. What I do know is that the industry is moving toward *exchange-traded derivatives*, where there are a few central counterparties. This isn't just some cosmetic hogwash. It can be seen clearly in the fact that non-over-the-counter (non-OTC) CDS contracts are being standardized. Standardization means that contracts are more like homogeneous transaction units, where the differences in circumstance are dealt with via an upfront payment by the buyer or seller. This makes contracts similar to each other and thus more amenable to secondary-market buying and selling.

Also, the contracts are written so the events that trigger CDS payouts are simpler and more straightforward to manage compared with OTC, so a clearinghouse can settle a contract easily. The central clearinghouse also will make counterparty exposures known, so you won't have entities such as AIG effectively taking on risk concentrations that make no economic sense. Far before a crisis happens, entities won't buy protection from counterparties with insane exposures.

Exchange-cleared CDS is huge because it means multiple layers of protection for transaction settlement. More important, it means that dealers that make the market are responsible for each other's failures. The clearinghouse is a business that survives or fails on the basis of its risk management.

There are different ways a clearinghouse does this, but the basic idea is to

- Create participant reserves requirements that can be tapped during stress
- Create participant cost sharing in the event that these reserves aren't enough
- Apply reinsurance and clearinghouse equity in a cascading fashion to absorb losses (Figure 28.1)

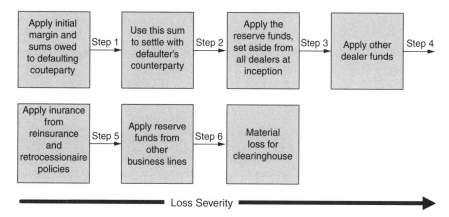

Figure 28.1 **Clearinghouse Process.**

All these financial architectures still do not mean that the system is unbreakable. In theory, though, it makes the situation better in an imperfect world. There is strong reason to believe that the clearinghouse idea will strengthen markets. Swapclear is designed to be extremely bulletproof. The Chicago Mercantile Exchange (CME) has never busted on an options meltdown or oil price spike.

But there is also reason for caution because exchange-cleared CDS simply haven't taken off. OTC CDS continues to exist for natural reasons. For now, *regulation isn't truly aligned with how this market operates.* Some parties need to have trigger events that are contingent on restructuring events, not just defaults. The motive is not speculation. It is pure insurance need. Most parties are happy with how things are in OTC land (more on this in Chapter 29).

THE SUN ALSO RISES

All the fear mongering facilitates a symbiotic victimhood simply because it is so paralyzing. It makes it easy to believe that never before has a society had to endure the trouble seen by *the unfortunates living right now* because of the abomination unleashed by those whom voters legitimately brought into power. The Great Depression needs its capital letters removed. Chairman Mao was a benevolent breeze of fresh air compared with George W. Bush or Obama. Ben Bernanke's blasphemous money printing is an obscenity, a kind of socioemotional hypocrisy.

Take comfort in knowing that Joseph Fourier showed (Riemann proved it) that everything can come in cycles, just like the sun coming up day after day on what is usually nothing new. And the sun will come up just like it always has independent of anything that happens on Wall Street.

The last thing fear spreaders want is calm acceptance of truth: They want control. It is truly debatable whether *anything* alive and feral like a financial market can be controlled. But this is precisely what one is supposed to believe: a pretense that everything is under control. Accept that the experts have it all worked out simply because they say so. Hear the call: Give in to policymaker demands, or risk that hellscape scenario again and again and again. And when the endgame finally vaporizes the illusions, regardless of any action or reaction done by regulators, the ruse just starts again with the hideously stupid formula: "We can get things back under control. Oh yes, we can!"

At their core, time-honored religious texts such as *Dao Te Ching* and Ecclesiastes contain the vision of an intrinsic moral logic in the universe that makes things right. Even if the *universe* rolls like that (debatable), convergence is slow and unpredictable. The support for *anybody* having anything completely under control is pretty flimsy. Ben Bernanke scarcely could control himself on a *60 Minutes* interview.[1]

BREAK ON THROUGH TO THE OTHER SIDE

So what to do? Let go of fear of the unknown, and try to make known what needs to be understood. Let go of easy, comfortable ideas that just can't stand up to news flow. Holding on to shimmering BS is a sham unworthy of the intellect. That is to say: *Communicate and engage.*

There's no going back because memory ensures that ideas aren't reversible. There never was a Golden Age when everything was clean and easy anyway because nothing has ever been easy or clean. So what if the 1950s didn't have derivatives. They had Jim Crow laws and H-bomb tests that literally annihilated pristine South Pacific islands instead.

Everybody needs containers to hold their insecurities, including the author of this joint. But I know enough to know I haven't figured it all out. And I never will. I will keep trying to figure out the nature of things, use the knowledge to make things better, and adapt when it all changes in an instant. This is the spice of life.

Living things don't stay still unless they are dead, so don't let your thinking stall out. Break on through to the other side.

CHAPTER 29

Are Swaps "Natural"?: Market Structure and Vietnamese Sandwiches

Some of the problems with swaps are independent of politics and policy. So it is opportune to leave swap politics aside for a time. One needs to separate the cronyism and potential wholesale corruption of political institutions by the financial entities that use swaps and the swaps themselves. The apparent corruption has done far deeper damage to modern finance than a mere political blame game that covers leniency and missteps. It leads to a common belief that credit-default and interest-rate swaps are artificial creations that fill no particular human need except greed. They are thought of as a modern equivalent of some financial plague, a blight on human history that ultimately will force all survivors into a Decameron-style exile.

I beg to differ. I submit that these swaps may well stand the test of time if market discipline is given a chance to work.

Swaps are a natural response to a challenging market environment. What makes the environment challenging is the Fed and other central bank policies. They keep interest rates too low for too long. This creates a lot of liquidity sloshing around and very forgiving credit markets. Companies with poor fundamentals and prospects get their debt rolled at what amounts to a subsidized policy rate. An interest-rate environment geared toward currency and price stability would signal risk so palpable that such funding would require much higher creditor compensation.

The free-flowing liquidity spigot isn't an issue of the last year or two. It's been the rule since at least 1998 and probably more like 1987. Everybody knows that it is going to end sometime: Interest rates must rise at some point, and credit risk will rise too. Credit-default swaps and interest-rate swaps were a natural creation to hedge these endgame risks.

They are new, but the level of recklessness we've seen by the powers that be requires something fresh. To hold that derivatives are nightmares and nothing more is tantamount to saying that innovation is wrong. The real issue is whether these derivatives are an innovation that will endure.

Whether they make it or not is an open question that depends on their effectiveness in hedging these risks in a cost-effective way. If central banks suddenly get prudent (the shock), they may be too costly given dramatically lower risk premia. Even if central banks remain utterly incompetent far into the future, these swaps may not survive simply because their mathematical underpinnings don't hold up to the resulting boom and bust cycles.

BACKGROUND AND VIETNAMESE BAGUETTE SANDWICHES

"Asian fusion" was all the rage a couple of years ago. When my friends raved about an exotic $50 menu, I recommended a $5 Vietnamese baguette sandwich instead. After all, the origins were the same: Some cook(s) wanted to do something different. The difference is the mode of creativity.

Baguettes are a crunchy, rustic, thoroughly French creation. Vietnamese cooks sandwich between this bread sweet, spicy, vegetable and meat combinations defined by the tastes of Vietnamese cuisine. The sandwich is a flexible medium that preserves two defining characters: One is freshness (raw vegetables) and crisp texture (good bread in the French style), and the second is an Asian balance in flavor profile (heat and aromatic flavor combinations).

What is important in style is that the cooking techniques enhance the Vietnamese flavor profile, and the ingredients need to be fresh. Beyond these aspects, there is great flexibility. The particular meat used is immaterial. It could be chicken or pork or beef prepared in multiple styles. I've even tasted jalapenos on these sandwiches. A jalapeno may not be particularly Asian, but when jalapenos are the freshest ingredient at hand, they impart authenticity. It is true to its roots by avoiding complication and embracing flexibility. This is the simplicity that makes it "natural." These sandwiches are truly a work of craftsmanship that absorbs environmental changes.

This approach is different from an Asian fusion of Swedish meatballs and root-vegetable curry in a coconut milk/peanut sauce. Asian fusion cuisine often glories in complication and has no ties to a particular *identity* at all. Such entrees aren't meant to work that way: The price alone makes it effete and rarefied. It requires a leap of faith untested by experience and is not defined by ingredients ready at hand. The size of the required leap of faith is what makes it "unnatural." It is more akin to a work of abstract art that belongs in a museum than to a sturdy instrument made with honored craftsmanship.

NATURAL REACTIONS TO PERVERSION

The Vietnamese baguette sandwich is *organic*: It turns ingredients and techniques necessitated by circumstance into something that "works." It works because it combines flavor (value) and attractive cost (price) using ingredients ready at hand. It ultimately works so well that it simply melds invisibly into the fabric of everyday life.

In contrast, Asian fusion cuisine requires consumers willing to stuff their face with curried Swedish meatballs mainly because it is different, mingled with some reputation effects. If it tastes good, there is a strong possibility that it will stand the test of time all the same. However, it is on some level *forced* because it has no historical precedent.

History's layers play a role. Original Vietnamese food has deep affinities with Cantonese cuisine in part because of the close linguistic ties that imply a similar material worldview. Vietnam received a deep impression from Chinese cooking techniques because it was a part of the Chinese empire for nearly a thousand years. It did not follow the path of Thailand in emulating Indian flavor profiles.

The colonial period resulted in an imposition of rich, earthy French cooking techniques on a wholly different tradition. It was these *Indochine* years that ushered in the Banh Mi, the baguette sandwich. The first such sandwich probably was as alien as a curry coconut Swedish meatball and required the same leap of faith. But it was cheap, more portable than a bowl of soup, and as far as conventional standards of taste were concerned, it had luck going for it.

Luck plays a role in everything. If the "time isn't right" or it just doesn't "taste right" according to conventional standards, then it goes the way of the dodo.

The question recapitulated: Are credit-default swaps (CDS) a fusion dish or more like the Vietnamese baguette sandwich? At this point in time, the question can only be explored, not answered.

CDS: Natural or Forced?

There is something of the craft and something of the art in a default swap. The financial engineers with the first recipe had no grand scheme to be different for different's sake. They simply pursued the logical conclusions of their understanding of markets. CDS are the product of mathematical ingredients at hand: the view that risk is a commodity that can be bought and sold.

Another important ingredient is cheap money. Historically, cheap money is an aberration that leads to asset bubbles with adverse consequences. CDS are simply a reaction to conditions within this frame of reference. Using that 150-year-long string of corporate bond default rates again, it is clear that credit risk is radically different from the past (see Table 29.1).

What cheap money provides is tighter control over the first and second moments of a distribution at the expense of higher moments, particularly kurtosis. What one gets in exchange for suppression of *perceived* credit risk is a much higher probability of extreme outcomes at the tails.

Table 29.1 Summary Statistics for Corporate Bond Defaults

Corporate Default Rates	Mean	Standard Deviation	Kurtosis
1866–1899	3.998	3.571	4.725
1900–1945	1.345	1.383	4.127
1946–2008	0.304	0.53	12.783

The greater propensity to extreme outcomes is the core weakness of selling credit risk through swaps. There are conditions under which selling CDS is roughly equivalent to holding the underlying cash bond in terms of performance. But stressed markets cause the relationship to collapse. On the short protection side, CDS spreads can move far more than the underlying bonds do. The equivalence breaks down precisely when it is most relied on. On the long side, a trader may face costly unwinds when markets are stressed, so he or she looks to buy CDS protection instead. However, CDS spread blowouts make them too expensive to purchase. In the extreme, traders may consider themselves well hedged in terms of risk, but a cascade of dealer defaults would make the payoff on their long credit protection impossible to collect. Traders often don't perceive the aggregate effects of stress on their own books. The perception of CDS traders is often limited to local conditions based on individual experiences and needs.

Suppressed interest rates carry equally serious risks because ultimately rates must rise to reflect reality. Such a rise affects funding costs and leverage in ways that cause asset unwinds. Interest-rate swaps work to hedge the effects of these rises, at least in a local sense. A swap requires counterparties that essentially exchange fixed payments for floating payments. Typically, a party can mitigate an adverse move in rates by entering an offsetting swap arrangement. However, if there is a large, discontinuous jump in rates, it is conceivable that there are no takers for an offsetting position. If the pain is concentrated in a few counterparties, it can be the start of some nonlocalized trouble that spills into other asset markets.

Not too long ago interest-rate swaps were novel and alien things, but that time is long gone. Interest-rate derivatives are now a cornerstone of risk management for banks, insurers, utility companies, and real estate investment trusts (REITs), among others. For large, complex organizations, it is like picking up the equivalent of a *banh mi* sandwich that hedges interest rate and credit risk.

CDS Coming of Age

In the large, it seems like CDS passed through its infancy in the 1990s, its adolescence up to 2008, but its coming of age is as yet incomplete. There are still significant infrastructure problems with CDS. These problems are not simply due to the endemic lack of market discipline. Another problem is market structure.

CDS are an undeniable child of the bond markets, and bond markets need OTC. There are about 7,000 equity names listed on the major U.S. markets. In contrast, fixed-income markets have far more complications. There are about 250 securities for Treasuries alone, more than 50,000 corporate bonds, over 10,000 asset-backed securities, and the number of mortgage-backed securities (MBS) dwarfs all the rest. The transaction size typically is more than $1 million.

There really is no possible way to provide continuous bid-offer quotes on products of this size without a supercomputer, near-complete historical information on mortgage pools, steep technical expertise, and a lot of risk capital. Only the biggest brokers have this kind of end-to-end execution capability, and they are happy with the OTC arrangement. Any continuous quotes they generate would be model-based because they don't trade continuously.

Further, the complexity of securitized and derivative products makes it difficult to value them. Adding transparency to such instruments will make interested buyers more willing to accept offers. Buyers are at an advantage as they make deals when the seller must move the security off his or her book. One could argue that this is the credit risk that CDS are meant to hedge. They began as a way to protect the stuff that just sits on dealer books.

If there is no way for a dealer to hedge his inventory, everyone will lose. The business won't be as profitable for dealers, and they won't make markets without bigger fees and premia from issuers. There will be even less liquidity, and the bid-ask-mid quotes will have less value. Complexity sometimes requires an OTC environment. OTC means that there is no obligation to buy or sell at quoted prices. Parties simply trade when it suits both parties to do so.

The downside is that OTC permits far more opacity. OTC has so few reporting requirements that specific exposures are unknown. CDS data are available publicly only in aggregate and fragmentary forms, and there are no public data about specific counterparties. But this is nothing compared with the games that can be played here. And for dealers, there is a definite gaming aspect to trading. They let offers hang out there the way fishermen drop bait into the water, with such comments as "I'm not sure how long this will be out there" and such. Dealers can bid and offer the same position to different counterparties at different prices. Dealers can mask a trade so that some counterparties can't see it.

This is the knock on the OTC market, but since the bulk of the activity is by dealers and large institutions, and for other reasons, it is muted. Criticism is somewhat muted even from end-user buyers of protection. These include insurance companies protecting their fixed-income book, some bond mutual funds with appropriate mandates and rules of operation, large hedge funds, and second- and third-tier banks and financial businesses. They want clear pricing, cheap reserve requirements, and less risk of being flayed alive at settlement. But they also depend on access to new issues, investment ideas, and the plug-in to a low-cost infrastructure that most institutional buyers can't afford. If they have to unwind a large block of bonds, they depend on their sell-side partner to do it. The OTC market as it stands allows more firms to have bond exposure because most can't afford in-house market making, risk management, and advisement of positioning and timing infrastructures.

So both sides of the trade may not love the current arrangement, but they clearly need it, even though institutional players are at an informational disadvantage and dealers face significant risk because their risk exposure is unclear. The result is a slow and clumsy evolution based on changing market needs. The clumsy solution is the clearinghouse.

The Clearinghouse Solution

Some clearinghouses serve dealer needs almost exclusively. The cost of entry is so high that only dealers can have a part in them. This is the solution that dealers want. It gives transparent counterparty risk exposure for dealers but leaves everyone else with the same advantages and disadvantages of the OTC market. Dealers are in many ways resistant to broad-based central clearing because it makes quotes and thus trading more transparent. This, in turn, preserves the latitude for mind games. But there are other legitimate reasons.

CDS have many nonhomogeneous parts and are not fully amenable to liquid trading and thus centralized clearing in principle. For example, CDS in the past have been valued by a number of different models. In fact, it is conceivable that a dealer can arbitrage the difference between valuation models of a CDS. Spreads change in time, and thus value depends on quotes at the time of the contract date. The triggering events can be different as well. One contract can be triggered by default, and another contract on the same name can be triggered by a "restructuring clause." There are a number of valid reasons for different triggers based on user needs.

Some clearinghouses think that CDS will grow exponentially in the future and that the market will be a significant source of future revenue with broad access, depth, and liquidity. These businesses focus on smaller end users in the belief that they will determine whether derivatives stand the test of time. They may be right. It is unclear why around 70 percent (possibly more) of interest-rate swaps go through SwapClear without a hitch, but somehow a similar arrangement for CDS is so hard to achieve.

It is a balancing act. Clearinghouses depend on dealer volumes, but they also want to grow the business by satisfying nondealer swap needs. There is a current tension going on between being very inclusive of other parties and making the clearing facility an exclusive place for dealers and other very large players. The tension is expressed through member reserve requirements. If the reserves are too high, only the biggest players can be a part of it. If reserves are too low, information on dealer flow will be available to many parties that can put dealers at a disadvantage. Lower reserves also impart more riskiness to the clearinghouse, making pooled reserves more at risk. This is a legitimate complaint. A real risk is that a large number of clearinghouses impose competitive pressure to lower reserve requirements and fees simply to draw customers. This could make the clearinghouse more susceptible to inadequate risk management and implosion.

NO EASY FIXES

Politicians need to show voters that "something has been learned from this mess" while at the same time preserving the essential status quo they don't really understand. So an answer to nonhomogeneity of contracts is to standardize contracts. For centrally cleared swaps, the valuation model for settlement is the one designed by the JP Morgan research desk. Differences in CDS spread quotes for contracts require an upfront payment sufficient to make contracts equivalent in value regardless of the strike date. The legal issues of swap triggers are streamlined by lawyers, and OTC is allowed for contracts with specific triggers that fall outside central clearing guidelines.

But it remains true that there are enough back-door ways to enable OTC transactions to ensure that the age of OTC is not yet over and probably won't be for a long time. There are also a number of functioning platforms for clearing and electronic trading of CDS, underused relative to the market size but ready.

In the beginning of modern finance, there was a need for bond dealers to hedge credit risk. The nexus of hospitable environment (ultracheap money altering credit risk) and efficient mathematical technique made CDS right for it. This environment may change so much that they aren't right for it. A clearinghouse does not necessarily make them better suited. There are no easy quick fixes to the problems we've made for ourselves.

CHAPTER 30

Twilight of the Models

There is nothing inherently destabilizing about a single credit-default swap (CDS). You are either in the money or out of the money: One side loses, and the other wins. This means that these derivatives transfer risk, not create it. What creates systemic risk is bad pricing, selective margining, and lack of netting, not the instruments themselves. A clearinghouse facilitates transparent pricing, netting, and straightforward settlement with fewer collateral squeezes.

So what's the problem? Many people think that Satan himself unleashed CDS on the world.

CDS AND INNOVATION

It is sometimes said that the sheer size of the CDS market is destabilizing in itself. Those gargantuan notional amounts are ambiguous, though. Swaps of any kind are not like bonds. There is little initial capital outlay to a swap, so you don't put down a million dollars to get a million-dollar CDS exposure. Also, there is a lot of double counting that occurs in those gross notional numbers. For example, when a $100 swap is way out of the money, an entity can buy or sell an offsetting swap of, say, $50 to reduce the risk exposure by half. The gross notional amount counts all $150 of exposure even though it is net $50 exposure to the entity. This is easy to do because at inception (when there is no upfront) the present value (PV01) of a swap is close to zero.

What is more informative is the netted amount. CDS account for around $3 trillion or so in netted exposure according to the Bank of International Settlements (BIS). Let's assume that this is too low because over-the-counter (OTC) markets can be difficult for a regulatory body to monitor and say that the total netted amount is $5 trillion. This is very small when considering that the underlying assets in the aggregate bond markets amount to more than $50 trillion.

The real systemic risk in the financial system is *insolvency*, which is a separate issue. In 2008, insolvency was little connected to the CDS written on underlying assets and strongly coupled to the underlying real estate securities. Insolvency means the destruction of aggregate capital: There is no winner in this scenario, only losers. A CDS is just another bill that a potentially insolvent bank can or can't settle. Insolvency can stress other entities by raising their counterparty risk.

A clearinghouse adds extra protection against counterparty risk, just as any type of exchange does. Further, a clearinghouse would signal a dangerous concentration of risk because transactions among members are more transparent than OTC transactions. Even more, a clearinghouse can more easily stop a line of banks from falling like dominoes because netting and reserves reduce the probability that the insolvency of a bank increases the counterparty risk of other trading partners.

Any innovation can be a double-edged sword. Think of atomic engineering: The same fundamental principles that inform weapons of mass destruction also create electricity and tools to cure terminal cancers. CDS are an instrument at the hands of people, complicated innovations that serve the ends of innovation. The outcome depends on the hands that use the innovation.

There is no possible justification for every reckless end to which people applied derivatives. There is no excuse for parabolic leverage ratios on bank balance sheets, nor is there one for the coddling approach that regulators and government institutions took to banks that enabled a decade of gross excess. There is no excuse for relying exclusively on highly assumption-specific models that excluded intuition, experience, and human judgment.

It makes sense to fear unchecked behavior and for taxpayers to be pissed when they have to write a blank check to clean up the mess. But the source of the problem is in two parts. A fraction lies with pricing models that fail to calibrate to reality. The other fraction of the problem is unchecked leverage—government capture. They add up to model failure and moral hazard.

MODEL FAILURE AND RISK

There is more to risk transfer than what at first appears. Derivatives indeed move risk from one party to another. A potential problem is that concentration of risk on one side makes for crowded trades. Under the illusion of adequate hedging, banks will hold similar portfolios of toxic subprime goo because the model-derived risk and reward favor it. Crowded trades are common to any asset market: The result is massive short squeezes and unwinds.

Further, when models do not price credit risk properly (jump to default), the risks of overleveraging are indeterminate. Whether you use a valuation or a pricing model, in the end it is calibrated to the market consensus. The market settles most disagreements when you unwind a trade. But what becomes clear is that the correlation risk inherent in any underlying credit portfolio is magnified by the derivative contracts on bank balance sheets by virtue of leverage effects. This is not because they are derivatives. It is because of the leverage deployed.

Crowded trades, correlation risk, and leverage—nothing new under the sun. When it looks like CDS constitute a perfect hedge, there are problems simply because illusion of control is created, causing people to take on more risk.

MORAL HAZARD AND FOOLS' ERRANDS

What is needed is strong resolve to control the moral hazard governments create and balance it with the need to preserve human ingenuity. This is the real human adventure—searching for something better through innovation. Success is defined by framing it within a prudent governance policy. Ideal polices are not patterns or structures embodied in some past golden age: Time is irreversible. Ideal policies minimize corruption, government capture, and moral hazard. If an institution fails to manage its embedded risks, it should fail, either by nationalization (so-called too big to fail) or by bankruptcy proceedings.

Of course, true and perfect ideals never have and never will exist outside imagination. Good policy is only a goal to strive for and work toward. When the chips are down, though, count on every government to protect itself to the end. Politicians don't want to lose kickbacks from dealers, and dealers don't want to lose fat spreads. Apply any BS title you wish to it—"socialist," "fascist," whatever. The only thing that matters is that people on top will protect themselves and their own prosperity.

Expect government lying, cheating, and stealing to deflect any blame from itself. It will give endlessly lenient financing terms to horribly insolvent banks. It will ignore the rule of law. It will allow deadbeat banks and squatters free rein to steal from everyone else. What this means for the governed in a crisis is a greater state of *unfreedom*—narrowed permissible ranges of action and a greater state of poverty.

Innovations challenge the status quo and break down hegemony. CDS are no different. No government truly wants a market of separate individuals making assessments of their true credit risk. This is precisely the disruptive potential of the CDS. Have CDS limited government freedom of action? Not yet. Those in charge want it to stay that way.

"Developed" countries may well intend to dispose of CDS because they pose a threat to their freedom to act irresponsibly or engage in untenable geopolitical projects. They will be unable to do so for reasons already outlined. Standardized contracts and central clearing will strengthen their signal. CDS generate a clearer upper bound on the extent of market impact of fiscal and monetary abuse.

BANNING INNOVATION IS A TYPE OF BAILOUT

Fearing derivatives won't make them go away. No winds of change will blow derivatives back in the bottle. Banning them will only relocate them. It won't take away why there is a demand for them: companies struggling to manage changing conditions, reckless fiscal and monetary policies, and perceived higher credit risk in general. They discipline companies as well as countries. Societies become stronger when they prevail over adversity owing to luck or hard work. They grow stronger even when they fail and accept the fundamental honesties of circumstance.

If governments ban or "regulate" exchange-traded derivatives, where does it end? Plain vanilla puts and calls on stocks fall into this category. It is more likely that such rules are used by insiders to keep the playing field uneven. And if you want to get to the brass tacks of the matter, there is an embedded optionality in just about every financial asset. For example, bank equity is a call option on bank assets. There is a repo optionality in government securities.

Banning innovation is just another type of bailout. A bailout for the status quo: for those ill equipped to prosper from change, making true success and true failure harder and atrophy stronger. Rewarding the unworthy and punishing the blameless makes honorable people predators. It makes dishonorable people sociopaths.

Chasing innovation into other ports of call can have dark side effects. In a not-so-distant future, what's to stop trading CDS in Shanghai or Mumbai on the Socialist Republic of the United States?

CHAPTER 31

Emerging Market Sovereign Credit Derivatives and Equity Markets

B oaz Weinstein came up with a terrific strategy called *capital structure arbitrage.*[1] The idea behind the strategy is that investors in bonds and investors in equities value a firm's liabilities and future prospects inconsistently. Depending on the view, one can short (buy) the bond and buy (short) the equity. Factors such as momentum for equity and interest-rate sensitivity for investment grade (IG) bonds make the strategy essentially short-long. It is conceivable that both assets could be purchased like a full basis trade.

Credit-default swap (CDS) spreads provide a useful tool to generalize this trade. The idea is to use CDS spreads to time a short equity in the emerging-market space as a hedge or speculative view. CDS spreads are more sensitive to new information than stocks, but stocks are more volatile. I tested this strategy using Barcap's Central Eastern Europe Middle East, andAfrica (CEEMEA) equity market subindices and Datastream's sovereign-debt CDS quotes. The CEEMEA subindices include bank, telecom, materials, energy, and consumer sectors domiciled in the following countries:

- Russia
- Turkey
- Greece
- South Africa
- Morocco
- Egypt
- Hungry
- Poland
- Israel
- Czech Republic

Datastream's sovereign-debt CDS quotes for

- Greece (wouldn't be a party without them)
- Russia
- Czech Republic
- Poland
- Hungary
- Turkey

The other member countries of the equity index had CDS quotes bordering on the nonexistent, so they weren't included.

This broad index of countries works best because equities in small markets can be illiquid. A big enough index is consistent with a diversified portfolio of emerging-market sovereign debt across a dedicated universe such as emerging Europe and the Middle East. This allows a dissection of specific subindices, as shown in Figure 31.1.

Selected CDS quotes from data streams for most countries are shown in Table 31.1. Not all countries in the CEEMEA have quotes at times.

CDS in illiquid emerging markets are used as a hedge mainly by big-money investors. These big-money institutions have informational advantages over everyone else, and thus CDS quotes can be a good signal of things to come.

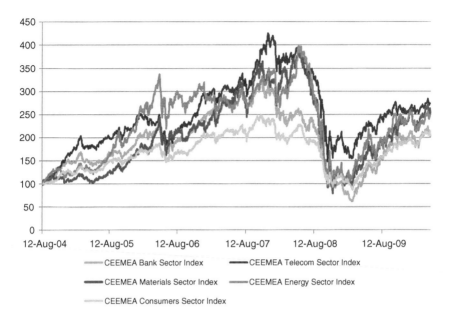

Figure 31.1 **CEEMEA Subindices, August 2004–May 1, 2010.**
Source: BarCap.

Table 31.1 CDS Quotes

| Date | CEEMEA | | | | | | |
	Czech Rep	Greece	Hungary	Poland	Romania	Russia	Turkey
Q4 2005	6	15	26	17	36	68	149
Q4 2006	7	8	21	13	20	43	160
Q4 2007	20	22	55	26	87	88	167
Q4 2008	174	232	419	245	635	744	411
Q1 2009	203	199	538	291	498	498	400
Q2 2009	109	131	360	170	392	341	261
Q3 2009	73	122	215	122	196	209	194
Q4 2009	93	263	238	132	279	185	183
Q1 2010	72	343	184	98	202	143	173
April 28, 2010	112	939	287	173	311	217	221

Source: Datastream.

In fact, there is a relationship between CDS spreads and some subindices. The correlations use CDS spread quotes interpolated to account for missing data from 2006 to May 2010. Correlations are run using contemporaneous CDS-index relationships, as well as lagged

CDS quotes from the prior quarter to the current index to determine to what extent changes in CDS spreads "lead" changes in equity (Table 31.2).

Table 31.2 Pearson Correlation Coefficients

	CEEMEA Bank Sector Index	CEEMEA Telecom Index	CEEMEA Consumer Sector Index
CDS basis-point spread leading by one quarter (unweighted by country)	−0.60168	−0.80466	−0.92141
CDS spread same quarter as equity subindex	−0.85787	0.32374	0.06199

Note that sovereign CDS spreads of the prior quarter have a strong negative correlation with current consumer-sector stocks in the CEEMEA Index. Bank stocks and CDS have an equally strong negative correlation with the CDS spreads during the same quarter. This makes sense because sovereign states and their financial systems are inseparably connected. Stress in sovereign debt implies sustained disintermediation on commerce and the labor market through its impact on the banking system.

In effect, a hedge on a long sovereign-debt position in emerging markets is a short on an index of bank and financial stocks associated with those countries. Monitoring CDS quotes provides a basis for when to be more aggressive in shorting.

Correlation indicates the strength of association, but a regression is a better way to indicate the best subindex to short because it provides an estimate of the magnitude of the changes.

The correlations indicate that consumer stocks have the strongest correlation with adverse moves in CDS spreads three months before. They are also a low-volatility equity trade in the CEEMEA region. They may work as a short candidate simply because there is less pain in shorting them, and the strength of connection between CDS spreads jumps and consumer stock drops.

It is visually clear from Figure 31.1 that bank and financial stocks began to break from the trend of other subindices and hit a lower bottom than all other sectors. The subindex provides a good short candidate simply because bank and financial stocks are much more sensitive to credit-market shocks, and they move contemporaneously with CDS spread jumps (Table 31.3).

Table 31.3 Linear Model with Lags Relating CDS Spreads and Equity Subindices

Model 1: CDS spreads$_t$ = α_t + $\beta_t \times$ bank stocks + ε_t

Model 2: CDS spreads$_{t-1}$ = α_t + $\beta_t \times$ bank stocks + ε_t

Independent Variable	Dependent Variable	Model-Adjusted R^2	Parameter Estimate	Pr > |t|
Same-quarter government debt CDS	Bank stocks	0.6982	−6.43832	0.0031
CDS quote a quarter before the index price	Consumer stocks	0.8238	−8.51289	0.0011

A SIMPLE HEDGE THAT REPLICATES A CDS SPREAD MOVE

The real utility in this exploration relates to how common carry trades are. The classic carry trade is borrowing at low rates in a home currency and lending long in a local currency in a target country that offers higher rates. This may work as a hedge on a carry trade, especially eclectic ones, where markets have little liquidity anytime. It is a simple, decent replication of a CDS spread move when everyone runs to the exits.

There are many nonclassic carry trades. Frankly, it seems that every asset on the planet is a beneficiary of the near-free money spewing out the front end of the Treasury yield curve. In essence, everything is becoming a carry trade.

CHAPTER 32

The Information Content of a Negative Swap Spread: Hedge Funds Turn Down Free Money

The interest-rate swap market is freaking huge and somewhat new (the first interest-rate swap was in 1981 between the World Bank and IBM[1]). The instrument itself is a weird animal in that its value derives from an offer rate and a bond yield, not an underlying asset. In this sense, interest-rate swaps are more like an asset (bondish) than a derivative. The most elemental parts of the economy—government debt and interbank markets—converge in interest-rate swaps.

Because the market is so big and used in so many different ways, swap spreads and swap volume are now arguably a central lynchpin of the interbank mechanism. In fact, swap curves are the benchmark for non-U.S. sovereign issuers and just about all spread investors too. As a result, swap spreads tell you a lot. If an economy's nerve cord is the Treasury market, then what makes it higher vertebrate is the swaps market.

Contemporary history has on tap a big swap-spread mystery: The 30-year swap spread went negative in early 2009 (Figure 32.1). That's right, negative. The long bond yields more than 30-year swaps.

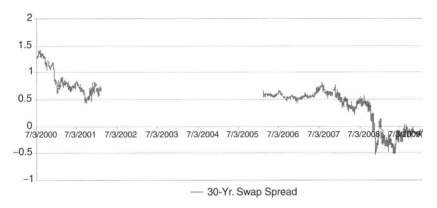

Figure 32.1 **30-Year Swap Spreads, June 2000–January 2010.**

Cool heads may say that this mystery is just the result of mortgage refinancing coming to an absolute standstill and hedge books spewing volumes of long-maturity swaps out their blow hole into a relatively illiquid 30-year market. Note, however, that swap spreads were negative when conventional wisdom says there was a big volume of refinancing going on. Further, U.S. Treasury swaps are not alone in this. I know that 20-year gilt swap spreads have been negative too. Most mortgages there are trackers. Nobody will refinance a tracker.

Swaps spreads say more than hedging: They tell a macro view that the final act of *Götterdämmerung* will have sovereign credit as the tragic hero. Swaps are ideal for examining this thesis precisely because they are the nexus of the two basic building blocks of organized civilization: government debt markets and core financial intermediation.

The innards of the negative-spread mystery revolve around how pricing is determined for swap spreads. As important as they are, quantifying what affects spread pricing is not adequately understood yet because bond and London Interbank Offered Rate (LIBOR) markets jointly determine the spread. Each market shares common drivers, making the mechanism complex and nonlinear. The pricing mechanism is also obscure because investors use swaps for many different purposes.

Even basic intuitions about swap mechanics seem to be square pegs in round holes. For example, it seems straightforward that the

LIBOR-to-repo spread would be a significant determinant of pricing. Swap dealers hedge their swap books by buying or shorting Treasuries and then conducting a repo (or reverse repo) over the term. If the dealer is the fixed-payer party, then the carry cost of its book is the LIBOR-to-repo spread (note that LIBOR is influenced by credit risk). Also, a low repo rate implies a steep yield curve, which makes the demand for the fixed side of a swap increase. So Lehman Brothers blew this intuition up in a thorough study[2] that showed that the LIBOR-to-repo spread was an insignificant predictor. Many stat models developed in the last five years don't even retain LIBOR-to-repo spread as an explanatory variable.

Let's look a little deeper at some suspects that play a role in making an interest-rate swap tick.

The Moving Parts Involved in Swap Pricing

- *Government deficits.* Deficits mean more government bonds; more supply means the yields go up. This directly affects the spread.
- *AA credit spreads.* What affects the issuer affects the swap to some degree, counterparty risk or no. Most banks issuing swaps are AA rated, and the perceived credit risk of issuers affects LIBOR, which affects swaps. Remember that Lehman left a massive overhang of swap structures when it cratered. This is a hotly disputed issue, honestly.
- *The repo rate.* See the discussion above.
- *The mortgage market.* Lower Treasury yields lower mortgage rates, which increase refinancing, which shortens mortgage-backed securities (MBS) duration. Swaps are a big part of the hedge book for those who hold MBS paper. Remember that negative swap spreads are more than a U.S. event. They happened to 20-year gilt swaps too.
- *The yield curve!?!* Given that the swap curve is inverted while 2s10s is at record width, I can't unscrew that. I believe that the curve is integral to the inversion story, but maybe not this mystery.

SWAPS ARE SCREAMING WHAT A BASIS PACKAGE WOULD WHISPER

A way to approach the mystery is to ask a commonsense question. Why would investors take swap positions when their return is less than longing same-maturity government bonds?

Perhaps in a climate of nationalization, ballooning debt, default fears, and bought-off legislatures, investors don't think govvies are safer than AA-rated banks anymore. Thus each leg of the swap has its own risky issues. Eyes wide open know that nothing—not even Treasuries—are completely free of default risk anymore. One could argue that CDS spreads on government bonds are hinting this—but not enough to explain a negative swap spread.

Note that this credit risk has little to do with the swap counterparties themselves. Think of the risk as a measure of aquarium acidity where they all swim around.

SWAPS AS AN INDICATOR OF TIGHT LIQUIDITY CONDITIONS

The other leg of the swap is based on LIBOR. LIBOR is a credit-risky proxy rate derived from a daily survey of offer quotes from big banks. LIBOR is the trimmed mean of these quotes.

Another commonsense answer to the mystery is that supply and demand conditions make the spread negative. Sure. But this only puts a different light on the same mystery. Why are supply and demand conditions like this? Arbitrage (free money) should fix the imbalance.

The arbitrage works like so: When swap rates are negative, there is free money in borrowing at swap rates and longing bonds. Just fund the swap with the coupon, and pocket the difference. This is free money! Where are the arbitragers?

Perhaps it's not so free after all. Possible explanations for why banks and hedgies would pass up "free money":

- Central bank discount window lending is the new LIBOR, but using it for such arbitrage is restricted by convention or stipulation.
- LIBOR is less than the actual interbank funding cost.

- They are severely capital constrained.
- A bank "solvent in name only" will have high borrowing costs that it wouldn't want reflected in LIBOR.
- They fear government quasi-default.
- The potential for a banking crisis can affect the payer of the floating leg of the swap.
- Any future banking crises would impair collateral embedded in the transaction.

If LIBOR isn't an accurate measure of funding cost, then the interbank market is dysfunctional, which should be scary to any rational person. On the other hand, if fear is so intense and pervasive in the core financial system that the arbitrage isn't a good risk, then take a swig of scotch or pop some Xanax because Ragnarok ain't over yet.

Another liquidity explanation is that many accounting methods put swaps off balance sheet, and as I wrote before,[3] they require no initial cash outlay. This makes them extremely capital efficient. It is difficult to overestimate just how important this is in an extremely tight credit environment. Maybe the people holding loan books resembling a cratered moonscape know the world isn't flooded with excess liquidity after all. Still, this doesn't explain people passing up low-risk arbitrage.

POSSIBLE IMPLICATIONS

More benign implications are that one or both of these markets are dysfunctional because things that feed them are used in an out-of-control way, but these will resolve themselves in finite time.

Such out-of-control factors include:

- unsustainable Treasury and other government security issuance.
- or suppressed discount window rates at just about every central bank in the world have made LIBOR cockeyed.

If the latter is the cause, then we have a laboratory in which to observe an experiment. Any Fed rate hike should pop swap rates. When the United States finally goes on its austerity budget, we'll see what the laboratory says about swaps.

A more negative implication is that stable processes cannot be predicted, and unstable processes can't be controlled, with all due respect to the genius of Janos von Neumann. Even hubris-riddled central bankers should know this because the central bankers' central banker, Charles Goodhart, qualified this.[4] He said that in a human system, using a measure of information as a lever to control behavior destroys that measure's information content. Controlled prices lose their signaling ability. Allocation becomes inefficient, and over time, these inefficiencies exponentially make for a shambling heap of ruin. Just ask the Soviet Union.

If this is the case, for the here and now of swaps, the message is

- The long bond is a pig with lipstick on it. And/or
- Lending is a corpse with lipstick on it. Or
- Maybe long bond spreads are wrong, the swap market is wrong, and only a few pilgrims are right about the Lllooonnnggg bond.

CHAPTER 33

For Those about to Swap (We Salute You)

Interest-rate swaps exist to hedge interest-rate risk. For example, a bond investor typically takes a position financed at a floating prime rate. If this floating rate rises, he or she is put in a tough spot where he or she has to liquidate his or her position. The same logic applies for any business that finances its outlays at a floating rate. If these rates rise too much, the company could go out of business. Swaps enable one to hedge interest-rate risk at every point on the yield curve. Even though they exist as a hedge, they also can be used to speculate on interest-rate movements. Everyday sensible reasoning using directly observed data leads to an understanding of the true nature of risks lurking underneath the surface of this speculation.

TAKE-AWAYS

- Perverse monetary policies including effectively zero interest rate policies (ZIRP) resulted in a radically steep yield curve.
- When policy normalizes and the yield curve flattens, it will lead to significant market dislocations.
- One dislocation will be in the interest-rate swap market. Losses could lead to massive swap unwinds.

- If losses related to unwinds are concentrated in primary dealer positions, this will carry illiquidity to other asset markets.
- Using the price of money as a control device destroys the information content of prices. Even marginal introduction of market forces into controlled price formation can lead to crashes.
- When government-administered backstops end or fail, risk reasserts itself. The most primordial risk is counterparty risk.
- There is a hedge, and a hedge in enough size becomes a trade.

WHAT IT MEANS TO UNWIND A SWAP

The net present value (NPV) of a swap is the key to any unwind decision. Possible ways to limit interest-rate swap losses include

1. Enter into a new interest-rate swap contract with another counterparty in opposite-ish terms.
2. Search the term clauses for a close option in the near future.

Entering an equal but opposite-term swap is a way to manage interest-rate swap losses. Basically, the swap has to mirror the original in all aspects, including legal documentation, but be the opposite in terms of receiver direction; for example, to offset a pay fixed, then the contract is to receive fixed. Getting the legalities exactly right could be hard to do, and your accounting system must recognize both swaps. If you do enter into a second swap to hedge the first, the perfect hedge is obtained from an identical offsetting swap. If the original swap has a nonzero market value, entering into the new swap will entail a cash payment *equal to the NPV of the swap* to reflect the new swap's offsetting market value. So you really haven't helped yourself much here, unless the interest-rate swap is a long-duration swap with no close option.

Closing out a swap is what is meant by unwinding a swap. The close option means contacting the original counterparty to see if the swap terms include a date that gives both parties the right to terminate the swap with a cash settlement *equal to the net present value (NPV) of the swap.*

In short, there is no costless way out of an interest-rate swap if you are on the losing leg. If you don't want front capital to unwind (close) the swap, then you enter into a new swap with terms that mitigate the loss. The sheer size of the interest-rate swap market implies that the latter is often the chosen option.

INTEREST-RATE SWAP MECHANICS: DERIVED NPV

Swap valuation requires

- Extrapolating a forecast of future interest rates to establish the amount of each future floating-rate cash flow
- Deriving discount factors to value the swap fixed- and floating-rate cash flow
- Discounting and present-valuing all known (fixed) and forecasted (floating) swap cash flows

These discounting techniques are the same ones used to establish the theoretical market value for any interest-bearing security.

Imagine a swap contract where you pay 6-month LIBOR in exchange for fixed Treasury yield. Table 33.1 lists the quotes you need and the calculations for the present value of that leg. I'm leaving details on the mechanics of using a few different yield-curve scenarios.

Given a contract of $100 million with these parameters, the summed risk-neutral expected cash flow present value amounts to around $4.2 million. Fixed receivers are in good shape if longer-duration Treasury yields widen and LIBOR stays constant. To illustrate this, I value the swap such that the curve steepens to an extreme level in Tables 33.2 through 33.4.

As yields decline, the fixed leg of the swap loses value. In addition, rising float payments are consistent with losing money on the fixed leg.

Table 33.1 Value of Fixed Leg Using Historical Data

Notional principal:	$100 million
6-Month LIBOR at last reset date:	0.00524 (semiannual compounding)
Continuously compounded LIBOR, 3 months:	0.0027
Continuously compounded LIBOR, 9 months:	0.00826
Continuously compounded LIBOR, 12 months:	0.01098
Fixed rate valuation:	0.0384

Time	Forward	Semiannual Forward	Term	Risk-Neutral Expected Cash Flow	Discount	PV
0.25	0.00524	0.00524	0.5	$1,658,000	0.99932523	$1,656,881
0.75	0.01104	0.011070527	0.5	$1,366,474	0.99382415	$1,358,035
1.25	0.01506	0.015116843	0.5	$1,164,158	0.98636876	$1,148,289
				Value of swap		**$4,163,205**

Table 33.2 Super-Steep Case

Notional principal:	$100 million
6-Month LIBOR at last reset date:	0.00524 (semiannual compounding)
Continuously compounded LIBOR, 3 months:	0.0027
Continuously compounded LIBOR, 9 months:	0.00826
Continuously compounded LIBOR, 12 months:	0.01098
Fixed rate valuation:	0.045

Time	Forward	Semiannual Forward	Term	Risk-Neutral Expected Cash Flow	Discount	PV
0.25	0.00524	0.00524	0.5	$1,988,000	0.99932523	$1,986,659
0.75	0.01104	0.011070527	0.5	$1,696,474	0.99382415	$1,685,997
1.25	0.01506	0.015116843	0.5	$1,494,158	0.98636876	$1,473,791
				Value of swap:		**$5,146,446**

Table 33.3 The Bear Flattener Case

Notional principal:	$100 million
6-Month LIBOR at last reset date:	0.0261 (semiannual compounding)
Continuously compounded LIBOR, 3 months	0.0215
Continuously compounded LIBOR, 9 months	0.031
Continuously compounded LIBOR, 15 months	0.0372
Fixed rate	0.03
Valuation:	

Time	Forward	Semiannual Forward	Term	Risk-Neutral Expected Cash Flow	Discount	PV
0.25	0.0261	0.0261	0.5	$195,000	0.99463942	$193,955
0.75	0.03575	0.036071428	0.5	–$303,571	0.9770182	–$296,595
1.25	0.0465	0.047044776	0.5	–$852,239	0.95456456	–$813,517
				Value of swap		–$916,157

Table 33.4 Swap Curve Inversion Case

Notional principal:	$100 million
6-Month LIBOR at last reset date:	0.0261 (semiannual compounding)
Continuously compounded LIBOR, 3 months:	0.0215
Continuously compounded LIBOR, 9 months:	0.031
Continuously compounded LIBOR, 15 months:	0.0372
Fixed rate valuation:	0.015

Time	Forward	Semiannual Forward	Term	Risk-Neutral Expected Cash Flow	Discount	PV
0.25	0.0261	0.0261	0.5	–$555,000	0.99463942	–$552,025
0.75	0.03575	0.036071428	0.5	–$1,053,571	0.9770182	–$1,029,358
1.25	0.0465	0.047044776	0.5	–$1,602,239	0.95456456	–$1,529,440
				Value of swap		–$3,110,824

Table 33.5 Outstanding Interest Rate Swap Notional Across the Swap Curve

	$ Millions in Notional			
Quarter Ending December 31, 2009	Interest-Rate Maturity < 1 Year	Interest-Rate Maturity 1–5 Years	Interest-Rate Maturity > 5 years	Interest Rate, All Maturities
Top 5 commercial banks	$79,924,622	$32,133,361	$25,489,845	$137,547,828
Other commercial banks	1,051,530	1,498,683	653,662	3,203,875
Total commercial banks	80,976,152	33,632,044	26,143,507	140,751,703

Source: OCC Quarterly Derivatives Report.

INTEREST-RATE SWAP MARKET DEVELOPMENTS

Given the size of the market and the leverage involved, the interest-rate swap market is a beast too big to tame. Because of this, major damage could stem from big derivative unwinds if they occur.

Most interest-rate swaps are contracted over durations of less than one year. Even so, huge notional amounts are contracted over the entire yield curve (see Table 33.5).

Trading revenues from these positions turned negative in the fourth quarter (Q4) of 2009, as shown in Table 33.6.

Table 33.6 A Taxonomy of Interest Rate Swap Trading Revenues in 2009

	Total Notional Interest-Rate Derivatives (Q4 2009)	Q1 2009 Trading Revenues from Interest-Rate Positions ($ Millions)	Q2 2009 Trading Revenues from Interest-Rate Positions ($ Millions)	Q3 2009 Trading Revenues from Interest-Rate Positions ($ Millions)	Q4 2009 Trading Revenues from Interest-Rate Positions ($ Millions)
Top 5 commercial banks	$137,547,828	$8,760	$1,691	$4,777	($1,472)
Other commercial banks	3,203,875	$339	($583)	$675	284
Total commercial banks	140,751,703	9,099	1,108	5,451	($1,188)

Source: OCC Quarterly Derivatives Report.

Note that these trading losses are not year to date; they are for Q4 2009. $1,472,000,000 is a lot of money to lose in one quarter. The data presented are insufficient to know with certainty bank interest-rate swap exposures, but such a loss profile is consistent with the top five banks paying fixed at durations less than one year. For longer-duration swaps, losses related to yield-curve changes could be even more pronounced because the swap could initiate before the zero-interest rate policy (ZIRP) began in 2008. In short, manipulation in the new normal (read: zero interest policies) or its reversal could decimate these positions. The monetary policy normalization and yield-curve flattening that will come with it could necessitate unwinding.

The situation is not without precedent: Reported interest-rate swap losses were worse in the fourth quarter of 2008 (Figure 33.1).

Those 2008 losses coincided with a reduction in interest-rate swap gross notional amounts, a major increase in counterparty risk (LIBOR-overnight indexed swap [OIS] spread widening), and a radical shift in the term structure. This is just the scenario identified in Figure 33.1. The easily satisfied conditions under which derivative

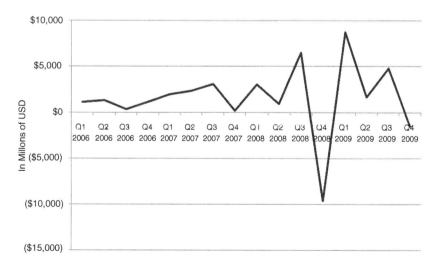

Figure 33.1 **Trading Revenue from Interest-Rate Derivatives for the Top Five Commercial Banks.**

unwinding would contribute to illiquidity and deleveraging of other assets include

- Unwinding losses are concentrated in prime dealers.
- The amounts unwound are sufficiently large.

Steep losses on interest-rate swaps could lead to closing of positions in a vicious cycle. Owing to the sheer size of the market, unwinding swaps could lead to seriously tight liquidity if settlement cash flows in a concentrated direction away from prime dealers. This is why long exposure to rising LIBOR-OIS is a good hedge against systemic meltdown.

A HEDGE POSITION IN SIZE BECOMES A TRADE

The essential hedge against a sizable interest-rate swap unwind is intuitive: Hedge a bear flattener or curve inversion. But this same hedge is also a useful hedge against more general systemic meltdowns. Here's why.

Markets crash because feasible time horizons of exposure to the market collapse: People want nanosecond maturity on the yield curve. Such crashes are phase transitions, fast adjustments to new credible information about reality. Counterparty risk affects time horizons. The Fed has powerful tools to affect investment time horizon, and it has used them as never before. However, these tools are limited in their ability to distort and transfer risk. Everyone has to believe in the Ponzi for the trick to work. At the epicenter, profiting from rising counterparty risk is a hedge.

The heart of the matter is that the basic foundation of society is exchange. Thus counterparty risk is the most elemental of all risks. This is why central banks have sunk so much capital into backstops of the interbank market. For good reason—society is very sensitive to prolonged counterparty risk. As an example, consider English common law, which is premised on trusting your neighbors more than government (trial by peers) as opposed to fearing your government less than you fear your neighbors (court of tribunal). No offense to *Code*

Roman and variations on the appeal to Caesar. Extreme and sustained counterparty risk hikes ultimately mean that trust between neighbors breaks down. What remains is a government that can turn justice into an iron fist.

The rising LIBOR-OIS spread is a clean way to capture the rising counterparty risk embedded in a crisis because it is market sensitive to systemic shocks. One can create a conditional spread trade that replicates a rising three-month LIBOR-OIS spread, and it could do this again. You could see LIBOR-OIS bucking in the 2008 meltdown. This spread is constructed by buying Eurodollar puts and selling OIS puts traded on the Chicago Mercantile Exchange.[1] There are expiration-matching issues involved in this hedge. Building the position is easy to fit into one's funding limits relative to lending proceeds.

CHAPTER 34

Notional Interest-Rate Swaps, Credit-Default Swaps, and Printing Press Irrelevance

A dark scenario I elaborate in this chapter is less about derivatives than it is about default. A prime dealer default will have massive effects on everything, and a big part of the channel will be derivatives. Here is an attempt to grasp what the world is really like—evolving, unpredictable, full of data that require constant translation and change context instantaneously. There are three possible scenarios.

1. The current playbook holds things together. A side effect is that the Fed's zero interest rate policy (ZIRP) will kill money-market mutual funds (MMMFs), and ultimately, the shadow banking system will "dehydrate." Death will be slow enough that society can adjust to the implied changes.

2. Accept another round of multi-trillion-dollar system backstops to save today, meaning that employment will not vaporize and life will go on with a lit fuse under it. The time bomb here is an impossibly large debt-service burden that will explode in some way in the future.

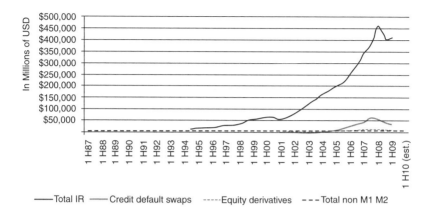

Figure 34.1 **When the Printing Press doesn't Matter . . .**

3. If another prime dealer goes under, there will be a shock so large that it will persist and absorb all other shocks into it, creating multiple failures in its wake. There will be no printing press(es) large enough or fast enough to fill the hole. Employment will vaporize, and life will change radically.

Nobody knows exactly how this surf will break. This is a worst-case scenario. The thesis here is simple: In the age of electrons as trillion-dollar transactions, the printing press can be irrelevant (Figure 34.1).

The world is third-eye blind to the real issue. With notional derivative amounts in the hundreds of thousands of billions, M1, M2, and a broader measure of money supply called money at zero maturity (MZM) don't account for much. Fed policy tools designed to jack up M-whatever aren't capable of doing what they used to.

THREE CONJECTURES

One of the biggest challenges here is that there are no ironclad certainties. There are events of varying likelihood, and even if an event is associated with high likelihood, precisely when it will occur is uncertain as well. Even if a wise person claims to know what is going down, he or she cannot really comprehend it all. What is important is to offer possibilities and ask questions that expand the realm of possibility.

Table 34.1 Irrelevance Incarnate: Causality, Over-the-Counter (OTC) Derivative Notionals, and Money Stock: Granger Causality Wald Test

Test	Chi-Square	Pr > Chi-Square
CDS notional change impacts interest-rate swap notional	6.27	0.0123
CDS notional change impacts M2 (less M1)	<0.00	0.9868
Interest-rate swap notional change impacts M2 (less M1)	8.75	0.0031

Conjecture 1

Changes in credit-default swap (CDS) notional are more volatile than changes in interest-rate swap notional, which, in turn, strongly affects traditional monetary aggregates. Because of the sheer size of the market, a contraction in interest-rate swap notional sounds real trouble.

CDS notional changes are strongly associated with later changes in interest-rate swap notional, CDS notional changes are not associated with later changes in M2 (less M1), and changes in interest-rate swap notional are strongly associated with later changes in M2 (less M1). I use Granger causality methods to determine this. Stats and *p* values are reported in Table 34.1.

Looking at relative change in Figure 34.2 provides a visual sense of what I mean by CDS and interest-rate swap notional volatility.

In the age of electronic money, notional amounts imply that quantitative easing (QE) is the only policy that can inject sufficient liquidity to counteract deflation. Treasuries imply liquidity, which imply collateral, which imply notional, which implies leverage.

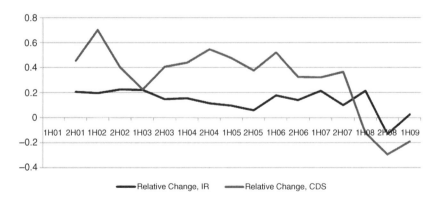

Figure 34.2 **Relative Change in Notional Value, 2000–2009.**

Conjecture 2

The galaxy's liquidity sump pump is the U.S. Treasury market. QE is the only effective vehicle of monetary policy. When exposures are this large. Rehypothecation defines current monetary transmission. It is money velocity at the top of the food chain.

After OTC interest-rate swap notional recovers, conventional monetary aggregates recover. SwapClear has better indicators of current monetary policy transmission than the Fed H.3. Swaps get valued by market-to-market methods (MTMed) very frequently, and collateral is adjusted based on these marks. This is a good thing because it makes them capital-efficient, reduces potential losses, and magnifies their information content. Frequent MTM demands high-quality collateral because almost all received collateral has been rehypothecated for other purposes. Rehypothecation is the transmission mechanism that diffuses Fed easing.

Has the *composition* of posted collateral changed in the past two years?

Conjecture 3

Credit easing is the way to get immediate monetary stimulus to diffuse down. But it is also implies a degree of nationalization.

Large and sustained notional contractions force radical monetary policy that has a direct impact on the real economy. The policy bypasses conventional intermediation and intervene directly in credit markets via the purchase of collateralized bond obligations (CBOs), collateralized loan obligations (CLOs), and collateralized debt obligations (CDOs), giving banks and businesses funding to operate despite negative cash flow.

THE IMPOSSIBILITY OF DEBT REPUDIATION

Everybody relies on the past to evaluate the present and the future. To some, the past is restricted to their own personal experience. To others, the past is generalized beyond the personal but limited in scope. Some people look in marginal places for unifying data. But sifting memories and history does not think through to black swans. These creatures necessarily must be extreme events. However, even this is insufficient: They also must defy any predictive past, reshape the present, and irreparably affect the future.

So perhaps we aren't thinking hard enough about the present and starting from the first principles of what is observed firsthand. Perhaps thousands of trillions of dollars in notional exposures in the age of stored electronic money have made debt repudiation in underlying liabilities impossible without setting off a chain reaction in the derivatives market.

Dollars can't be so easily discarded when nearly every player in the financial system holds staggeringly interlocked debits and credits. Interlocked debits and credits means that nearly every institution that matters holds at least some vested interest in keeping the system alive. They win some and they lose some, but most important, the majority remains vested in the casino's blackjack table.

Interlocking denotes net (gains added and losses subtracted) as opposed to notional (all of it aggregated) exposures. These gains and losses from derivatives exposures are not concentrated in a handful of institutions. They are distributed across the majority of institutions. There is just too much to lose by walking away. So the casino will continue operating as long as there is enough skin left in the game— or until the building catches on fire and everyone runs for safety, screaming all the way.

According to the Bank for International Settlements (BIS), the June 2009 gross market value (net notional) for interest-rate swaps alone was $13,934,000,000,000 (see Table 34.2 for more information). Now imagine a liquidation of only a *fraction* of these positions because a series of sequential bond auction failures squeezed the collateral requirements or because mortgage foreclosures blow up a shark's hedge book. And then comes the chain reaction of liquidation in derivatives that most will never know is imploding until it shows up in the volatility index (VIX) or in implied correlation.

Possible result: Imagine a squeeze strong enough to make $1 buy 15 loaves of bread. How about the dividend yield on that $50 stock you bought yesterday going from 6 percent to 0.1 percent? How about

Table 34.2 BIS, Table 19: Amounts Outstanding, OTC Derivatives, December 2009

Risk Category/Instrument	National Amounts Outstanding					Gross Market Values				
	Jun 2007	Dec 2007	Jun 2008	Dec 2008	Jun 2009	Jun 2007	Dec 2007	Jun 2008	Dec 2008	Jun 2009
Total contracts	**516,407**	**595,738**	**683,814**	**547,371**	**604,622**	**11,140**	**15,834**	**20,375**	**32,244**	**25,372**
Foreign exchange contracts	**48,645**	**56,238**	**62,983**	**44,200**	**48,775**	**1,345**	**1,807**	**2,262**	**3,591**	**2,470**
Forwards and forex swaps	24,530	29,144	31,966	21,266	23,107	492	675	802	1,615	870
Currency swaps	12,312	14,347	16,307	13,322	15,072	619	817	1,071	1,421	1,211
Options	11,804	12,748	14,710	9,612	10,596	235	315	388	555	389
Interest rate contracts	**347,312**	**393,138**	**458,304**	**385,896**	**437,198**	**6,063**	**7,177**	**9,263**	**18,011**	**15,478**
Forward rate agreements	22,809	26,599	39,370	35,002	46,798	43	41	88	140	130
Interest rate swaps	272,216	309,588	356,772	309,760	341,886	5,321	6,183	8,056	16,436	13,934
Options	52,288	56,951	62,162	41,134	48,513	700	953	1,120	1,435	1,414
Equity-linked contracts	**8,590**	**8,469**	**10,177**	**6,159**	**6,619**	**1,116**	**1,142**	**1,146**	**1,051**	**879**
Forwards and swaps	2,470	2,233	2,657	1,553	1,709	240	239	283	323	225
Options	6,119	6,236	7,521	4,607	4,910	876	903	863	728	654
Commodity contracts	**7,567**	**8,455**	**13,229**	**3,820**	**3,729**	**636**	**1,898**	**2,209**	**829**	**689**
Gold	426	595	649	332	425	47	70	68	55	43
Other commodities	7,141	7,861	12,580	3,489	3,304	589	1,829	2,141	774	646
Forwards and swaps	3,447	5,085	7,561	1,995	1,772					
Options	3,694	2,776	5,019	1,493	1,533					
Credit default swaps	**42,581**	**58,244**	**57,403**	**41,883**	**36,046**	**721**	**2,020**	**3,192**	**5,116**	**2,987**
Single-name instruments	24,239	32,486	33,412	25,740	24,112	406	1,158	1,901	3,263	1,953
Multi-name instruments	18,341	25,757	23,991	16,143	11,934	315	862	1,291	1,854	1,034
Unallocated	**61,713**	**71,194**	**81,719**	**65,413**	**72,255**	**1,259**	**1,790**	**2,303**	**3,645**	**2,868**
Memorandum Item:										
Gross Credit Exposure						2,672	3,256	3,859	4,555	3,744

Source: Bank for International Settlements.

a squeeze making every corporation on the planet default on its debt? Cheap bread sounds nice, except you won't have a job when human society is in full cardiac arrest.

However, even seemingly innocuous tampering with underlying assets holds grave risk. Taking creditors' rights of recovery as in the General Motors bailout and by the constant meddling in established court procedures to deal with foreclosures have unintended consequences that make things worse for everyone. These free rides given to banks, businesses, and households as a part of political calculations destroy the liquidity necessary to avoid the implosion mentioned previously. It is difficult enough to unwind a distressed equity tranche. How can it avoid becoming worthless if the holders have no rights to exercise collateral?

The problem is beyond a single democracy because exposures are global in scope. What matters are institutions with exposures several times the size of their sovereigns' gross domestic products (GDPs) built over the course of decades by easy money with momentum like a Juggernaut—and almost all of it collateralized and denominated in U.S. dollars. Warts and all, this is globalization, baby.

The big predators will be the ones that starve when things get bad. Smaller, nimbler, and unobtrusive organizations will suffer but will fare better. The poorest and least privileged on the bottom of the financial food chain will suffer the least.

There has been much fear of explicit dollar devaluation, but dollars are not tied to a commodity standard any more, and there is a derivatives market too big to conduct new currency experiments without immense risk. How do you devalue the dollar on command when it is a convertible currency? *Devaluing dollars with a printing press when quintillions of dollars worth of derivatives are being vaporized would be like trying to hold an Apollo rocket launch down with your bare hands.*

Perhaps the reality is more frightening and inescapable than we are willing to admit. Perhaps things are now so new and novel that no one knows how the system will behave. I suspect that there is a Newhouse theorem and a Palis conjecture for the financial system:

There are an infinite number of possible disaster and salvation scenarios, but only a finite number of them can be attained no matter what policies are taken and what people do. Just about any outcome is possible.

DOMESTICATION FAILURE

Because of the two-steps-forward, one-step-back cycle of human existence, we are all conditioned to attempt the domestication of everything. Because we turned wild grasses into grains, tamed the wolf into Fido, and live well enough in a hive community, we delude ourselves into thinking *everything* can be domesticated.

But domestication efforts fail in two ways:

1. When they suffocate
2. When they fail to defend the perimeters against exponential scale effects

The financial system is engulfed by a massive scale effect, a malignant appendage grown so large that it no longer serves its intended purpose and function. Its only internal logic is to nourish itself, to draw liquidity wherever it can be found. If growth stops, then the current system fails.

Regulatory strategy is an attempt to manage the by-product but not essential problem of derivative notional growth being too big to handle. *No one knows how to tamper with notional growth without causing phenomenal collateral damage.* With the printing press irrelevant, then the center cannot hold,[1] and extremes will be the new normal.

On the other hand, tinkering with the underlying could have destructive unintended consequences. Providing targeted liquidity to the real economy or interfering with established rights of liquidation will put a leaden hand of overcentralization on everything.

Failure is an essential part of existence: It can be managed and must be accepted. But societies fear it, and governments take great pains to deny it. This is why governments stepping outside their defined role (apex predators) and suppressing natural selection has heightened extinction risk for the entire ecosystem. Not only does the apex predator change, but all species in the ecosystem also change in morbid ways. Know that ultimately budget constraints must be made binding again, and the elements that have grown too large must be surgically corrected. If policymakers don't accomplish this, then these two failures will self-correct. Even though the wild corrections nature selects are the stuff of nightmares, this too shall pass.

CHAPTER 35

The Structure of Future Finance: Lessons from a Mathematical Landscape

Underappreciated volatility and overreliance on imperfect models are the scum floating on the swimming pool of "Meltdown 2008." While this statement may deflate some self-important egos and infuriate math phobes alike, what quants do wasn't really central to the meltdown at all. Such things as copula arguments are mere technical adornments to a collateralized debt obigation (CDO) feeding frenzy.

Sort of. All the "mathiness" signifies a deeper issue: the habit of grabbing hold of ideologies and running as fast as we can with them, right over the cliff. There is a stubborn inability to see beyond preconceived notions, a faith that the part of the iceberg we see is symmetric with the hunk lying underwater. Devotion to a cult of certainty always leads to overextension. And it is a part of human nature. These are the weaknesses in human nature that play a deep role in what went wrong—what continues to be wrong—with the global financial system.

That is to say: Excessive risk taking and leverage aren't the only problems. In fact, taking risk and calculated gambles on the state of the future drives progress. The biggest problem is an inadequate representation of what risk really is. The inadequacy makes progress a *lurching ride* forward that crashes in unexpected places and times. This is the ironic way of all financial markets.

As a result, even the notion of progress itself is opaque. Progress has become a gigantic, somewhat pathetic war of ideas. The objective is to propose coherent systems that unify and compartmentalize absolutely everything. Although some battles are won, the war is a hopeless cause. There is no grand unifying theory of everything. Even so, people won't stop. Perpetual motion is ingrained in how we think, and how our brains work.

GEOMETRIC AND ALGEBRAIC INTUITIONS

Whether you liked math in school or not, people tend to think logically and mathematically. The brain is split between geometric intuitions and algebraic intuitions. The right side of the brain is geometric, comparative. It operates based on pattern recognition, visual acuity, and comparisons with known categories. The left side of the brain is algebraic, linguistic. It manipulates symbols governed by explicit rules. The interaction of symbols and rules is the very essence of language, meaning communication derived from the combination and decomposition of symbolic data. Most people instinctively dislike algebra because most brains naturally favor geometry. Speaking in averages, the brain processes symbolic information (algebra) at about 10 bits per second, contrasted with the 10^7 bits per second for subconscious visual processing (geometry).[1] This is why algebraic arguments seem cold and alien.

Nevertheless, algebra increasingly dominates mathematical research and applications. It is well on the way to taking preeminence from geometry and maybe everything else. This is nothing to fear necessarily—it is what it is. In fact, the logical consistency it imposes on thinking is, in the large, beneficial. Some caution should be exercised, though, because that otherworldly precision creates some serious mirages.

One of the illusions of algebra is its almost magical symmetry: Knowledge of the iceberg tip extrapolates to the part that lies underwater. There is a stasis in algebra that does not unfold or change: Its gaze assumes that market behavior is not a work in progress but rather the product of distinct elements interacting with fixed rules. Algebraic method applies itself to such well-defined, understandable problems but leaves problems of high importance yet not amenable to its methods to gather dust. As with any established subject, it tends to kick the can down the road.

Why algebraic methods have grown so common is conjectural. It certainly wasn't that way for the last few centuries. Perhaps computer-aided math processing is more than an aid in computation and is more symbiotic. This cannot be the entire story because the rise of algebra began well before computers. Further, math overlord Alexandre Grothendieck's work cements this domination, and it is unassisted by even a simple calculator. Perhaps "algebraization" is the next step in cerebral evolution.

No doubt, though, computers play a big role in how quickly algebraic methods expand into diverse areas such as finance. Its greatest impact is in algorithmic trading, computer execution of trades at lightning-fast speeds (called low-latency trading). Computer-driven trading is just one step away from algebra because it is a formal language of precise definition and rules of operation. While computer trading is constituted symbolically like algebra, its application goes far beyond the traditional limits of algebra. Functioning code often does not conform to the usual definition of mathematics. It uses symbolic constructions far beyond the limits of their proven validity: In fact, proofs are not used at all. Instead, there is validation based on consistency checks or even by plausibility based on limited observation. Here is really where intuition and algebra come together. I'm going to call it "algebraization."

The idea behind "algebraization" is simple. Algebraic statements are a kind of software code—logical, precise instructions. This algebraic code works as a set of instructions that outputs a replica of a geometric object—or any object, for that matter. Algebra replicates increasingly diverse types of things, and the algebraic developer's toolkit is more and more complex. Although these tools lend themselves to generalization and extension, algebraic machinery doesn't always generate a good replica of the original. In some settings, it is unclear how accurate the produced replica actually is because the object of replication is misunderstood. Algebra here leads to representation failure. Quantitative finance and algebraic trading should be taken into account.

"Algebraization"

In highly stylized settings, "algebraization" works pretty well and is a driving force behind a lot of current math research. As a starting point, consider the continuous functions of geometry and the polynomials of algebra. Note that every real polynomial is a continuous function, but not every continuous function is a real polynomial. The Stone-Weierstrass approximation theorem implies that algebraic polynomials and the continuous functions of geometry are not far apart at all. It states that there are suitable structures or symmetries where the closure of polynomials and the closure of continuous functions are the same. *Therefore, any continuous geometric function on a closed and bounded interval can be uniformly approximated on that interval by algebraic polynomials to any degree of accuracy.*

The implication is that if one can represent something from a geometric standpoint, then it can be equally well represented by an algebraic copy. From this basic starting point flows a mathematical trend that reconfigures anything countable, orderable, or in any way quantifiable into an algebraic argument. "Algebraization" is at its core a deep change in representation, and as a result, it changes how things are conceived in equally deep ways. It is the transformation of everyday concepts into abstraction.

Risk Becoming Abstraction

The very notion of risk becomes an abstraction. Measures of risk such as the second moment of a return distribution (the variance) really only approximate risk, but the logical consistency of the measures reshapes thinking about risk to the extent that risk is volatility. Risk is no longer a somewhat unquantifiable category to hedge or avoid. The representation itself becomes something to be bought and sold. Risk, the historical scourge of humankind, is thought of as an insignificant residual in a formula. The drive for inner consistency becomes a refusal to admit obvious inconsistency.

Similarly, financial models take derivative contracts, whose price is truly determined by a buyer and a seller of the *embedded optionality* in financial assets, and convert those contracts into a stylized identity that can symbolically reconstruct the financial assets themselves. This repli-cation is measured by the basis, which has a clear algebraic connection.

Basis trading puts a kind of straitjacket on how to think about valuation. Derivatives become defined by an internal logic sufficient within themselves. Since this logical mechanism of derivatives is well understood, the inner consistency of these replicating objects defines value for the mass of buyers and sellers. Under these conditions, notional derivative exposures can be greater than the underlying cash assets they attempt to replicate, and the underlying assets become dominated by an abstraction from organic perceptions of asset risk and reward.

SYMMETRY AND BASIS-TRADING BREAKDOWNS

Algebra conceives of this consistency as *symmetry*. Symmetry can be found in many places. For example, Fourier series enable mathemati-cians to break down complex functions into constituent parts, just as music can be decomposed into a sum of notes on a scale. In fact, the gen-eral use of Fourier series is called *harmonic analysis* because of the clarity that this musical analogy provides. Harmonic analysis exposes symme-tries in areas like acoustics, ballistics, quantum physics, engineering, finance, and probability. Quantitative finance uses harmonic methods on diffusion equations to replicate assets with derivative contracts.

The basic building blocks of harmonic analysis are algebraic groups. Groups classify complex structures by decomposing them into their simplest components. The periodic table is the irreduc-ible class of basic elements from which all matter is formed. The prime numbers are the basic irreducible factors that generate the whole numbers under arithmetic operations. Groups define abstract symmetry.

Groups first appeared as devices to determine a formula for find-ing solutions for polynomial equations of degree greater than 4: $ax^5 + bx^4 + cx^3 + dx^2 + ex + f = 0$. Group theoretic arguments showed that a solution for all classes of such equations does not in general exist. There can be no solution formula that applies to all cases because the possible symmetries (called *permutations*) of the solutions are more complex than the symmetries that can be represented by an algebraic formula. Algebraic operations to solve equations fail because there are solutions that escape known categories. In a similar way, group-theoretic methods applied to differential equations (called *Lie groups*) explain why some differential equations can be solved and others cannot. A basic insight of the study of symmetry is that symmetries may fail. *There are categories we know and categories we will never know.*

Lie groups are particularly interesting because they link discrete permutations with the continuous variation of differential equations. This interplay between algebraic groups and geometric objects altered both subjects. The process of algebra absorbing geometric concepts, in turn, enriched the algebraic notion of symmetry. Symmetry emphasizes structure identification when applied to geometric concepts.

On a Lie group, both continuous geometric procedures such as integration and discrete algebraic procedures such as rotations are possible, and this is reflected in their structure. The simplest Lie group consists of all points on the real plane. These same Lie groups have a discrete substructure made up of the collection of integer coordinates on the real plane as a subgroup.

The grid that these integers make on the real plane is called a *lattice*. This structure shows that the plane of real numbers is structured like a sheet with a repeated dot design defined by the lattice points. The structure of this lattice subgroup defines the structure of the whole Lie group. Algebraic method conveys information about a small area of the subgroup and extrapolates it to the entire Lie group.

This kind of extrapolation is often assumed in finance, with profound implications. If one knows something about the model-implied behavior of a derivative contract (called *synthetic*) that replicates an underlying (called *cash*) asset, then structural symmetry implies that you know something about the cash asset itself. For example, one can purchase a bond that pays a fixed coupon. Equivalently, one can sell credit-default protection and receive a fixed payment. Structural symmetry implies that they are the same, and deviations in price from one another indicate that one is priced rich to the other and can be traded in expectation that the prices will converge in time. Because of small random factors such as measurement error, among other things, they will never be exactly the same. But *the principle implies that a synthetic derivative replicates a cash asset less some random noise.*

This equivalence relationship is called the *basis* in quant vernacular. Because cash and synthetic do move in a synchronized way, and because divergence from this behavior often disappears during "normal" times, structural symmetry seems reasonable. The reasonableness of the observed relationship leads to the belief that the logical symmetry adequately captures financial reality. The trade "disappears" into a routine. Symmetry holds until it doesn't. Basis breakdowns are not uncommon in the presence of unanticipated events such as illiquidity and counterparty risk.

Finance Can Learn from Algebra

Even in pure algebraic research, symmetries are handled with caution because there are algebraic objects that defy characterization, symmetry, and structure. Groups incorporate basic behavioral features of functions and operations, but many artifacts are irreducible. They are what they are, and that is all you can say about them because they can't be decomposed into smaller parts. Symmetry in groups is like the symmetry of integers. Just as each whole number can be expressed as a product of prime numbers, each finite group can be expressed as a combination of certain factors known as *simple groups.* These simple groups correspond to prime numbers because they cannot be factored: They are the irreducible constituents of all finite groups. All other finite groups are the product of simple group combinations by a process analogous to multiplying the prime numbers to get all other integers.

Most simple groups belong to one of three families: cyclic groups, alternating groups, and Lie groups. *Cyclic groups* consist of cyclic permutations of a prime number of objects. *Alternating groups* consist of permutations that are formed by interchanging the positions of two objects an even number of times. *Lie groups* form 16 subfamilies, each associated with a particular family of continuous groups associated with the solutions of differential equations. But some simple groups do not belong to the cyclic, alternating, or Lie families or any family at all.

These simple groups that defy characterization are *sporadic*. Some sporadic groups contain many other sporadic groups as subgroups, suggesting a family structure for sporadic groups not yet discovered. These sporadic groups are the fascinating, unexplained rogues of algebra. They show up in weird places, like the study of sphere arrangements in a 24-dimensional space. Even within algebra itself, there are objects that defy characterization, symmetry, and structure. The only structure they have is *no known structure*.

Further, symmetries may exist, but their complexity disposes of any understanding of their meaning or even why they exist. The Monster group provides an example. This sporadic group is almost unimaginably big: It contains 8×10^{53} elements comprising the group of rotations in a 196,884-dimension space. At the same time, certain coefficients in harmonic analysis correspond to the dimension of the Monster. Namely, in the Fourier expansion:

$$j(\tau) = q^{-1} + 744 + \sum_{n=1}^{\infty} c(n)q^n$$

where $q = e^{2\pi i \tau}$, and one confines τ to the half-plane. Solving for the integer coefficients $c(n)$ yields $c(1) = 196{,}883 + 1$ (the addition corresponds to the one trivial representation). No one knows exactly why such symmetries exist.

The good news is the promise of finding surprises in fundamental structures. This is like figuring out a pattern that permits fitting a bunch of known pieces into a puzzle. People stumble onto new objects outside of known preconceptions all the time. This is akin to finding new puzzle pieces (such as the Monster) that can fill many gaps in a puzzle. To look outside a prevailing worldview, to think about something that everyone else thinks about and find something different from everybody else, requires a serious dose of luck.

The peril is the assumption that some observed regularity implies a pattern that always works when it actually doesn't. The virtues of models can be so convincing to our convictions that a puzzle piece is forced into a place where it doesn't fit. It may be healthy to suspect that the puzzle board changes from time to time for no apparent reason, and the number of pieces grows at an exponential rate.

THE "ALGEBRAIZATION" OF EVERYTHING

To recapitulate: Mathematics is a natural mode of human thinking. The primary type of mathematical thinking is geometric; another mode of thinking is algebraic. Geometric thinking is about space and generalization of size, shape, and what is the same and what is different about objects. Algebra explores time or, more to the point, sequential resolutions over time. There is a tension between the two, sometimes reflected in subtle snarkiness between geometer and algebraist communities.

Everyone uses both intuitions, but there is seldom a perfect harmony between the two. One mode of thinking generally prevails over the other. Looking at mathematical history, when geometric thinking prevails, proofs are less rigorous, more exploratory, and given to wilder ideas that damage the internal consistency of mathematics: It often defines an age of forward discovery without regard to the gaps left in its wake. When algebraic thinking prevails, it is an age of criticality. The focus is on consolidation of progress and organization of existing knowledge through classification, symmetry, and structure identification.

We live in an age of criticality. Although there will always be renegades who do their own thing independent of taste and convention, in broad brushstrokes, the current trend is to take intrinsically unique objects, disregard the intrinsic properties that make them unique, and remold this stripped-down essence into algebraic terms.

The basic idea is Hermann Schubert's.[2] Start with algebraic software, such as a finite sequence of Aristotelian questions of degree and kind. The assumption is that a finite number of kind questions such as "What is it/what is it not?" and degree questions such as "How much is it/How much is it not?" is adequate to characterize *anything*.

Formally, one represents an arbitrary condition by algebraic symbols and then attributes two independent conditions with symbols such as x and y. Represent that a condition holds given an operation on x and y with the symbol $\sim$ (the symbol choice is arbitrary). Represent that a condition holds simultaneously by another operation on x and y with the symbol $\wedge$. Consider the symbols x and y equal if all the conditions $\sim$ and $\wedge$ applied over an adequate sequence are equivalent. This algebraic "code" outputs a structure amenable to algebra tools.

Alexandre Grothendieck, a twentieth-century genius on par with Gauss and Newton, added the essential steps that make algebraic abstractions conceivable just about anywhere. In fact, his innovations made total abstraction so successful that physics, number theory, and topology increasingly fall under the sway of algebra. It is easy to think of Grothendieck as an algebraic totalitarian, but his writing and methods are direct, intuitive, and profoundly creative.[3] It's weird how this works in math.

Before Grothendieck, there was no adequate way to capture the idea of an open neighborhood around a point using algebraic language. As a result, the described algebra "programming" approach didn't work well. To remedy this, Grothendieck designed an algebraic plug-in called a *covering*. A covering is equivalent to imposing a substitute structure, implying that the internal features are frequently irrelevant. Whether or not some of these internal features are identified adequately is minimized by the theoretical apparatus itself. Just like the basis trade, sometimes the covering is a nice copy and sometimes not.

ALGEBRA AND "PHYNANCE" (PHYSICS + FINANCE)

The fundamental problem of logical representation in an amorphous, ever-changing context such as financial markets remains open, but prevailing mathematical trends always seep into finance. Mathematical finance imposes consistency and order on markets and instruments with inherent *inconsistency*. Successful conversion of intractable things into tractable abstractions requires precise definitions and immutable rules of behavior. This implies a shift from representation by notions of change (derivatives) and accumulation (integrals) to a focus on structure and order properties (groups).

But even the most fundamental financial concepts *resist* immutable rules of behavior. I touched on the difference between risk and risk measures already: Here I delve further.

The VIX and Volatility Representation

Volatility serves as an approximation of risk or a measure of risk. Volatility is similar to the standard deviation imposed on a given asset or index. The Volatility Index (VIX) contract is a traded synthetic volatility instrument on the Standard & Poor's (S&P) 500 Index. As such, the VIX contract is a representation of equity risk at given points in time. Risk is far more than volatility, though, and the information content of any tradable quantity is further obscured by intrinsic counterparty and other risks.

In fact, the VIX is even inadequate to conceive of volatility because different asset classes, by virtue of how they trade, have different kinds of volatility. Commodities (in general) run up fast and break down fast. Their volatility follows the same spiky up and down pattern. Equity volatility declines slowly, reflected in how equity prices rise in incremental steps. When equity prices crash, volatility is like a mirror image that spikes suddenly higher. Fixed-income volatility is more symmetric than the other two, with more gradual up and down movements than other asset classes.

The behavior of volatility can change in time. Asset classes have "regimes" of volatility where the governing rules change unexpectedly. There can be periods of flat volatility, periods of heightened volatility, and periods of depressed volatility. Determining a regime depends on hindsight: You know what volatility is like after the fact, but this tells little about the present. *Volatility approximates risk, but it is not risk.*

In essence, volatility is the product of observed past data. Other models generate *implied volatility*, a theoretical value implied algebraically by all the other given terms. These two quantities, one from the past and the other a "guesstimate" consistent with an internal logic, make possible a type of trade that gets to the core of quantitative finance—historical volatility versus implied volatility.

One side of the trade presumes that the past is the same as the present and no events are truly game-changing—the essence of mean reversion. The other side of the trade presumes that, at least in a local sense, deviations can and will persist. This appears to define a fundamental symmetry: One side wins, and the other loses. However, there is an asymmetric possibility where both sides lose due to counterparty risk. If the loser puts on the trade in size and is bankrupted by it, the winner may not get his or her winnings or may find his or her winnings so impaired that it wasn't worth the time to trade.

ABSTRACTION AS A WORLDVIEW

Abstractions amass to the point that people accept the replication of reality as reality itself. Abstraction becomes a pathology that limits thinking when fixed categories remain unchanged even as underlying reality continues to evolve.

Consider the evolution of the risk-free rate concept. Financial models depend on a rate of return that carries no (negligible) risk as a basic reference tool to decompose risky rates into more basic components. Government securities, particularly those denominated by entities with a reserve currency, provide such a risk-free reference rate. However, the circumscription where these securities provide a meaningful reference rate is increasingly narrow.

This situation was due to persistent fiscal and trade imbalances and central bank policies that subsidize interest rates on sovereign securities. The subsidy distorted interest-rate risk, which, in turn, strengthened the need to hedge interest-rate risk. The market response was interest-rates swaps, typically issued by large dealer banks and complex financial institutions. When interest-rate swap spreads, whose rates float and are not fixed like a bond coupon, indicated that government securities were more risky than swaps, floating interbank rates such as the London Interbank Offered Rate (LIBOR) supplanted government securities as the risk-free reference rate used in financial models. In 2008, the Lehman collapse elevated counterparty risk, and LIBOR spiked in response to the elevated counterparty risk. With counterparty risk front and center, overnight secured lending rates such as the overnight indexed swap (OIS) rate are increasingly the risk-free reference rates.

The ultimate result is that today's financial system has few comparable reference points with the past. A new toolkit of replicating instruments such as basis spreads, swaps, forward interest rate agreements

(FRA), and other forward rates are the foundation. These instruments transfer risk, hide risk on the footnotes of balance sheets, and depend in complex ways on collateral, counterparty stability, and liquidity. A generation ago, these risks didn't exist. This fluidity makes it difficult to know what works financially and what doesn't, what endures and what fails the test of time. Healthy, incremental returns for five years are no guarantee that year six will not wipe out all gains and then some.

There are no proven rules that govern complex financial phenomena. Few people even take a shot at this endeavor. Instead, you have symbolic constructions that interact with reality in fascinating, profitable ways. However, because the explanation is based on local data, it is subject to change. *Luck combined with prudence is the best way to manage reality shifts that blowtorch our thinking.*

Derivative instruments are more than complements to simple cash flows and tangible stores of wealth. They serve as replacements. The proliferation of these financial instruments, combined with changing environments, creates an inherent challenge. They are so new that it is unclear whether these instruments are robust to extreme changes in market conditions and policy stances. Their market volumes are so large that there is no way that they can fail without bringing everything down with them.

CHAPTER 36

The Reasonable Ineffectiveness of Mathematics in Trading

Mathematics affords virtually unlimited precision, but is limited in its scope.

—PARAPHRASE OF EUGENE WIGNER, "THE UNREASONABLE EFFECTIVENESS OF MATHEMATICS IN THE NATURAL SCIENCES"

Is mathematics a quantum leap forward compared with other methods of thinking? Sure. Its precision beats every other possible "system," and human intuition is limited by experience. One cannot "see" curves without tangents or intuit an n-dimensional space, but one can study such objects mathematically. Successful trading is about buying cheap and selling dear: Mathematical thinking is an indispensable means to that end. But it also can obscure intuition that necessarily deals with the inexact definitions of everyday life. Further, a mind-set wholly engrossed in the mathematical development of an axiom base can take one far from practical relevance.

DON'T BE A (NORBERT) WIENER

Janos (Johnny) von Neumann reinvented himself multiple times before he died of cancer. He was a key contributor to the foundations of mathematics, was the pioneer of ergodic theory (Birkhoff tried to cheat von Neumann here), did some slick investigation on the invariant subspace problem, was the expositor of the underappreciated subject of continuous geometry, was the one who systematically investigated game theory, was the human calculator behind components of the first nuclear weapon, and was considered the father of machine computing. These achievements don't even cover all that he did, much less capture their depth. He knew how to party too, but that comes further down.

There was nothing superhuman about him: He just had a solid, thoroughly normal personality with a tremendous work ethic. If there was any genius in him, it was his instinctive drive to stay close to directly observed facts and applications. This is not to say that he didn't theorize. In fact, his axiomatization of quantum theory is still one of the best reads on the subject because his axioms are stylized from observation, are straightforward, and are easy to relax and restrict depending on where you want to go.

His approach stands in stark contrast to that of Norbert Wiener in constructing a view of the world. Wiener was the first to rigorously characterize Brownian motion, but he exclusively used a (then) challenging and formal measure-theoretic construction. Wiener avoided drawing connections to probabilistic methods because probability theory had a bad reputation among his mathematical colleagues. Probabilistic intuition and measure theory truly reinforce each other: Many who could have benefited most by Wiener's advances were left out of the discussion.

Perhaps these differences in approach are based on personality. Von Neumann was reasonably courteous, somewhat intolerant of pretension and illusions of superiority, generally friendly, and a fun-loving people person. Wiener was by accounts childish, overly sensitive, self-absorbed, and difficult to be around. The divide between their personalities was diametric.

The current divide between mathematics and hard sciences couldn't be much wider either. Mathematicians talk among themselves.

Engineers talk among themselves. As the respective dialects grow mutually unintelligible, both tend to ignore natural problems that anyone can understand. Instead, both delve into their own franchised abstractions. For example, Lie group representations permit an abstraction of Fourier methods for solving differential equations, but the generalization is, with some exceptions, limited to equations amenable to separation of variables. Lie groups do provide a vantage point where one can survey interesting mathematical vistas, but for close-up details, one often has to fall back on solution methods engineers use routinely. These methods also fail to overcome current challenges. Engineers busy themselves in altering one assumption after another to gain slightly more general solution methods (or accuracies) that persistently fail to adhere to the demands of some real-life problems.

Long gone are the days when Isaac Newton built the foundations of calculus by observing the effect of gravity on an apple or a wave equation to measure the speed of sound. Laplace corrected Newton's work not based on symbolic manipulation but because of the values his experiments yielded. Cauchy elaborated Newton's theory of light dispersion using the same prism as a starting point. Well into this century, Born, Heisenberg, and Schrodinger used harmonic analysis merely as a tool to substantiate quantum observations.

Von Neumann followed this tradition and modeled experimental statements via a Hilbert space and deduced how the statements connect logically. Wiener refrained from deploying an expository method for common use and wide relevance because it was distasteful to his colleagues. Everybody loses when experts write mutual admiration notes to each other coded such that they either bore others to death or exclude them from grasping the point.

This relationship is just the tip of the iceberg. If one thinks the difference between mathematics and engineering is huge, then consider the difference between them and softer subjects such as economics (no offense meant). Isolation leads to shallow thinking and research in narrow settings, and mathematics needs relevant practical problems to renew itself.

When the Emperor announced the Japanese surrender to the Allies after World War II, his subjects couldn't understand what he was saying. After centuries of distance from his subjects, the Imperial court no longer spoke common Japanese. The recording preserves a jumble of lilting tones and strange cadences that left everyone but a handful scratching their heads.

ACTION PRECEDES DATA

Johnny von Neumann was terrible at poker. This wasn't because he got too drunk during the games: Polish mathematician Stefan Banach once got Neumann so drunk on vodka that he had to run to the toilet to puke. After the purge, he reentered the Scottish Café and resumed his functional analysis discussion without missing a beat.

The point is that a human calculator with unrivaled skills of preparation such as von Neumann easily could compute the highest-probability opportunities of a poker hand, but if your hand sucks, it sucks. Sometimes all options are bad, and the lesser evil is still disaster. The only option: action. But sometimes nothing is a pretty cool hand.

Poker involves human interaction and strategy, which means, above all, mind games. Mind games, as their name implies, are designed precisely to throw reasonable thinking out of whack. Must there be head games? Well, basic reality is described by the observable arrangements of particles governed by replicable physical laws of motion (classical and quantum). These laws are understood imperfectly, conditioned on a limited knowledge of the world. But it is unconscious bits of brain matter that cause unobservable consciousness and interpret meaning.

Consciousness is subjective; conscious interaction with others shapes society. Society in increasing complexity brings with it money, property, government, and standards of right and wrong. Yet the foundation remains utterly subjective: It exists because enough people believe that they exist in a reasonably concrete way. The changing quantum of *enough people* determines the basic building block of *value*—what is desired. Value presents itself when enough people who see it accept it. Price presents itself as attractive when an individual accepts the offer. The price is the price.

People can anchor their perceptions of value based on the prices of things now. Valuation becomes a part of the *gestalt*, something given, not something for which to search. Subjective consciousness and basic reality dissolve into a unity because an unchangeable worldview is assumed. Those who fail to "get it" simply do not understand the obvious. There is little place for rational disagreement because it is arguing against what the crowd finds to be self-evident. While the financial motivation for trading remains sure—the commitment to survive and thrive—there are opportunities within established parameters for anything and nothing. All action is channeled into modes of "not missing out" and, alternatively, "not rushing in where fools tread." For a time, just about everyone thought equity tranche mortgage-backed securities (MBS) were "good enough" and that super-senior tranches (the segment of these securities that would lose money only if all other less senior tranches had horrendous losses) were bulletproof. Now only braver souls sniff nonagency securities.

Action precedes data. What drives price *action* is trading. Without trading, or in an illiquid market, no one knows how an asset is valued. Trading in a liquid market provides approximate knowledge of value up to an interval in which price fluctuates around the bid-ask spread needed to fund market making. Valuation is always dynamic. Data that inform models come after.

By virtue of their beauty and elegance, mathematical methods can make even things with thoroughly unobservable foundations seem natural, realistic, and inevitable. People manage voluminous information and complexity by sticking to a view of the world no matter how shaky that outlook is. This is an illusion that breaks down easily.

Predictive mathematical models provide a rigorous justification for behavior *based on hindsight*. They reinforce the belief that the world cannot change materially from the present (stationarity) and in so doing obscure the distinction between the subjective and the objective. Mathematics does have unparalleled precision, but unquantifiable events fall outside its scope. There is a place for thinking outside the data at hand and exploring whether never-seen-before scenarios could make models fail.

Using mathematics to model what is essentially subjective and intractable is like playing poker: It can identify high-probability strategies to play, but one has to work the table. This is why the sell side and forecasters exist. The outcome of a bad hand is determined by how you play it as well as what's in it.

POKER OR BINGO

The current antidote to this endless cycle of falling blindly in love—not with an asset, but with a dubious axiomatization that shapes how the world is perceived—and the inevitable bitter, disillusioning breakup is called *risk management.*

Oversimplification alert: The focus here is on hedge funds that make money by taking residual risk, not on making money through the flow business. Risk management is different for the two. Dealers need risk models that calibrate to daily markets because tomorrow the position will be unloaded to another customer. Risk management for those taking residual risk is managing liquidity (cash/near-cash provisioning), reducing return volatility (diversification), and hedging nonstationarity (cheap exposures to the other side of crowded trades).

At the end of the day, though, what good does a reasonably self-funding but imperfect instrument such as the Volatility Index (VIX) call spreads really do in the face of a meltdown? Risk management that depends on VIX depends on the same worldview that leads to melt-downs in the first place. Take value-at-risk (VaR), for example. VaR works like it should only when a book is liquid. One is once more forced to concede that liquidity simply means that you know what your book is worth. Illiquidity means that you can't price it.

In addition, one has to take into account the size of the players at the table and the types of trades they make. Small investors are price takers and not price makers—they are able to enter the market, trade in the volume they choose, and leave without disturbing the market price (however, any trade can shift the price to some degree under a microscope). In contrast, large investors are price makers because the sizes of the trades they make inevitably shift market prices (thus they lack the anonymity of small traders, and this can be seriously damaging, especially when a trader is forced to trade through visible weakness). Considering that just about everything is a short-end borrow, the effect of illiquidity on prices can be as extreme as a surfer swallowed by a tsunami. It doesn't matter how the hand is played in this case. You take what is given.

Illiquidity is nonstationarity. Are there trades such that nonstationarity can be exploited? These types of trades carry inherent risks still, but a floating component moves with nonstationary shocks. Meaningful diversification is a mix of receive float/receive fixed positions.

For a fixed receiver example, consider a 13-month reverse convertible note paying 6.5 percent. You lose money only if the index drops approximately 80 percent. Synthetics also allow you to customize exposure with no float caps: Take a bond, buy protection on it, and then swap the cash flow for a floating rate. A simple concrete example: Buy a 10-year Japanese government bond with protection, and pay fixed rates on a 10-year interest-rate swap. Pocket the bond coupon and any floating rate (less funding, protection costs, and fixed swap payment).

TWO KINDS OF DIVERSIFICATION

In general, appropriate risk taking comes via diversification, and there is *deep* diversification and *naive* diversification. In deep diversification, a portfolio structure receives some fixed cash flows and some receive floating cash flows. The float adjusts to multisigma moves and discontinuous jumps—the extremes. Diversification of this kind smoothes net asset values relative to discontinuities and infinite distribution moments. Buying a rental property is a pay fixed, receive float investment. So is buying stocks on margin. Buying a bond at par with London Interbank Offered Rate (LIBOR, like an interbank prime rate) funding is a receive fixed, pay float exposure. Naive diversification is easier: It is expressed by buying multiple equities within a given sector or buying an index instead of a name. It smoothes net asset value relative to local noise by exposure to mispriced idiosyncratic risk, but it cannot diversify enough to escape systemic problems.

Beware of these risks as well as classic paralysis by analysis. Dangers grow as one broods on them. In the concrete example using the IOY japanese bond, there is an implicit assumption that the credit-default swap (CDS) contract has a near-perfect inverse relationship with the underlying bond. Even if the trade is well within one's risk tolerance, serious leverage has to be deployed to make money. This leverage increases mark-to-market risk via funding pressure. There can be upfront issues with a dealer. There is counterparty risk on the float proceeds and the protection. Relatively inexpensive counterparty risk hedges such as exposure to rising LIBOR-OIS spreads replicate the risk inefficiently. CDS on the protection seller is costly and self-defeating. Even then, there is counterparty risk on that protection too. There are currency risks: Cash serves as a reference point, but it certainly isn't a risk-free one.

Liquidity and diversification increase the chances for getting lucky, and luck matters a lot because only trivial axiomatic worldviews are consistent: There will always be problems that cannot be resolved in a closed-form way. The closer one looks, the more hedge needs come into view. It can become like plugging holes in a Cantor set. There are contingencies where hedging is futile. There are times when precision is needed, and there are times when precision gets in the way.

CHAPTER 37

A Characterization
of Dark Risk

The difficulty with modeling markets in a dynamical way is that their essence is free human choice, whereas the central core of dynamical systems is determinism. *Determinism* means that the past determines the future and, as will be demonstrated, vice versa. This definition implies that zero topologic entropy is a requirement for predictability. This will take some unpacking.

THEOREM (KAMINSKI)1

A system (X, T) is *topologically predictable* if for every continuous function f in $C(X)$ we have f in $<1, T, f, T^2, f, \ldots>$ where $<F>\subset C(X)$ denotes the closed algebra generated by a family $F \subset C(X)$. (X, T) is topologically predictable if and only if every factor of (X, T) is invertible, where a factor is a system (Y, S) and is continuous onto map $\pi X \to Y$ such that $\pi T = S\pi$.

What this means for a class of functions $F: X \to F(X)$ is shown in Figure 37.1.

In both scenarios, the system consists of a set of past-present states X and future states $F(X)$ defined by rule F governing time evolution from past-present states to future states. Crucially, for each rule

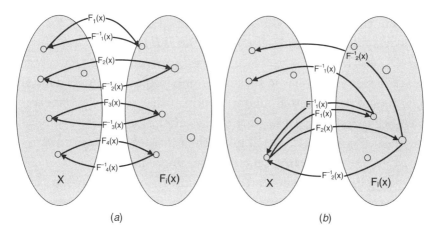

Figure 37.1 **Predictability and Determinism:** (*a*) **Deterministic, Topologically Predictable System,** $F_i(x)$; (*b*) **Topological Unpredictability,** $F_1(x)$, $F_2(x)$.

governing past to future, there is an inversion of the rule that determines how present-future states relate to the past.

In the deterministic-predictable case on the left, (*a*) of Figure 37.1, the mapping of past to present is clear and one-to-one, corresponding to an "if A happened, then B will happen" logic. Further, the present can be used to determine past values, validating the premise of backtesting models based on historical data. The "if-then" logic combined with the ability to invert time evolution rules to return information about the initial state is a powerful concept. This idea ensures that the system can be understood at all points in time (within a tolerance) and that the rules governing evolution are unchanged over time.

Topologically unpredictable systems imply that there is no one-to-one correspondence from the past-present to the future: The rules governing the transition from past do not map to unique future states. This situation is not insurmountable; it just makes prediction more imprecise. The real problem is that the inverse of transition rules (mapping the present-future to past states) is nonunique as well.

This problem is what makes deterministic models break down. It implies that well-worn "if-then" logic and intuitions don't work because in this setting knowing where you are now offers little indication of where you were. It is equivalent to saying (in the case of $F_2(x)$ and its inverse) *if A in the past, then B or C, but if B now, then either A or D, and if C now, then either A or E*. Confused yet? As the number of states and evolution rules grow in size, it becomes difficult to understand the dynamics of the system. Roughly speaking, when complications exceed tolerance thresholds, we say that the system has *positive entropy*. So the presence of noninvertibility implies the presence of positive entropy, which implies complexity, which implies unpredictability.

This intuition is behind Kaminski's theorem, implying that a starting criterion to determine unpredictability lies in noninvertibility. At the extreme, if each point of a system has multiple preimages, it is totally noninvertible. In a totally noninvertible system, there is always an open set of points whose preimages—the $F^{-1}(x)$'s in the figure—are bounded below by some positive constant. Therefore, putting things in reverse, a topologically predictable system has zero topologic entropy, every invariant measure on it has zero entropy, and the system is invertible.

Predictability means that there is information from the past embedded in the present (determinism), and the relationship among the past, present, and future is simple enough (zero topologic entropy) that rules governing how the system evolves over time can be known. Thus there are two senses in which a system is unpredictable.

> *Type 1:* The transition rules can be known, but knowing them requires infinite time or computational resources that no one has.
>
> *Type 2:* The transition rules cannot be known because they are indeterminate.

Unpredictability of the second type is equivalent to the concept of "dark risk" introduced by Stuart Turnbull.

INCOMPLETE INFORMATION INDUCES DARK RISK

Type 1 risk is premised on a partition of unknown future sets and completely known past states. A class of dark risk stems from incomplete information. Incomplete information implies that not only are future states unknown, but also a subset S of past states is unknown. Incomplete information could be because of bad ticks thrown out, measurement error, or just because everything about everything isn't captured.

Incomplete information enables a characterization of some types of dark risk. Assume a simple system possessing the following type of determinism: A future state $F_1(X)$ of the system is not affected (it is independent) by any other past states outside the past state X_1. The implication is that there are only a finite number of past states that matter in figuring out the transition path from the past to the future. Thus prediction depends on particular past states, and all other historical data is irrelevant from a model perspective. Missing or incomplete data can make it impossible to model the system correctly even if it possesses such a dependence structure.

Under incomplete information, rational people under a pretty wide set of circumstances use sufficient statistics—they include all historical observed information—in their decision making (proving this requires some special sauce that is rather complicated). In effect, missing data limit model choice to models that make prediction a function of the entire past history of observed values. Even if better models require less data to capture system behavior, the fact that data are missing makes their outputs very sensitive. Thus data limitations force model choices where prediction outputs perform poorly out of sample.

This dark risk is prevalent for a wide class of systems because differential information is a commonplace kind of incomplete information. For example, since some traders can have different information than other traders, sufficient estimates that drive decisions can differ.

Even if the underlying dynamics of a system possess the determinism described earlier, there is no substantiation for assuming that the influence of the past decays quickly in the case of incomplete information. Positive entropy implies complexity, but they are not the same things, so entropy measures are not adequate. Needed is a measure of the minimal information such that all past data with predictive content are incorporated in model. The efficacy of such measures is subject to debate.

IMPLICATIONS FOR BACKTESTING

Since such measures are equivocal, rough techniques applied to back-tests are a possible way forward. Backtesting typically withholds a subsample of the data and uses it to measure prediction against observation, usually with held from the most recent past. This subsample choice implicitly assumes that the influence of the distant past decays quickly, or essentially the same information is embedded in all times. If this implication is wrong, backtests may indicate good training period performance against simulation data, but the model will have poor trading performance in even the immediate future.

The following backtest procedure provides some insight into the degree of unpredictability, if the conjecture holds. First, create two simulation buckets. One bucket contains data from the recent past, whereas the other bucket contains data from further back in time. A stationary process implies that model simulation is equally good (statistically speaking) for both buckets given appropriate sample size and model selection. If the converse true, it has far-reaching consequences.

If model simulation is equally good for both buckets, then the underlying process is stationary. Quants can wear it out with all their wiles.

CHAPTER 38

Stop Chasing Tails: Some Long-Only Opening Lines in Portfolio Theory

The two most basic investment concepts are the following:

- Investing returns requires risk taking.
- The humble realization that you can't predict the future means that you must diversify.

CENTER BETS VERSUS FAT TAILS: THE TOPOLOGY OF "EXTREMISTAN"

Everybody knows what fat tails are, even if just vaguely. They refer to a higher probability of extreme events embodied in thicker tails of a distribution when compared with the Gaussian distribution. Fat tails imply the relevance of the extreme events in life. Specifying the exact distribution is often unimportant because the distribution evolves over time. What *is* important is recognizing

1. The grave error in making assumptions based purely on linear cause-and-effect constructs
2. The fact that most predictions underestimate or overestimate risk and reward

Statistical models such as regression analysis are particularly prone to the defect of linear thinking because they assume normality or near normality that does not factor in extremes, putting weight on the body of a distribution and assuming that the shape of the distribution doesn't evolve over time. Even well-worn tools such as correlation are inadequate in capturing a nonlinear reality.

That said, you can only hedge linear events: You can't hedge non-linear events effectively. So the tools in the statistical arsenal do have a useful place: They are ways to categorize thought, and they work well when the tail risks are small. Just like anything that maps human systems, they don't work well when tail risks are large.

There it is. The issue is not about a proper choice of probability distribution. It is not about human inability to find the "right" distribution because it slips out of our fingers as it evolves. The issue is about reality constantly reinventing itself. All probability distributions are derived from an underlying dynamical system, which, in turn, can be unstable. This instability introduces the potential of constant change at any given time and state because the world undergoes phase transitions. It is not an issue of finding the unknown— it is an issue of accepting the unknowable.

Instability is why all predictions fail and why everyone is eventually wrong. Not even the simplest processes can escape this graveyard. Consider the simple example of a coin flip off your thumb. One asks, "How can the probability of a head or tail ever be appreciably different from 50 percent?" Well, if you flip a coin a million times off your thumb, that thumb will be rubbed to the bone and eventually will fall off. You will be forced to flip the coin in a different way that ultimately can affect the probabilities of heads and tails.

The world does not resemble anything as simple as a coin flip anyway: Predictions are exponentially harder. All you can do is base decisions on available data, use models that accommodate the widest range of potential states of the world, and recognize that as the time frame gets longer, the forecast error grows exponentially.

Who knows . . . you may even get lucky.

HUMAN LIMITS AND PROBABILITY UNPLUGGED

> My daughter was telling me about an Adonis who lives in a fraternity house opposite her school. "He's so handsome, Muddy," she sighed. "So handsome! Why his face is simply carved with dueling!"
>
> —"Time Mellowed Germany," *National Geographic*, 1934

Years after first reading it, I never forgot this quote. It is a classic example of the divergent errors of estimates compounding exponentially, not arithmetically, over time. The man with the carved-up face in 1934 may well have been driving a tank in Kursk in 1943. What a wildly different opinion she would have, given the perspective of time!

Probability is just a rule-based way to organize what we observe. Since probability distributions in general are unobservable, often one starts with some prior distribution based on intuition and then modifies it based on evidence. Thus, if an event is repeated often enough, the evidence will give "shape" to a distribution, and most people will agree on what it should be. Only people with very different starting intuitions will disagree significantly. Even though their prior is different, given enough time, even diametric views will converge (more on this later).

Owing to measurement error and other practical limitations, it is seldom possible to prove that something is 100 percent correct or 100 percent wrong. A probability distribution functions as a measure of belief based on supporting evidence. The degree of successful prediction is often due to the starting intuition, the hunch that is your prior assumption. In a sense, alpha can be the pure luck of your assumptions being better than others at the start.

Distributions can evolve, starting off flat like the uniform when all outcomes are equally uncertain. Over time, recurring sample properties make outcomes look normal. Then way-out-there extremes that come out of the blue make the tails fat. To borrow Nassim Taleb's terminology, reality fluctuates between "Extremistan" and "Mediocristan" depending on sampling and time horizon (see Figure 38.1).

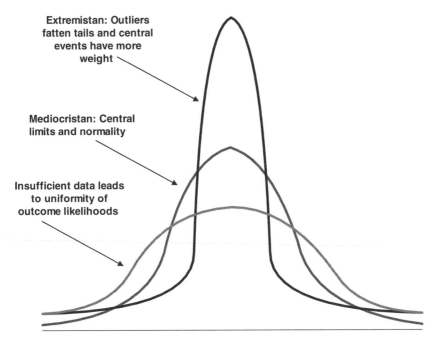

Figure 38.1 "Extremistan" and "Mediocristan."

The figure shows that over time, the distribution fluctuates between flat and extreme as the underlying dynamical system changes.

SOURCES OF UNPREDICTABILITY

Thus, given this reduction of probability to degrees of belief, the essential issue would seem to be one of convergence—it is not. The real issue is that the unobserved probability distribution is unstable. History is a dynamical system that produces bad events when it "breaks down" and good events when it starts "working right" again. Bad events are associated with uncertainty. In extreme uncertainty, our perception tends to weigh possible events with the unique distribution with the most entropy and the most symmetry—the uniform distribution.

In terms of statistics, this reduces to drawing observations from a rapidly changing distribution—what is observed comes from a distribution that changes at points in time (the extreme case). Take this thought back to the coin-flipping example: Flipping a coin produces very stable outcomes and probabilities over a long time period, but

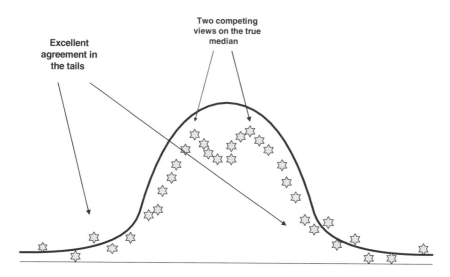

Figure 38.2   **Missing the Center for the Tails. Significant Discrepancies in the Bulk Imply an Undecided Market.**

ultimately, your thumbnail will rub down to the quick, and you'll flip the coin in an outcome-altering way.

Note something about the fat-tail distribution: The center is even more concentrated than under the assumption of normality. Thus, if you believe in fat tails, then it is more important to find the precise center than anything else. Worry about the tails after you focus on the center. You may risk manage those tails beautifully, but if you manage reward poorly, you lose big. Often when market sentiment is divided, the center bet is bimodal. Don't lose sight of the importance of adjusting risk *and* return (see Figure 38.2).

If your portfolio doesn't cover the center adequately, the tails don't matter at all. This is the pain of the permabear. Everything is concentrated on one tail.

FAT TAILS, RISK AVERSION, AND LEVERAGE: SOME LONG-ONLY OPENING LINES IN PORTFOLIO THEORY

I've thought about portfolio building under alternative assumptions, and I use the Mediocristan-Extremistan shorthand employed in Taleb's book *The Black Swan.*[1] Here positions are long-only: there is no selling or shorting of positions. The result is something with analogies to hypermodern chess theory.

Mediocristan

Mediocristan is the same as assuming normality, and the tails are not as "fat". Here, you don't need to worry about extreme events. This is not uncommon. News about municipal bonds is dominated by true fiscal basket cases such as California and Illinois, but behind these headlines are the vast majority of states that take responsible steps to repair their balance sheets. Mediocristan often saves the day.

One's portfolio options seek alpha and get exposure to a wide center. You pick solid companies across sectors and hold varying positions across their capital structure. Bank debt is a strong center bet, but their common stock is more exposed to negative tail shocks. Their senior debt is more robust against shocks in the extreme because of government guarantees. Technology stocks are more exposed to positive shocks because technology companies innovate. Ownership of these companies is desired; being a creditor to technology companies is less possible, because they don't issue as much debt.

Stock ownership doesn't insure against extremes such as really high inflation or financial systems collapse, but when normality prevails, there's no need. If you think of this in terms of chess strategy, it is like the concept of centralization (Figure 38.3).

Leaving aside the optimal level of liquidity (a separate issue all on its own), good and bad tail events require diversification. The portfolio in Figure 34.4 holds more senior debt, which is a choice, not a stipulation. There is a place for subordinated debt when the price is right.

This isn't a radical idea. There is an ancient rule found in the Talmud about investing: In a nutshell, it says that the optimal portfolio is diversified equally in cashlike assets and risky business ventures. Figure 38.4 shows how such a rule looks given the expanded set of portfolio choices in modern times.

The essential point is diversification by indexation across the capital structure. Hold a diversity of debt from lower-risk high-grade (HG) bonds to higher-risk, high-yield (HY) bonds. Preferred shares

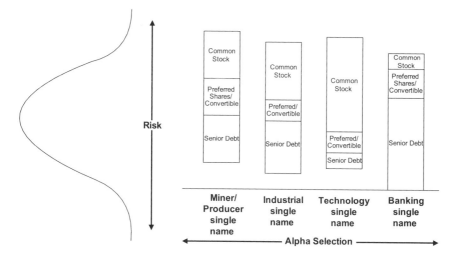

Figure 38.3 **Centralization in Mediocristan.**

for maximum yield. Less diversified large caps because they have less room to grow. Midcaps and small caps to get exposure to growth and general positive shocks.

Extremistan

Someone who believes in really fat tails believes that there will be either a very small move or a very large move and not much in between. I'm

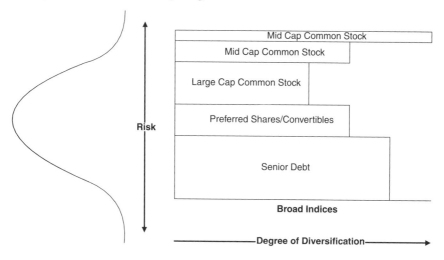

Figure 38.4 **The Talmud Rule in Mediocristan.**

a believer in these extremes to some degree: No matter how long we collect observations, something will come along that will surprise us if we look over an ever-longer time frame. The central issue is that no one knows when they will occur.

Thus we need both insurance and low-probability/high-reward bets far from the center to protect some part of our plans if things go wrong. Still, you must play the center because money concentrates on assets with more likely outcomes. There is more stability in investments when the vast majority of investors are more prepared for "center positions," especially if you beat them to it. You will lose loads if you bet entirely on the fat tails.

It is ironic that the safest possible assets are difficult to identify, so be invested in black swan hedges and melt-up positions, objectively based on random selection, with one caveat: Buy tail exposure when it is cheap. Crashes are not always moments of clarity for risk. They are places where the markets incorrectly overemphasize bad tail outcomes. Melt-ups in equities are often where to pick up cheap insurance. The center is where you accumulate safe yield. See the diversification in Extremistan in Figure 38.5.

Good and bad shocks can't be predicted, so smart people have little advantage. There is little alpha in Extremistan.

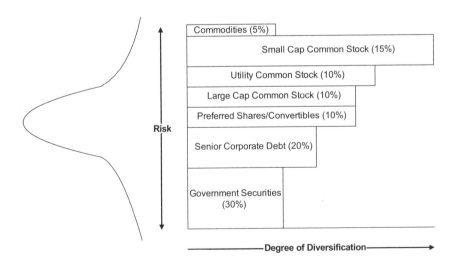

Figure 38.5 **Diversification in Extremistan.**

SOME TAIL MEASURES

There is some profit in playing with tails because tail risk is often underpriced and overpriced, and people's fear and greed are best gamed here. This kind of trading is a combination of mind games and psychology, because positive tails are more often than not overpriced. So is buying puts. Buy underpriced tail risk, and sell overpriced tail risk. Some indications of such mispricings are:

- Wide differences in inflation breakevens across maturities
- Low volatility (which implies perception of thin tails)

Maximize your exposure to positive tails, and minimize your exposure to negative tails—this may be obvious to the trader who buys low and sells high, but tails are hard to price for even the best traders.

CHAPTER 39

Financial System Resonance and Complexity

The wonder of financial crises is how events can move straight from impossible to inevitable, without ever passing through improbable.[1]

—ANATOLE KALETSKY

Dynamical systems are a refinement of our hunter instincts. We focus on motion, and dynamical systems capture motion. In the most general setting, it is a space X equipped with a geometric structure called a *topology* and a function μ mapping across transformations of X called a *measure*. When X is of manageable size—it is compact—we can normalize $μ(X) = 1$, making it equivalent to a probability. Often in practical applications, $μ(X)$ is iterated to model the passage of time.

Take, for example, a system composed of a huge number of small particles or a market composed of many small investors. Each of these small agents acts under a large number of random and largely unknown forces so that following each of them is practically impossible. However, there are conditions where all investors converge to a state of rest called *equilibrium*. In this case, the distribution of the particles throughout the system can best be represented by some measure μ. This measure is used because the huge number of particles are hard to track individually, but their behavior in aggregate unfolds over time randomly, settling on a path that is independent of the beginning point of the particles.

However, it is quite possible that the system will not settle at a state of rest. In fact, it can behave like a perpetual motion machine, something slightly more complex, or even so intractably complex that it is hard to understand its behavior at all. The flux between stability and instability is the key idea: There are conditions under which a system generates simple behaviors only to collapse into behavior so complex that it looks random. This chapter delves into just how difficult the primal motive of extracting order from apparent chaos can be.

THE CONNECTION BETWEEN DYNAMICAL SYSTEMS AND PREDICTION

It is human instinct to find order and her elusive sister, predictable behavior. Nonlinear dynamics—popularly called *chaos theory*—provide some new avenues for prediction and some hard bounds on unpredictability. It is an important conceptual tool because it demonstrates that even relatively simple nonlinear wrinkles produce complicated dynamics across multiple time scales that challenge probabilistic *laws of average*.

The introduction of nonlinear equations into models can generate time series that look like random noise even though the generating mechanism is completely deterministic. Nonlinearity introduces a basic challenge for determining the nature of the dynamical system—whether generated phenomena are the product of essential randomness or other high-dimensional complexity or a low-dimensional chaotic attractor. Very long data series with no secular trends in underlying dynamical system parameters imply that the time series is stationary. Scaling-law techniques are a way to determine whether a time series is driven by random factors or complex deterministic laws of motion.

One such technique is the Lyapunov exponent. This technique compares predicted values with observed time-series measurements, the degree of divergence makes distinctions between dynamical chaos and random noise. It works like this: For a low-dimensional chaotic time series, the accuracy of a nonlinear forecast falls off as the horizon increases, and determining whether accuracy diverges in an exponential or some other way is the simple intuition behind the Lyapunov exponent. Nonlinearity limits the forecast horizons because nonlinear model forecast error grows in an exponential way for a very long time series.

The meaning of *very long* for a time series is contingent on the time horizon of a forecast and the number of data points. You can't predict deeper into the tails than the length of the time series permits. Outside the measurement interval, extrapolation with a model is no better than extrapolation without a model. Thus, if there are five years of observations, prediction is invalid (much less any good) more than five years into the future at a constant time scale. In the same way, 100 observations means that the 99 percent confidence level is a hard bound on precision, given one degree of freedom. Beyond this basic idea, technical considerations regarding the minimal data needed are functions of specific techniques employed.

The lack of secular trends over a forecast interval means that the measurement errors generated by a given model are uncorrelated. For uncorrelated noise, a forecast horizon is valid across the entire time series given that the series is sufficiently long. For short time series, it is more difficult to distinguish between low-dimensional chaos and autocorrelated noise. Some forms of high-dimensional chaos may even be low-dimensional chaos *plus* autocorrelated noise.

Given that one has a viable model that generates uncorrelated noise, and that there are sufficient data for the forecast horizon, other practical difficulties exist. Prediction can fail when abrupt changes in the underlying dynamical system's parameters produce divergent behavior from the behavior implied by the model. There may be structural changes in the dynamical system equations such that the laws of motion governing a system behave in a completely different way.

Aggregating data too coarsely can obscure the true nature of the dynamical system and lead to model errors. Low-dimensional deterministic complexity is especially sensitive to random sampling error, making it difficult to calibrate a model. These limitations reduce prediction to pattern recognition, quantitative or qualitative, based on a vocabulary of experience. Because time and chance generate outliers—no one has "seen it all"—predictions fail.

DYNAMICAL PATTERNS

A dynamical system is a way to describe how these states of the world are attained in time and is a representation of the "machine" that determines how reality evolves. This system is the underlying data generator that we can observe only approximately at distinct points in time.

Definition

Let (X, d) be a given metric space, and suppose that to each point p of this space and moment of time t in $\mathbf{R}^2$ there is a set correspondence into a nonempty compact subset $f(p, t)$ of X whereby if we let $f(A, K) = U_{(p \text{ in } A, t \text{ in } K)} f(p, t)$,

1. $f(p, 0) = \{p\}$ for every point p in X.
2. If $t_1, t_2 > 0$, then $f[f(p, t_1), t_2] = f(p, t_1 + t_2)$ (linear transformation in t).
3. If q is in $f(p, t)$, then p is in $f(q, -t)$ (invertibility).
4. $\lim_{p, p_0, t_0} D[f(p, t), f(p_0, t_0)] = 0$, where D is a Hausdorff metric (continuity).

Then $f(p, t)$ is a dynamical system.

Think of the global economy as a complicated machine. The machine's products (gross domestic product) can be sampled at discrete points in time. The sampled sequence of, say, gross domestic product (GDP) observations from the economic dynamical system can be considered random variables. So given a dynamical system, an $f: X \rightarrow X$, and a function $\varphi: X \to \mathbf{R}$ that is the measurable or observed GDP, then the sequence of functions

$$\varphi, \varphi \times f, \varphi \times f^2, \ldots, \varphi \times f^n, \ldots$$

can be analyzed like genuinely random stochastic processes.

Dynamical systems have interacting parts that influence the dependencies of these processes as they evolve. The strength of these dependencies depend on how fast memory of the past is lost by the system as time evolves. A key issue is to what extent observations made in the present φ are affected by observed initial values in the past ψ. This is expressed by the familiar statistical concept of correlation:

$$C_n(\varphi, \psi) = \int (\varphi \times f^n) \, \psi \, d\mu - \int \varphi \, d\mu \times \int \psi \, d\mu$$

The function $C = 0$ depends on $(\varphi \times f^n)$ and ψ being independent random variables when the value of $\varphi \times f^n$ becomes less and less dependent on the value of ψ as time goes to infinity.

When the decay is exponential, then the dynamical process can be said to display *ergodic* behavior. Ergodicity has useful properties for modeling and prediction. It makes possible the concept of predictability where the past determines the future because the past, present, and future are essentially the same. Such processes are predictable in the following sense: If we know the entire past history of the process before time t_0, then we can predict the outcome at t_0 with probability 1. Similarly, if we know *enough* of the history before time t_0, then we can predict the outcome at time t_0 with arbitrarily high probability.

Structure of Ergodic Processes

Stochastic processes generate random outcomes. The most important ones for financial modeling are indexed to time. For example, stock prices evolve in time, and at certain intervals in time there are measurements of the price system. Such processes can be partitioned into subsequences defined by a finite number of mutually exclusive "bins."

For stocks, the "continuous" movement of a stock price during the afternoon can be divided into movement above the opening, below the closing, and the same as the closing.

Formally, an ergodic process (ρ, F) is an invertible, measure-preserving function F acting on a space X of measure 1 and a partition ρ of X into a finite number of disjoint sets (the "bins" in the finanacial example). Any measure of this system with a finite number of outcomes corresponds to a partition ρ of X. Starting with a process and constructing (ρ, F), the space X can be thought of as a system evolving according to F for some ρ measurement. Birkhoff and Shannon showed that there are two useful properties about processes of this type.

The Birkhoff ergodic theorem[2] states that if we look at enough of a process's history, any fixed string will occur with a fixed frequency. *Thus, if F is ergodic, we can recover all the information about a process from almost every instance of the process, and probabilities can be identified with the frequencies.*

The Shannon-McMillan-Breiman[3] theorem states that most strings of length n generated by the process have roughly the same probability. If one ignores subsequences that arise with small probability, then one has only to code $2^{E(\rho, F)n}$ messages of length n.

Further, consider two ergodic processes (ρ, F) and (σ, G). If they are isomorphic, then they can be realized as measurements on a system, each of which determines the other. If (ρ, F) is a measurement in a real system, then (σ, G) can be realized as a measurement on the same mechanical system that determines and is determined by the ρ-measurements. When two independent processes have the same entropy, they can be obtained as measurements on the same system, each of which determines the other. Therefore, there is one generating function and two generating partitions, each representing one of the two original processes.

A deterministic system gives rise to a measure preserving transformation on a measure space (called a *phase space*). Processes of 0-entropy are nonergodic and completely deterministic, meaning that there are special cases where any event can be determined by what a process does in the arbitrarily distant past with probability 0 or 1. There are also completely nondeterministic processes in the sense that no event can be predicted from an arbitrarily distant past. These processes inform the intuition of the Kolmogorov and Levy 0-1 laws, where things either happen or don't, and there is little possibility of knowing which.

STABILITY AND INSTABILITY

The interplay of ergodicity and probability enriches dynamical systems. When the long-term evolution of many systems depends sensitively on the initial state, this implies that the behavior of individual trajectories is complicated and unpredictable. In other cases, though, the statistical properties of the phase space orbits contain meaningful information.

Uniformly hyperbolic systems are such a case because they are *structurally stable*. This means that the statistical behavior of these systems can be described in terms of a finite number of outcomes like a steady-state: There exist invariant probability measures such that the time average exists. Other systems can be persistently nonhyperbolic—*persistently unstable*. For this reason, uniform hyperbolicity falls short of a general theory of dynamical systems. Unstable systems include those with infinitely many periodic attractors,[4] as well as chaotic systems rooted in physical models such as the Lorenz attractor[5] and the Henon attractor,[6] among others. The core problem for understanding nonhyperbolic systems is homoclinic tangencies—nontransverse intersections between stable and unstable manifolds of a periodic point.

Structural stability implies that a dynamical system is governed by fixed laws of motion. However, these fixed laws of motion may be so complex that they are intractable. The simplest dynamical behavior comes to a state of rest in finite time. The actual point of rest is called a *fixed point*, and the convergence to this point is fast.

Other laws of motion generate periodic orbits of a dynamical system. The generated orbits are a two-dimensional circle. They can be more complex and generate an annulus of periodic orbits that looks like a doughnut in three (or more) dimensions. The former are called *limit cycles*, the latter *quasi-periodic cycles*. If all orbits in a given neighborhood converge to a limit cycle, then the system is stable or attracting. If all the orbits diverge, then the system is unstable or repelling. If some orbits converge to a limit set and other orbits diverge, then the system is semistable.

Orbits can be even more complicated. More complicated orbits are described as chaotic.

Chaotic Behavior

When the orbits of a system

- Have a limit set in a neighborhood for almost every initial condition, the limit set is not periodic or nearly periodic.
- Have orbits that show sensitive dependence on initial conditions, the limit set has a dense orbit.

Then the system carries such complexity that it is called *chaotic.*

Much chaotic behavior is a result of noninvertibility. In fact, noninvertibility is a requirement for chaotic behavior in one-dimensional systems. However, everywhere invertible maps in two or more dimensions also can exhibit chaotic behavior. This is because as time proceeds, the trajectories of multidimensional systems may become trapped in bounded regions of the state space of the system. These types of systems are classified as dissipative or conservative. Dissipative systems tend to collapse to sets of measure zero (as opposed to conservative systems, which do not). Dissipativity indicates that systems tend to come to a state of rest unless acted on by outside force. A consistent result of these two tendencies is for the dissipative system orbits to be attracted to an infinite singular set of Lebesgue measure zero (a fractal). Sets of this type are called *strange attractors.* Conservative systems can display chaotic behavior by having a different type of attractor—one that is like a space-filling curve or similar structure.

The Palis Conjecture

Brazilian mathematician Jacob Palis proposed a conjecture that, if proven true, would make a very large class of dynamical, well-behaved systems understandable and predictable. Here it is:

Palis conjecture[7]: Every surface diffeomorphism can be C^k approximated by another that is either hyperbolic or has a homoclinic tangency.

It is typical to assume that the conjecture is true because it limits the behavior of dynamical systems to hyperbolic systems or homoclinic tangencies, systems that are easily analyzed. The conjecture is proven for $k = 1$. In higher dimensions, it is known that some attractors satisfy the conjecture but these attractors are little understood.

Palis's conjecture is really an attempt to rescue general dynamical systems from intractable complexity. It is not proven in general, although recently a special case was proven by Golubitsky.[8] Something quite the opposite of the Palis conjecture could be taking place in general. If so, then there exists a nonempty open set of diffeomorphisms on M and a set S in M with Lebesgue measure > 0 such that if x is in S, the time averages

$$1/n \ \Sigma_{n-1} \delta_{fkx}$$

do not converge when $n \to \infty$. Nothing is known that would prevent this from being generic behavior in dynamical systems, and this has profound implications for prediction.

Newhouse's Infinite Sinks

Despite the convenience of the Palis conjecture, sudden changes in laws of motion can induce sudden jumps and radically different trajectories and attractors, including transient chaotic behavior that comes and goes, cascading behavior, and other variations that are "messy" compared with structurally stable systems.

Sheldon Newhouse demonstrated that such systems exist and have an infinite number of attractors—meaning there are an infinite number of points to which the system can come to rest. Further, Newhouse showed that these systems are dense—meaning that such systems not only exist, but they also dominate in number all other types of dynamical systems.

This means that the system may exhibit unpredictable behavior: Instead of fixed-limit cycles or quasi-periodic behavior, an orbit can converge to infinitely many different points. As a result, it behaves like a random walk. Such behavior could very well be common in the world of smooth dynamics. This is the darker side of dynamical systems.

NEWHOUSE AND "HISTORICAL BEHAVIOR"

Newhouse's characterization of systems with an infinite number of attractors opens up profound implications. An infinite number of attracting sinks implies that the paths through are attracted to an infinite number of sets and, as a result, travel through the system in a way that appears persistently random, like, for example, Brownian motion. This nonrecurrent behavior is of a special type. Combining this nonrecurrence with measures of infinite limit generates the historical behavior: As time tends to infinity, the trajectory has no obtainable decision rule to govern it. Historical behavior ends up being as unpredictable as completely random behavior.

Predictability implies that any diffeomorphism mapping dynamical behavior tends over time to an attracting periodic orbit. Historical behavior doesn't imply that the diffeomorphism is divergent. It implies that there are infinitely many points to which it can possibly converge.

The Newhouse theorem states is that there are possibly an infinity of fixed points to which $f(n)(x)$ will oscillate. A dynamical system with an infinite number of attractors can be either structurally stable or unstable. A trajectory can oscillate ever more slowly between two fixed points, but the effect can disappear given small shocks to the system. It is equally plausible that a system can be deterministic, have similarities to smooth systems, and at the same time behave persistently like a random walk. There are simple dynamical systems with such time evolution, cellular automata, for example.

LARGE DYNAMICAL SYSTEMS

Cellular automata are an example of a large dynamical system that displays interesting behavior. Cellular automata are systems that constitute networks of coupled oscillators usually finite in size. They have many small constituent parts adding up to large dynamical systems.

Consider a large cellular automata system composed of a very large set of investors of type N in a region Ω. In this setting, the types of investors are a smooth function of space and time $N(x, t)$. These investors relate to the environment as random diffusion owing to the information they process in choosing asset positions. Richer dynamics can be overlaid by introducing signals that make the investors respond by buying or selling stocks. This example is called an *interacting-particle system*.

Such systems can be represented by partial differential equations of the elliptic-parabolic type. Given a stopping time T and index time such that $(\Omega \times 0, T)$ is the bound on the region Ω with a smooth boundary $\partial\Omega$ on $\mathbf{R}^2$ or $\mathbf{R}^3$, the system becomes

$$u_t = \nabla \cdot (\nabla u - u\nabla v)$$
$$0 = \Delta v - av + u$$

where Δ is the Laplace operator, $a \geq 0$, ∇ is the spatial gradient, and the unknown functions u and v are nonnegative. The system can be solved by substituting $v = (-\Delta + aI)^{-1}u$ from the second equation into the first and treating it as an initial boundary value problem in u.

The diffusion (newsflow driven) component of this system is

$$I_1 = -D\nabla_x N$$

where D is a constant that is interpreted as particles move from high density to low density. The interaction signal consists of forces that govern buy and sell signals based on whatever investor momentum is present. These interactions can be represented as

$$I_2 = N \sum_{i=1}^{m} {}_j(\vec{W})\nabla W_i$$

W works opposite to the diffusion effect unless Ψ is negative; then it reinforces the diffusion effect. If newsflow trading dominates momentum trading, then we can rewrite the system as:

$$\frac{\partial N}{\partial t} = D\nabla \cdot (\nabla N - N\nabla W)$$
$$\frac{\partial W}{\partial t} = \alpha N - \beta W$$

Given an assignment of states s_x and s_y to x and y, these interaction effects can be a part of Hamiltonian $H(s) = -\Sigma_{\{x,y\}} \mathcal{J}_{\{x,y\}} b(s_x, s_y)$, and these laws of motion can be substituted into the dynamical system. When the interaction effects themselves are random, the system is called *disordered*.

PROBABILITY FOR TIME-DEPENDENT DYNAMICAL SYSTEMS

Chaos is an extreme case where complex systems exhibit sensitive dependence on initial conditions, whatever the initial conditions may be. Chaotic systems are everywhere unstable, and the time evolution has limited or negligible predictability. Chaotic systems lose memory of the *recent* past quickly. This is not because they converge to a unique state of rest or asymptotically coalescent trajectories but because of their sensitive dependence on *initial* conditions. Small measurement errors at the outset multiply quickly in time so that, in practice, it is virtually impossible to track a specific trajectory in a chaotic system. In effect, there is only a random chance to make accurate long-term predictions by virtue of the sensitive dependence on initial conditions. Since we cannot measure the starting point with infinite precision, we cannot predict long-term behavior.

Sensitive dependence on initial conditions sets fundamental limits on prediction. There is a deep implication in this statement. One must pass over in silence even speaking of the past of such systems unless the past can be observed to such a degree that model outputs estimate it well. Further, the model can't depend too much on insignificant details of assumed earlier states; otherwise, infinitesimally small errors lead to ruin.

The only chance of saving the idea of predictability given such complexity is to make statistical predictions when suitable assumptions hold. If we measure the values of some observable, it remains impossible to predict exactly its long-term fluctuations, but ergodicity makes it possible to predict the limit of its time averages almost everywhere.

The *functional central limit theorem* is the limit of time averages and is known to hold for processes with a finite variance that are much more general than an independent, identically distributed (i.i.d.) sequence. If the stationary process is ergodic, then the sample standard deviation is a consistent estimator of the population standard deviation. The sample standard deviation converges to the population standard deviation as the sample size increases with probability 1. For structurally stable systems, Anosov diffeomorphisms, and axiom A attractors, correlation decay is exponential, and the central limit theorem always holds. Outside of axiom A systems, little is known in general.

The key is ergodicity. Ergodicity lends itself well to this context because of the rapid memory loss of complex systems. Ergodic machinery expresses itself through natural probabilistic tools, so this complexity, in turn, necessitates a probabilistic description of the world. Such approaches are of great interest in complex dynamics.

A Blackfly in the Chardonnay

Prediction can be significantly more difficult than anticipated because of an additional complication. Not only are there practical problems with measuring initial conditions of a system. Calibrating the parameters of the dynamical mapping cannot be accomplished with arbitrary precision either. Dynamical systems not only can be sensitive to initial conditions, but they also can exhibit sensitive dependence on parameters. Arbitrarily small changes to these parameters can result in significant changes in the averages of the observable and predictive outputs.

To characterize this phenomenon, consider a compact metric space (X, d) and a continuous map $f: X \rightarrow X$. The pair (X, f) is a dynamical system; the space X is a phase space. It is illuminating to compare the phenomena to dependence on initial condition.

Sensitive Dependence on Initial Conditions

The dynamical system (X, f) has *sensitive dependence on initial conditions* if there is a set Y subset of X of positive measure and $\varepsilon > 0$ such that for any x in Y and neighborhood U of x there is y in U and $n \geq 0$ with $d[fn(x), fn(y)] > \varepsilon$.

Consider a family of maps $f_t\colon X \to X$ parameterized by some element t in T. T has a topology and a reference parameter measure.

Sensitive Dependence on Parameters

The dynamical family (X, f_t) has sensitive dependence on parameters if there exists an observable $\varphi\colon X \to \mathbf{R}$, a set S a subset of T' of positive measure and $\varepsilon > 0$ such that for any element s in S and a neighborhood U of s there is an element t in the intersection of U and T' with

$$\int \varphi d\sigma_s - \int \varphi d\sigma_t > \varepsilon$$

LONG MEMORY AND THE OPPOSITE OF ERGODICITY

Some systems generate processes that possess long memory, meaning that correlation does not decay, or it decays very slowly. Long memory is connected to the lack of ergodic properties in the underlying dynamical system that generates the stochastic process. A nonergodic process has infinite memory, meaning that the result of a single coin toss will contribute to the outcome of all future coin tosses.

Long memory processes have long stretches of time when the process tends to be above the mean outcome and long stretches when the process tends to be below the mean. From a practical standpoint, this often justifies an assumption of nonstationarity. Thus it makes sense to talk about stationary processes as having finite memory and nonstationary processes as having infinite memory. However, the relationship between long memory and nonstationarity is delicate in a number of ways. There are stationary long memory processes, which are a class of stationary processes that also closely resemble nonstationary processes.

Stationary long memory processes are unusual stationary processes, and phase transitions can be a useful concept to understand them. Phase transitions represent shifts from short memory to long memory. If one knows when these shifts happen, prediction is possible in some intervals of a process. Heavy tails in the distribution are the practical consequence of long memory. When the marginal tails of a stationary process are heavy, extreme values have more weight and are more important. As the marginal tails of a distribution get heavier, concentrating on the partial sums of the process, particularly on their rate of growth, to identify the boundary between short and long memory becomes less useful.

A useful concept to determine long memory is the property of fractal, or self-similar, behavior. A process is *self-similar* if there is an H such that for all $c > 0$ one has

$$[Y(ct), t \geq 0] = {}^d[c^H Y(t), t \geq 0]$$

The number H is alternatively referred to as the *exponent of self-similarity*, the *scaling exponent*, or the *Hurst exponent*. Self-similar processes have the property that a scaling in time is equivalent to a scaling in space. The connection between the two types of scaling is determined by the Hurst exponent. The value of this exponent determines whether or not the increments of a self-similar process with stationary increments possess long memory.

COMPLEXITY AND RESONANCE

Complexity is often why thinking about things linearly and deductively doesn't work well. Logic is deductive—reasoning that depends on definitions, sequential progressions, and constancy of rules. When underlying laws of motion change, institutions reconstitute/reorganize, feedback times aren't constant, and logic that depends on cause and effect fails. This doesn't mean that reason is irrelevant or even flawed. It just means that sometimes the world isn't up to the standards logic requires.

Such changes are called *phase transitions*. Phase transitions occur when the constituting properties of a system undergo fundamental and abrupt change. Water undergoes a phase transition with the introduction of heat—from ice to fluid and then from fluid to vapor. Identifying the "natural" state of water depends on conditions such as the temperature and the chemical compounds it contains. If the temperature drops below a threshold, then fresh water freezes. However, ocean water doesn't freeze at the same temperature because of the compounds present. When water freezes, it takes on a different personality.

Phase transitions can occur in complex systems like bond markets. The "natural" state of such things as asset valuation is subject to a complexity of influences. Because there are so many factors and the interrelationships are complex, it is in some cases problematic to speak of "fundamentals." Valuation is sometimes as fluid as water, as ephemeral as steam, or as cold as ice. It depends on momentum—what others think about future prospects—and on positioning—if it is trading at a 52-week low or 52-week high, as well as the strength of balance sheets.

Valuation is difficult to ever be precise about because there is a divergence in opinion of proper value among different market participants. Thus valuation really implies prediction of others' expectations, and this type of prediction is hard.

If you wake up at 7 a.m. and you see lightning and hear thunder among dark gray skies, then a good forecast for that morning is rain. If someone were to ask you about the weather next week, that information is of little use. This is the nature of prediction in systems with nonlinear effects. Time makes prediction with reasonable tolerance impossible. The dominant factor contributing to success reduces over long timelines to blind luck. The Lorenz attractor models convection so that meteorologists can grasp the nature of sudden, unpredictable shifts in the weather, but these models don't add much accuracy to the weather forecasts. One could in fact say the same for a lot of financial models.

Phase transitions in financial systems are complicated to conceptualize and more often than not hard to observe—incalculably many factor effects cancel each other out, or the factor effects are nonlinear and remain so under the vast majority of cases. When they don't cancel each other out or are nonlinear, the coincidence of different factors acting simultaneously can create feedback loops that induce systemic nonlinear, nonperiodic behavior and phase transitions. This speaks to *resonance*. Here's an example of how complicated these dynamics can be:

Consider the smooth coupled oscillator system:

$$x_1' = f_1(x_1) + \varepsilon g_1(x_1, x_1', x_2, x_2')$$
$$x_2' = f_2(x_2) + \varepsilon g_2(x_1, x_1', x_2, x_2')$$

where $x_i \in \mathbf{R}^2$, $i = 1, 2$, and $\varepsilon \in \mathbf{R}$.

The solution set of the unperturbed system has the following characteristics:

1. The plane autonomous system $x_1' = f_1(x_1)$ has an invariant annulus A consisting of periodic solutions, and every periodic solution in A has the same period $n_1 > 0$, meaning that the period annulus is isochronous with period n.
2. The plane autonomous system $x_2' = f_2(x_2)$ has a periodic trajectory Γ with period $n_2 > 0$ such that either Γ is a hyperbolic limit cycle or Γ belongs to a period annulus, and the derivative of an associated period function at Γ does not vanish.
3. The trajectory Γ is in resonance with the period annulus A; that is, there are relatively prime positive integers S_1 and S_2 such that $S_1 n_1 = S_2 n_2$.

Parameter values for this model are such that several periodic solutions can coexist. These periodic solutions in the four-dimensional phase space are all sinks or saddles.[9]

The basin of attraction for a periodic solution consists of a sink in a region of phase space "captured by resonance." There are many variant behaviors of this system: Saddle periodic solutions may have one-, two-, or three-dimensional attractors. Solutions starting near the stable manifold can vacillate near the saddle periodic solution for a very long time only to leave the vicinity of the saddle periodic solution along its unstable manifold. It may appear to be captured and then pass near a second saddle or perhaps become captured by a stable periodic solution. Perturbations of the system can radically affect system evolution. If there are several such saddles, behavior may become very complex. There is an open question as to whether periodic sinks coexist with more complicated attractors, generating historical behavior.

Financial System Resonance

The financial system has been susceptible to such resonant effects and wide variation in behavior over the past two decades because innovation and deregulation blurred the organizational lines between hedge

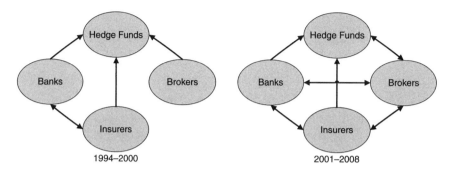

Figure 39.1 **Changes in Financial System Interconnectivity, 1994–2000 and 2001–2008.**
Source: Monica Billio, Mila Getmansky, Andrew W. Lo, and Loriana Pelizzon, "Measuring Systemic Risk in the Finance and Insurance Sectors"; unpublished working paper available at http://papers.ssrn.com/sol3/papers.cfm?abstract_id=1571277.

funds, mutual funds, insurance companies, banks, and broker/dealers. The Granger causalities shown in Figure 39.1 suggest how interconnected the financial system is. The arrowheads show causality and the direction of contagion risks.

From 1994 to 2000, monthly returns of hedge funds were influenced unidirectionally by the monthly returns of banks, brokers, and insurers (one-sided arrow). Banks and insurer returns influence each other simultaneously (two-sided arrow). Hedge funds can sell off equity holdings in a liquid market. Not so banks. Because bank loans are illiquid, banks are not designed to withstand rapid and large losses. They are the natural repository for systemic risk in the ecosystem. From 2001 to 2008, the relationships are more interconnected, and there is little unidirectional impact. Changes in one component affect other components. An implication of this is that illiquidity now affects all financial assets and thus all financial institutions.

Bank capital requirements and risk-management practices attempt to mitigate these liquidity problems. Standardized methodologies such as value-at-risk (VaR), and recent modifications like conditional value-at-risk (CVar), and expected shortfall don't work. If the riskiness of assets held by one bank increases owing to heightened market volatility, then the bank is required to sell some of those risky assets to maintain its VaR. In effect, this is VaR acting as a stop-loss rule. This stop-loss liquidation restores a bank's financial soundness in isolation. However, when all banks liquidate assets to maintain VaR standards, a self-sustaining positive-feedback loop requires all banks to continue selling even more assets.

Khandani, Lo, and Merton (2009)[10] show how resonant effects can arise in residential housing markets from the simultaneous changes in three factors: rising home prices, falling interest rates, and increasing efficiency and availability of refinancing opportunities. Each of these factors in isolation has minimal adverse impact and often contributes to economic growth. When all three factors prevail at the same time, however, it creates system resonance that tears valuations apart. Home owners synchronize home equity withdrawals via refinancing, ratcheting up home owner leverage simultaneously without any means for reducing leverage when home prices eventually fall, ultimately leading to waves of correlated defaults and foreclosures. Bad lending practices, procyclic regulations, and government policies feed excessive risk taking.

Fraud and deception lead in the worst case to extinction events when institutions become too large, exhaust loan demand, and then slowly starve to death as a result. At best it fosters a kind of innovation that mingles greed with power. It takes good ideas, swallows them whole, and then pukes up a disgusting version of the original.

UNBALANCED INNOVATION AND SECURITIZATION

Unbalanced innovation infected the beautiful idea of securitization. Securitization converts small-denomination loans into larger yield-bearing securities that are more liquid. This good idea was taken to excess, and securitized paper became a voracious loan-eating machine. The demand for loans stemmed not from organic lending needs but instead solely to seed securitizations, and it mutated the financial system into something ill-equipped for survival. While lending standards have improved, it remains to be seen whether the institutions that still walk among us are anything less than the living dead.

The modern fractional reserve banking system uses money deposits to create loans. This exerts a telescoping effect on the supply of money because deposits can be used as loans, a portion of which is redeposited and loaned out again. Thus the money supply is controlled by the bank requirement to limit lending to only a (large) fraction of deposits and keeping the rest as a reserve in case of drawdowns. The fundamental brake is this: Reserve banking controls individual loan growth and limits the total amount of bank credit available to the economy.

Securitization allows banks to sell loans that would otherwise stay on their books and prevent them from generating more loans. Because this process destroys the link between risk aversion and loan creation, banks vastly extended their lending capacity and altered the mechanism that governs the rate of growth of credit. *This is immensely inflationary until the capacity of borrowers or buyers reaches a critical point.*

Since an increase in loans to the economy functions in the same ways as an increase in the supply of money, the things that typically are purchased with credit, such as houses, commercial real estate, and stocks, increase in price as the credit supply increases. Assets created out of credit, traded, and used as collateral on other loans create a virtually unlimited credit growth. The only real limit is finding borrowers to lend to and purchasers to buy the securitized loans.

But there is a hard limit on the amount of debt and compound interest accrued that can be supported by available banking deposits—there can only be so much borrowing. When loans decrease, this implies that the demand for things purchased with credit, such as real estate and financial assets, deflates. As defaults increase and the value of existing securitizations takes haircuts, the demand for future securitizations vanishes.

Securitized paper has no explicit required reserves set aside to cover losses. Cover for losses immediately comes out of what reserves exist and profits, which also restricts the supply of loans. The restriction of credit causes even more defaults, and the debt-deflation cascade repeats itself. At this point, there is really nothing left for the reserve banking system. Central planning has to step in to fill the void by monetizing debt. Quantitative easing (QE) injects liquidity that circumvents the risk aversion of banks and organic loan demand degeneration. This liquidity may arrest the price decline of assets typically bought with credit, but it clearly inflates the price of assets insensitive to loan demand, such as food and fuel.

CHAPTER 40

Robots and Reptiles

Financial markets are about optimism, forward thinking, and the peddling of hope. They epitomize the great strength and great weakness of hope. We remain positive despite Pandora's miseries. In the next moment, we believe things are fine even as the canoe goes over the waterfall. The huge difference between how humans think and how machines compute deserves some thought.

As discussed earlier, there are two basic logical intuitions of the human mind: the geometric and the algebraic. People are more prone to process data geometrically. They process what they see and develop rules that interpret the data as they go to make comparisons. This is the most basic geometric intuition. It is behind financial methodologies such as technical analysis and momentum trading. Machines process data in an algebraic way. They start with an inventory of facts and sequentially build a structure connecting them together according to *preestablished rules*. When a machine's database or vocabulary becomes very large, it can synthesize interconnections in unexpected ways.

People use their reptilian id and machines use their literal precision for a common purpose—pattern recognition. Recognition is built on the hard-won human experience of pleasure and pain or a good set of specification codes for machines. This highlights a weakness of robot processing. Robust pattern recognition requires *context*. For example, prior to an Federal Open Market Committee (FOMC) meeting, money can be made by putting tight stop losses on a simultaneous purchase of $3 \times$ long and $3 \times$ short Standard & Poor's (S&P) exchange-traded funds (ETFs). A rule can be built for computer implementation to mimic this, but the rule is unsuitable without context (for lack of a better term) that imparts a high probability to an FOMC meeting actually meaning something compared to a trivial FOMC meeting. Situating a context is the distinctive human method of thinking through intractability.

Trading based on a context isn't perfect by any means. Context is only relevant in the intervals between liquidity breakdowns when some type of "normal" prevails. The process of history is a period of reasonably predictable normal, a crisis that eliminates predictability and resets correlations, and then a slow process of figuring out the new normal. Thus trading based on a context works only in a "local" sense, but outside a given neighborhood, both visual pattern recognition and explicit programming fail. Survival takes thinking outside the model and recognizes nonstationarities where the context is vague. A large part of this is liquidity management. For example, the relative difference between a pricing-model output and a valuation-model output becomes irrelevant in the face of panic and liquidation.

Using the working notion of liquidity as the interval between infrequent crises, it is clear that liquidity stopping times vary by asset. For example, complicated securities like collateralized debt obligations (CDOs) combine complicated cash flows that are hard to price. Their valuation can become very sensitive to the assets they include and how they are combined in the security.

A way to gauge this sensitivity is with a statistical concept called the *ratio of signal to noise*. It describes how well one can confidently determine the performance of a CDO given the performance of the assets that comprise the CDO. The between-asset variation is the signal. The within-CDO measurement error is the noise, which is measured on a scale of 0 to 1 (0 = all variability is due to noise or measurement error; 1 = all variability is due to real differences in asset performance).

The ratio lies somewhere between these signal extremes and defines the reliability of the CDO. Reliability in this case is a function of asset variation and the number of assets bundled in the CDO.

CDOs can take on different behaviors when within-asset error is increased and between-asset variation is reduced. Put simply, when all assets within a CDO are strongly correlated, the CDO is subject to big swings up and down. When the combined assets have limited or negative correlation, the CDO is more stable. Performance is hard to estimate when the distribution of returns is radically different for assets combined in the CDO.

The iron rule of financial markets is that you buy assets when they are cheap and you sell them when they are rich. But the structure of securitization assets makes implementation never as easy as it seems.

Supercomputers can conduct a sensitivity analysis (allowing some moving parts to change while holding other moving parts constant) for literally millions of mortgages (and their historical attributes) in a CDO. Humans can't possibly do this. They value things by finding the most closely related asset with a liquid price, determining relevant differences, and factoring in risk premium based on the differences. This is complicated enough, and it works pretty well.

Can a human and robot love connection fuse these latent and formative approaches?

I'LL GET BY WITH A LITTLE HELP FROM MY ROBOT

There are no fully functional "learning and autonomous" robots yet. I won't jump into the associated philosophical issues of artificial intelligence here. At present, computers are largely servants to the logical instructions that are designed to enable machine performance. By implication, their performance is based on a programmer's ability to develop and formulate code for a given problem. Whether computers become sentient is irrelevant because this category isn't necessary. Computers have already evolved to the point where the problem posed can be quite general and that is in most ways good enough. What is decisive is whether they operate with an order of complexity that *mimics* sentience at some level of tolerance. Deep Blue beating Gary Kasparov[1] is an example of this "good enough" mimicry. This example itself highlights the strengths and weaknesses of human and machine reasoning.

How human reasoning sucks compared to that of robots:

- People forget too often. Sometimes we remember bad things too much, sometimes not enough.
- People think slowly.
- People lack formal precision. One wrong step at the beginning screws the whole thing.
- Human brains get tired, and we lose concentration. Then we screw up long, complicated logical tasks consistently.
- People are emotional. We think with our genitalia and other biologic imperatives when other organs would serve better. Our reptilian id gets in the way.

How unimpaired human reasoning busts a cap in computer reasoning:

- People learn by identifying regularities; computers must have a "regularity" defined before they can recognize one.
- Related: People *visualize*; perhaps this is the hallmark of context.
- People synthesize; to avoid their weaknesses, humans adapt seemingly unrelated solution methods to problems we think are interesting.
- People can amend the central categories of their reasoning. They step outside the box and create unity from the broken pieces.

In some ways these differences are neither advantages nor impairments. In another sense, our strengths can be reduced down to an understanding of that hard-to-define word *context*. And in other ways, we have decided disadvantages.

A ROBOT APPROACH TO SECURITIZATION

Start with a basic formulation of asset securitization through robot eyes. Actuaries were the first to design securitization methods using the well-known (to actuaries) office model. Consider that the random variable $P(t)$ representing a single mortgage can be aggregated into a very simple security $P(t)$ using the following cash-flow-delinquency process:

$$P(t) = \sum_{s=0}^{\infty} \sum_{j=1}^{N(i-s)} K_S^P A_{i-s,s}(\mathcal{J}) I_{i-s,s}^s(\mathcal{J})$$

where K_s = cash flow at duration s per mortgage

A = delinquent payment or obligated payment less than required per bond

I = default indicator (0 if in default at time t, 1 otherwise if $x_{t-s,j}$ is not in default).

The issue here is ensuring sufficient computational resources. However, as $P(t)$ becomes more specified, indeterminacies arise that can make the summations involved in computing $P(t)$ intractable. To ensure tractability, technical conditions have to be imposed on the model that may cause it to diverge from reality. Here is where human creativity can aid brute-force processing, as shown in the following example.

Risk Management

In simple terms, the Gorton Model evaluated the risk of losses on the super senior portion of the CDO bonds; the Gorton Model did not measure the market value of the super senior portion of the CDO bonds, only the risk or likelihood of a default of each of the underlying reference obligations.

The default rates in the Gorton Model were based upon severe recessionary market scenarios that were modeled to be worse than the worst post–World War II recession.

From the Gorton Model, AIGFP [AIG Financial Products] determined the attachment point for the super senior tranche of the CDO, i.e., the point where the model determined that there was sufficient subordination to adequately protect against credit losses, with an additional cushion built in for more protection. AIGFP would only write protection on deals where the Gorton Model showed that the risk of credit losses above this attachment point would be remote. At the time, *the Gorton*

Model gave us confidence that there was an extremely small risk that any of our positions in the MSCDS portfolio would ever experience any sort of loss.

. . . in July 2005, I questioned whether in our modeling we needed to consider additional analysis of deals containing large amounts of interest-only loans, deals that were biased toward low FICO scores, and deals that were heavily concentrated in particular geographic regions. Further, I asked whether we should strengthen the process used to evaluate the CDO managers who were in charge of these deals, particularly in non-static deals where the managers had the ability to add and remove collateral within certain limits.

. . . the problem that we at AIGFP and many of our counterparties faced is the simple fact that by the fall of 2007, there was no longer an existing market, much less a liquid market, for the instruments we were trying to price.

—Andrew Forster, executive vice president, testimony
before the Financial Crisis Inquiry Commission[2]

Was the Gorton model wrong? No. The Gorton model evaluated the default risk embedded in securitizations. As such, it worked in the local intervals between crises when liquidity was sufficient. It wasn't designed to cope with contingencies outside that domain.

The italicized testimony above points out both the eagle-eye power of human foresight about what can go wrong (it did) and the fragile foundations of confidence in rigorous models. If anything, the testimony shows that adherence to models without a robust view of the technical assumptions, the methods used, and the nature (forget probabilities) of adverse contingencies is disastrous.

THE FUTURE: LONG LIVE SECURITIZATION

There was a time when banks lived off the spread between deposits/wholesale fund rates and loan rates less default costs. There were good times and bad. Due diligence in a loan book was time-intensive but manageable. It was time-intensive because banks held on to their originated loans, and monitoring costs were lower. Taking more term risk on government securities was a very good hedging option.

Banks will not go back to loan-holding, Pleasantville-style institutions. Nor will they continue to leverage up to the gills with collateralized collateral on collateral. They will continue to move loans off book and securitize, but CDO structures will be simpler so that they will remain tractable. Transparent mechanics implies easier pricing.

CDOs aren't going away because they are just too good an idea.

The most interesting part of future securitization is conditioned on whether a wholly different type of reasoning emerges that incorporates the best elements of the human and machine—reasoning that is intuitive and geometric and able to usefully integrate techniques from unexpected sources. At the same time, it would be reasoning that is computationally mistake-free and able to crunch through a multitude of special cases with raw, brute-force computation. Sign me up!

A marriage such as this is interesting because neither approach works perfectly in all contingencies, but together they would work *better* for all contingencies. Some problems don't have a solution. Some problems have solutions, but one can never derive them. Some have a solution, but getting to them is extremely hard. Some are tractable, manageable problems. Computers and humans can both solve tractable problems in different ways, but no reasoning of any type can solve truly intractable problems.

Humans *manage* intractable problems. They fool other humans into thinking that there is a solution. The fooler then can manipulate the resulting herd while acting rationally himself or herself. Intractable problems can even be overcome by self-delusion. This is a common problem when reputation has strong connections to income and social status.

The Future of Fixed Income: Past as Prologue?

If there is one thing I've learned in my few years on this planet, it is that ultimately we are all full of it when it comes to predicting how markets will move in the future. Yet we continue to make predictions over and over again about how political, social, and economic events affect these markets, simply because it gives us some sense of control and justification for our actions.

Just as prediction is the sibling of control, so the need for control is the driving force that spurs the transformation of more and more of finance into mere adjuncts of mathematical discovery. This is because natural selection has chosen reason, logic, and the scientific method as the best way to go about predicting the future. The shaman and fortunetellers are relegated to the margins now.

But math isn't enough to guarantee making money. There is no reason to rule out that the rules determining how the world turns can change. In fact, you see rules-in-flux all the time in nature and elsewhere. Take a simple example[1]. Fungi are well-established scavengers. But some fungi are known to trap prey and to be predators when times get tough for them. They deploy sinister looking nooses to strangle microbial prey, hooks that snag them, and secretions that attract and glue them in place. When there is a lack of living prey, the fungi reverts back to the "normal" methods of fungal nutrition, absorbing decayed remains. You see these kinds of changes whenever you deal with situations where agents can learn and adapt—living systems and anything that humans have a hand in shaping.

Extreme behavior complements normal behavior, and the shift constantly hamstrings our predictions. When environmental factors change, the rules governing outcomes change. This builds a largely unobservable instability into human systems. No use denying it: the rules of living spontaneously evolve when under stress.

So do the rules of finance. In fact the outer contours of the financial world change so much that it is scarcely recognizable compared to twenty years ago. But at its core it hasn't changed so much. Bonds have been around for a long time, and stresses here always indicate impending turmoil and possibilities for significant change. Government bonds are so closely connected to the health of the state that the yield curve corresponds to the spinal cord. There are new things too, derivative instruments that, for a seller, sit higher on the capital structure than bond, and permit the buying and selling of future risk. And therein is the rub. You have bonds, which have stood every conceivable stress-test of time, subordinate to a liability that has been coddled from its outset.

That is to say: we really do not know if one can adequately price credit and interest-rate risk over an extended period of time. There is a legitimate need and reason to hedge credit and interest-rate risk, and there is no reason to begrudge anyone for taking a speculative view on the price of these risks. And I concede that clearing and settlement structures in place for interest-rate swaps like SwapClear do mitigate their inherent risks much more than credit default swaps. *But again: we really do not know if one can adequately price credit and interest risk over an extended period of time.* Every time you had a busted market for these risks, central banks rushed in to supply enormous liquidity to shore up the short side, and guarantee credit default swap protection. Absent these artificial stimulants while the market was small, if it blew up, parties would lick their wounds, and while a few might go the way of the dodo, the mass would move forward wiser for the pain. The market itself would adapt to changing conditions and resize itself. What we have now is a market that may very well be inherently infeasible and scaled far too big to fail without apocalypse.

This is what is so disturbing about the Fed and politicians so much. Tampering with market mechanisms leads to disaster. And let's cut the unicorns and glitter about the implications of financial failure. There is no magic reset button that will take all our interconnected obligations painlessly away. Pulling the plug on a market with so many interlocking claims on funds just isn't feasible. And in a complex adaptive system with large banks connecting everything together, a major default will lead to another, and another, on into a financial disaster.

The interacting nature of the system contributes to the problem of risk pricing, because the interaction itself spawns new modes of behavior that amplify ever more risks. Interaction obscures good measurement and makes models collapse. The genuinely new things that have never occurred before make the entire system unstable.

This runs counter to how people assess risk, and assuming distributions with fatter tails are only a partial resolution to the underlying problem instability poses. There is a prevalent, implicit assumption of normalcy bias: that the future will be by and large like the past if only because the past is all that we know. This is how we typically assess risk, allied with probability to determine likelihoods. But rules governing the assignment of probabilities are static. And a reality capable of extreme readjustments can diverge to the point where our models implode.

How things change.

Fixed income is dominated by "contextual" trading now. There are iBoxxx and CDX indices amenable to computer trading just like stocks, which just serves to add yet more noise into the calculations. You buy bonds financed at a prime rate, but you can hedge the interest-rate risk with an interest-rate swap at just about any point on the yield curve. So there is less need to be concerned about liquidity. Because you can sell an arbitrary amount of the credit risk on a reference name with a credit default swap, you don't care so much about the quality of the bond itself. Of course this last depends as much on the ability of short counterparties to pay out on claims when you need them honored the most.

All the hedges give the appearance of being fool-proof. Trading this way is not superior to good fundamental analysis where you are paid to determine if a bond is money good over its life. At their best, swaps make trading more logically precise and mathematically sure, but in the end it just enables speculation on what seems a high percentage shot. It's like introducing seat belts when there are no speed limits. Under certain conditions, they do the opposite of saving lives. They make people act even more recklessly.

And it is all dependent on ever-increasing liquidity. Liquidity in fixed income lies in the nanosecond ability to drop practically unlimited capital in the Treasury market free of transactions cost and get it out equally fast. There is no way of knowing how sensitive the architecture of modern finance is to the decades-long bull market in Treasuries. It may not be robust to changes to this bull market and may collapse like a sandcastle when the tide comes in.

A bear market in treasuries is outside of the experience of most. I know it will eventually happen. Low volume, grinding losses, and illiquidity, which ensure that you don't know how much what you have is worth—it's a metaphor for a mode of existence. I know that the financial system today is almost entirely speculative, as opposed to driven by fundamentals. People will adapt and revert back to more stable ways of doing business when the Treasury bull market ends.

Whether for good or evil, the financial system now is the most efficient thing humanity has ever constructed, like a cheetah. The question is whether a cheetah made for the savannah will die off in the swamp or the desert before it can adapt.

Notes

Introduction

1. www.springerlink.com/content/713j0q7333620tp2/.

Chapter 2

1. www.cbo.gov/ftpdocs/105xx/doc10521/budgetprojections.pdf.
2. www.moneynews.com/StreetTalk/Treasury-China-Sheds-US/2011/06/06/id/398915.

Chapter 3

1. Meir Kohn, "The Determination of Exchange Rates," in *The Origins of Western Economic Success: Commerce, Finance, and Government in Preindustrial Europe*, Chap. 4, p. 31; available at www.dartmouth.edu/~mkohn/Papers/99-04.pdf.
2. Edwin S. Hunt, *The Medieval Super-Companies: A Study of the Peruzzi Company of Florence* (Cambridge, England: Cambridge University Press, 1994).
3. C. Desimoni, quoted in L. T. Belgrano, *Della vita privata dei Genovesi*, 2nd ed. (Genoa, 1875). The author indicates that the silver ducat experienced a consistent secular debasement trend. Compared with the dollar, it was nothing. The ducat was amazingly sound currency, losing only 20 percent of its value in 100 years. On the other hand, the Genoese pound commonly had only 40 percent silver content in its coinage.
4. Reinhold C. Mueller, *The Venetian Money Market: Banks, Panics, and the Public Debt 1200–1500* (Baltimore: Johns Hopkins University Press, 1997). The author notes that thirteenth-century bank certificates of deposit had typical returns of 8 percent per annum, simple (noncompounded) interest.
5. www.bis.org/statistics/derstats.htm.

Chapter 4

1. For a discussion of immiserization, see http://www.cnbc.com/id/43441924/ How_Miserable_Index_Says_the_Worst_in_28_Years.
2. www.universa.net/.
3. The Royal Bank of Scotland, "Guide to Inflation-Linked Products." Booklet for Risk magazine (2003).
4. www.scribd.com/doc/19586729/Barclays-Capital-Global-InflationLinked-Products-A-Users-Guide.
5. www.icap.com/markets/interest-rates/inflation-swaps.aspx.

Chapter 6

1. Barrie A. Wigmore, *The Crash and Its Aftermath: A History of Securities Markets in the United States, 1929–1933* (Santa Barbara, CA: Greenwood Press, 1985).

Chapter 8

1. R. H. Stroup and R. G. Marcis, "Income and Expenditure Patterns in Rural South Vietnam." *Economic Inquiry* 6:52–64, 1967. doi: 10.1111/j.1465-7295.1967.tb01175.x.
2. www.youtube.com/watch?v=cKUvKE3bQlY.

Chapter 9

1. http://search.japantimes.co.jp/cgi-bin/nb20080401a3.html.
2. www.reuters.com/article/2009/05/18/us-financial-japan-idUSTRE54H2RW20090518.
3. www.jstor.org/pss/4200233.
4. http://socrates.berkeley.edu/~hdreyfus/pdf/HdgerOnArtTechPoli.pdf, p. 11.
5. www.washingtonpost.com/wp-dyn/articles/A1911-2005Mar2.html.

Chapter 10

1. http://blogs.wsj.com/economics/2010/07/22/bernanke-lowering-interest-rate-on-excess-reserves-could-threaten-market-functioning/.
2. http://macromarketmusings.blogspot.com/2011/06/what-successful-and-unsuccessful.html.

Chapter 12

1. www.stanford.edu/dept/MSandE/cgi-bin/people/faculty/giesecke/pdfs/glss.pdf.

2. J. G. Dercksen, "Silver and Credit in the Old Assyrian Trade," in *Trade and Finance in Ancient Mesopotamia* (Leiden: the Netherlands: Nederlands Historisch-Archaeologisch Instituut te Istanbul, 1997), pp. 55–84.

Chapter 14

1. Naohiko Baba, Shinichi Nishioka, Nobuyuki Oda, Masaaki Shirakawa, Kazuo Ueda, and Hiroshi Ugai, "Japan's Deflation: Problems in the Financial System and Monetary Policy." BIS Working Paper No. 188, 2005; and Nagahata, Takashi and Toshitaka Sekine, "The Effects of Monetary Policy on Firm Investment after the Collapse of the Asset Price Bubble: An Investigation Using Japanese Micro Data." Bank of Japan Working Paper No. 02-3, 2002.
2. Ibid., p. 15, footnote 43.
3. Ibid., p. 14, §3.1.
4. Ibid., p. 19, §3.3.3.
5. Takashi Nagahata and Toshitaka Sekine, "The Effects of Monetary Policy on Firm Investment after the Collapse of the Asset Price Bubble: An Investigation Using Japanese Micro Data." Bank of Japan Working Paper No. 02-3, 2002, p. 26.

Chapter 18

1. www.federalreserve.gov/monetarypolicy/tslf.htm.
2. www.bis.org/statistics/otcder/dt1920a.pdf.
3. www.bis.org/statistics/otcder/dt1920a.pdf.

Chapter 19

1. www.eraider.com/images/articles/0211_brown.pdf.

Chapter 20

1. K. Ito, "Poisson Point Processes Attached to Markov Processes," in *Proceedings of the 6th Berkeley Symposium on Mathematics and Statistical. Probability*, Vol. 3 (Berkeley, CA: University of California Press, 1971), pp. 225–240.
2. http://arxiv.org/PS_cache/hep-ph/pdf/9910/9910471v1.pdf.

Chapter 21

1. http://arxiv.org/abs/1102.0683

Chapter 22

1. Simeon M. Berman, "Limit Theorems for the Maximum Term in Stationary Sequences," *Annals of Mathematical Statistics* 35/2 (1964), 502–516.; http://projecteuclid.org/DPubS?service=UI&version=1.0&verb=Display &handle=euclid.aoms/1177703551.

2. K. Ito, "Poisson Point Processes Attached to Markov Processes," in *Proceedings of the 6th Berkeley Symposium on Mathematics, Statistics, and Probability*, Vol. 3 Berkeley, CA: University of California Press, 1971), pp. 225–240.

3. B. Maissoneuve, "Exit Systems." *Ann Prob* 3:399–411, 1975.

Chapter 23

1. www.orie.cornell.edu/orie/manage/people/upload/The-Final-Meltdown.pdf.

Chapter 25

1. G. Polya, "Herleitung des Gauszschen Haflergesetzes au seiner Funktionalgleichung." *Math Z* 18:96–108, 1923.

2. J. Marcinkiewicz," Sur une propriete de la loi de Gauss." *Math Z* 44: 612–618, 1939.

3. V. Ju, I.Linnik, and. I. V. Ostrovski_, "Decomposition of Random Variables and Vectors," in *Translations of Mathematical Monographs*, Vol. 48 (Providence, RI: American Mathematical Society, 1977).

4. P. Levy, "Sur les integrales dont les elements sont des variables aleatoires independents." *Ann. R. Scuola Norm. Super. Pisa, Sei. Fis. e Mat.*, Series. 2 (1934), Vol. 3, pp. 337–366; Series. 4 (1935), pp. 217–218.

5. H. Cramer, "Uber eine Eigenschaft der normalen verteilungsfunktion." *Math Z* 41:405–414, 1936.

6. D. A. Riakov, "On the Decomposition of Poisson Laws." *Dokl Akad Nauk SSSR* 14:9–11, 1937.

7. P. Barfai, "Die Bestimmung der zu einem wiederkehrenden Prozess gehorenden Verteilungsfunktion ais den mit Fehlern behafteten Daten einzigen Realisation." *Studia Sci Math Hungary* 1:161–168, 1966.

8. Halasz and Major, "Reconstructing the Distribution Form Partial Sums of Samples." Ann Prob 5(6):987–998, 1977; available at http://projecteuclid. org/DPubS?service=UI&version=1.0&verb=Display&handle=euclid. aop/1176995665.

9. http://projecteuclid.org/DPubS?service=UI&version=1.0&verb=Display &handle=euclid.bams/1183524998.

10. www.amazon.com/Topics-Noncommutative-Geometry-Yuri-Manin/ dp/0691085889.

Chapter 26

1. www.telegraph.co.uk/finance/economics/8029560/Brazil-warns-of-world-currency-war.html.

2. www.telegraph.co.uk/finance/comment/ambroseevans_pritchard/8182605/ Chinas-credit-bubble-on-borrowed-time-as-inflation-bites.html.

Chapter 28

1. www.cbsnews.com/video/watch/?id=7117930n.

Chapter 31

1. www.supercc.com/presentations/CapStrucArb.pdf.

Chapter 32

1. www.ericbenhamou.net/documents/Encyclo/swaps%20development% 20of.pdf.

2. http://faculty.insead.edu/peress/personal/Lehman%20swap%20spreads.pdf.

3. www.zerohedge.com/article/guest-post-swap-spread-puzzle-and-some-thoughts-time-being-different.

4. www.apeaweb.org/confer/sea06/papers/takeda-ueda.pdf.

Chapter 33

1. Details on these products can be found at www.cmegroup.com/trading/ interest-rates/.

Chapter34

1. William Butler Yeats, "The Second Coming."

Chapter 35

1. "Mathematics under the Microscope"; www.maths.manchester. ac.uk/~avb/MMW.pdf.

2. www.gutenberg.org/ebooks/25387.

3. http://library.msri.org/books/sga/from_grothendieck.pdf.

Chapter 37

1. Brunon Kaminski, Artur Siemaszko, and Jerzy Szymanski. "The Determinism and the Kolmogorov Property in Topological Dynamics." *Bull Polish Acad Sci Math* 51(4):401–417, 2003.

Chapter 38

1. Nassim Nicholas Taleb, *The Black Swan: The Impact of the Highly Improbable* (New York: Random House, 2007).

Chapter 39

1. www.theaustralian.com.au/news/markets-crisis-could-get-much-worse/story-e6frg9mx-1111117674864.

2. www.math.sunysb.edu/~jack/DYNOTES/dn9.pdf.

3. www.math.brown.edu/~timaustin/ETnotes11.pdf.

4. S. Newhouse, "The Abundance of Wild Hyperbolic Sets and Non-smooth Stable Sets for Diffeomorphisms." *Math de L'IHÉS* 50(1):101–151, 1979; available at www.springerlink.com/content/713j0q7333620tp2/.

5. http://arxiv.org/PS_cache/nlin/pdf/0406/0406031v2.pdf.

6. http://arxiv.org/PS_cache/nlin/pdf/0510/0510061v1.pdf.

7. Enrique R. Pujals. "From Peixoto's Theorem to Palis's Conjecture: Dynamics, Games and Science I," in *Springer Proceedings in Mathematics*, Vol. 1 (Amsterdam: Springer, 2011), pp. 743–746; available at https://springerlink3.metapress.com/content/n36v518510181110/resource-secured/?target=fulltext.pdf&sid=pqhchk452bgubo55lcm1ey45&sh=www.springerlink.com.

8. A. Gorodetski and V. Kaloshin, "How Often Surface Diffeomorphisms Have Infinitely Many Sinks and Hyperbolicity of Periodic Points Near a Homoclinic Tangency." *Adv Math* 208(2):710–797, 2007; available at www.its.caltech.edu/~asgor/Sinks_final.pdf.

9. Chicone, 1993; "Periodic Solutions of a System of Coupled Oscillators Near Resonance" SIAM J. Math. Anal. 26, pp. 1257-1283 (27 pages); available at http://arxiv.org/abs/chao-dyn/9305007.

10. Amir Khandani, Andrew W. Lo, and Robert C. Merton, Systemic Risk and the Refinancing Ratchet Effect. Unpublished working paper; available at: http://papers.ssrn.com/sol3/papers.cfm?abstract_id=1472892.

Chapter 40

1. http://college.cengage.com/psychology/shared/exercises/nl/nl-why_did_deep_blue_frame.html.
2. www.fcic.gov/hearings/pdfs/2010-0701-Forster.pdf.

Conclusion

1. http://www.virtualmuseum.ca/Exhibitions/Mushroom/English/Science/Lifestyles/predators.html

Index

Figures are indicated by *f* and tables are indicated by *t*.